It Takes More than Love

A Practical Guide to Taking Care of an Aging Adult

by

Anita G. Beckerman, A.R.N.P., C.S., Ed.D.

&

Ruth M. Tappen, Ed.D., R.N., F.A.A.N.

HEALTH PROFESSIONS PRESS

Baltimore • London • Winnipeg • Sydney

Health Professions Press, Inc.
Post Office Box 10624
Baltimore, Maryland 21285-0624

www.healthpropress.com

Typeset by Barton Matheson Willse & Worthington, Baltimore, Maryland.
Cover design by XinaDesign, Baltimore, Maryland.
Manufactured in the United States of America.

Cover photograph: Photo credit Comstock, Inc.

"Father Time," by Christopher de Vinck, appeared in *The Wall Street Journal*, June 17, 1994, p. A14.
Republished with permission of Dow Jones & Co., Inc.; permission conveyed through Copyright
Clearance Center, Inc.

Figures 2 and 3 in Chapter 11 by Juanita Wassenaar-Beggs (from *Falls in Older Persons: Prevention &
Management*, 2nd edition, © 1998 by Health Professions Press, Inc.).

Library of Congress Cataloging-in-Publication Data
Beckerman, Anita.
    It takes more than love : a practical guide to taking care of an aging adult /
by Anita Beckerman and Ruth M. Tappen.
        p. cm.
    Includes bibliographical references and index.
    ISBN 1-878812-50-5
    1. Aged—Home care Handbooks, manuals, etc. 2. Caregivers Handbooks,
manuals, etc. I. Tappen, Ruth M. II. Title.
HV1451.B419   1999
362.6—dc21   99-28049
                                                                                      CIP

British Library Cataloguing in Publication Data are available from the British Library.

For my husband Herb; our eight children, Sylvia, Miriam, David & David, Ruth & Andrew, and Michelle & Lawrence; and five grandchildren, Matthew, Lenny, Alex, Molly, and Mayann.

For my mother—may she rest in peace. Thank you for being my role model.

—Anita G. Beckerman

For my parents, Edna and Gerard Marchand, who never questioned
that they would care for each other; and for my grandparents, Gertrude and
Oswald Marchand and Dorothea and Daniel Reichelt, whose strength and courage
have always been my inspiration.

—Ruth M. Tappen

Contents

Acknowledgments

We thank our editors, Mary Magnus and Anita McCabe, for understanding and supporting the meaning of what we wanted to convey in our book. Their comments and suggestions always took into account our objectives for the book, and for that we are very thankful.

Special thanks go to David D. Wexler, whose untiring efforts facilitated the process that enabled us to publish this book.

1   Introduction

No person was ever honored for what he received.
Honor has been the reward for what he gave.

Calvin Coolidge

Your 70-year-old mother could be living alone for the first time in her life.

Your husband, who has always been the backbone of the family, could be unable to speak or feed himself after a massive stroke.

Your brother or sister, best friend, or neighbor could have cancer and no one but you to turn to for help.

At one time or another, most older people find that they need help from others. This help may come in the form of advice and counsel, emotional support, financial help, or what health care professionals call "hands-on help" taking medications, changing dressings, or performing personal care. You chose or have been chosen to provide that help to the older adult in your life, and you'd like to learn more about giving care to him or her. This book can help you.

As shorter hospital and nursing facility stays continue to be emphasized and costs continue to rise, more and more family and friends are called on to provide the type of care that once was the province of paid professionals. Few people are really prepared to provide this kind of care to an older person. The responsibilities can be complex and time consuming and can encompass a wide range of tasks that the ordinary person has probably never performed.

Beyond learning specific caregiving tasks, a caregiver needs to realize the wider ramifications of his or her role. You'll be called on to give your time, your energy, and maybe even your physical strength to caregiving. Being a caregiver also may involve your financial resources, your ingenuity, and your problem-solving skills. Demands are placed on your emotional and psychological resources.

There is both joy and pain in being a caregiver. Your feelings will swing between the two. You'll feel

> *satisfaction* from having made a difference
>
> *sorrow* that a loved one may be suffering, that a future together could be compromised
>
> *pleasure* from seeing relief on the person's face when you lend a hand
>
> *worry* when your loved one refuses needed help or his or her condition requires that extra safety measures be taken
>
> *warmth* from the affection shared
>
> *anger* at another friend or relative who won't help

Caregiving can bring a lot of satisfaction from doing something selfless and important, but it's also stressful for the person giving the care. You already may be overwhelmed by family and work responsibilities, uncomfortable with the idea of being a care provider, or even ill and disabled yourself. The older person you're trying to help may be angry or depressed because he or she needs help and can no longer manage independently.

One of the stresses of caregiving is the distress that you feel when you see what has happened or is happening to the older adult in your life:

> *Mom was a proud, dignified woman. Now she messes in her pants. I know it upsets her even though she never says so. It upsets me, too.*
>
> *He is in pain most of the time. I can't bear to see him suffer so much.*
>
> *He's dependent on me for everything. He always hated having to ask other people for help. Still does.*

> *She's despondent since the last amputation. Doesn't think life is worth living anymore. Her despair gets me down. I don't know how to help her.*

Another source of stress is giving the amount of time and energy that caregiving often demands. It's relatively easy to provide an occasional hand with housecleaning or a ride to the doctor. However, some older people need far more help, sometimes around the clock. These demands can be difficult for caregivers to manage:

> *I have three kids, a demanding job, and a husband who can't help much either. How much more responsibility can I take on?*

> *My own health isn't so good either. I have cataracts so I can't drive anymore, at least not until I can have them removed. And my blood pressure is out of control. The doctor said it was stress.*

> *My marriage is already strained, almost to the breaking point. Adding caregiving responsibilities right now is too much for me to handle.*

Sometimes it's the emotional strain rather than the demands on time that is a caregiver's primary concern:

> *We never got along well. What makes you think it's better now just because he's sick?*

> *She was supposed to take care of me. Now I have to take care of her. I wasn't prepared for this.*

> *He yells at me if I don't do something exactly how he wants it done. It's getting on my nerves. I'm eating too much, and I started smoking again. At night I'm exhausted, but I can't sleep.*

Caregiving confronts caregivers with their own vulnerability. "This could be me," is a thought that occurs to many caregivers.

For some, that thought is all the more reason to be as caring as possible, whereas for others, the thought is so uncomfortable and frightening that they want to run away from the situation, pretend that it's not happening, that it couldn't happen to them.

Caregiving can create serious strains within families. Many times, when decisions are being made about who will provide care and how it will be provided, issues that have been suppressed or ignored for years may be reignited: Old resentments resurface, ancient slights are remembered suddenly, and undercurrents of conflict are brought into the open. The atmosphere can become emotionally charged and difficult to handle without some guidance, such as what this book can provide.

The physical care of the older adult in your life may require you to get some "how-to" knowledge. Many physical changes take place as a person ages, changes that are considered "normal" aging. Separating these normal changes from health problems that need attention is something that even physicians are still learning to do well. There are still many misconceptions about older people's needs for continued activity, a healthy diet, and preventive care, such as flu shots, mammograms, and prostate examinations. Although we can't provide details on managing every health problem that could come up, we'll share the fundamentals of providing hands-on care for an ill or disabled older person, including some important principles for using medications.

In most communities there are many services available to older people who need help, but finding the right services and ways to pay for them can be quite a challenge. Even aging services professionals have trouble keeping up with the changes in what's available and in the rules concerning whom is eligible for them. With even more changes in benefits being debated at state and federal levels, we don't expect this situation to improve soon. In fact, it may become more confusing, maybe even more difficult, to arrange needed services.

There is good news, however. Once you've learned the basic terminology—for example, the difference between Medicare and Medicaid and what each will pay for—you'll be able to ask the right questions and help the older adult in your life find the services that he or she needs. How important is this aspect of caregiving? The following examples may give you an idea of what a difference locating the right services can make to you and the person you're caring for:

> *Dad's eyesight is so poor and his hands are so unsteady that he can't cook for himself anymore. But with home-delivered meals and housecleaning help, he does just fine on his own. I call him every evening to see how he is and visit him once a week. He really prefers to live in the home he and Mom shared for so many years, and these services make it possible.*

> *Without the Alzheimer's day center, I would've had to put Ralph in a nursing home a long time ago. While he's there, I can run errands, have lunch with friends, or go home and take a nap without worrying about what he's doing. It gives me a time of peace and quiet that refreshes me, and then I'm ready to take care of him again. Ralph enjoys getting out and seeing people. He's usually tired but happy when he comes home in the afternoon, so it works for both of us.*

You may have to make some very difficult choices along the way. These choices often revolve around how much and what type of help you can or should give, how to balance everyone's needs, and how to be helpful without creating unnecessary dependence. Here are a few examples:

> *Should I encourage my mother to move in with us, or should I encourage her to try to manage on her own? We would be happy to have her here, but is it good for her?*

> *I can either reduce my work hours in order to stay home and care for my wife or I can hire help and continue to work. Which one is the right choice?*

> *I have very little free time. Should I spend it with my children, my husband, or my parents, who are both really frail?*

> *The doctor gave my father three choices: radical surgery, conservative surgery, or chemotherapy. Each has risks and*

each has benefits. Which is best for him? Should I help him decide?

None of these questions has easy answers. Open, caring conversation between caregiver and care receiver can help everyone to feel more comfortable making choices. It's so important that everyone be genuinely involved in the decisions, especially the older person. Many of these difficult decisions are discussed in this book.

We also offer suggestions about the concerns that many of you have; for example, how to balance caregiving with other responsibilities and how to meet your own needs as well as those of the older adult in your life. We speak from our own experience as specialists in the care of older people as well as from the knowledge and experience of other experts in the field. It's our hope that what we have to share with you helps to lighten the load for you both physically and emotionally and to make the caregiving experience more rewarding for you and for the older person you're caring for.

1

Becoming a Caregiver

2

Caregiving Challenges

Caregiving encompasses any type of help that one person gives another person. No matter how independent we are, all of us need help sometimes, and the amount of help can vary a great deal. In this book, we focus on the type of help that's commonly provided by family members and friends to older adults. This help may consist of advice and counsel, or it may involve hands-on help with remembering medications, changing dressings, or performing personal care.

Caring is the emotional component of caregiving. It encompasses the positive feelings we have for a loved one that lead us to provide care when it's needed. Sometimes, though, a sense of obligation and guilt rather than love leads one person to help another.

The *primary caregiver* is the person who has the main responsibility for providing care to the dependent older adult in his or her life. If the dependent older person is married or is involved in a long-term relationship, then the spouse or partner usually is the person who assumes the role of the primary caregiver. If the dependent older person doesn't have a spouse or longtime companion, a son or daughter often becomes the primary caregiver. If there are no adult children or they are unable or unwilling to provide care, other relatives or friends may step in to help.

Caregiving responsibilities are easier to assume when the primary caregiver can rely on others to share the responsibilities or to provide *respite*, a break from caregiving. Too often, however, one person is left with total responsibility for caregiving, which we'll discuss in later chapters.

The care that's provided may be mainly *psychological*—for example, listening to the older person's concerns or helping him or her work through a problem—or it may be *physical*—for instance, repairing a leaking roof or helping the person to bathe. Sometimes an older person's care needs are only temporary. Maybe a serious injury has made it impossible for the person to continue to live alone without assistance. After several weeks of recuperation during which care is provided by part-time or live-in care providers, the older person may be able to resume his or her active, independent lifestyle. At other times, the person and his or her family conclude that he or she won't recover or regain the ability to function independently. Family members may then decide that they'll provide the long-term assistance that's required.

All old people aren't alike—one person may not want or need the same kind of help as another older person. In fact, some older people don't want any help at all, even when they need it. To complicate matters further, many caregivers—even spouses—fail to ask the older person what type of assistance he or she wants. The following scenario illustrates the importance of asking such questions.

Mary

Mary is an independent 75-year-old widow who fell and broke her hip on an icy sidewalk. After being hospitalized for a week, she was transferred to a rehabilitation hospital to regain strength and balance so she could walk independently again. Mary's friend, Isabel, was concerned that Mary would be lonely in the hospital, knowing that she had no family nearby. When she visited Mary in the rehabilitation hospital, she promised, "I'll come every day. Then you won't feel alone."

"Oh, I'm fine," Mary responded. "My family calls me every day and the nurses are really nice. In fact, my

Care Commonly Provided by Family or Friend Caregivers

Emotional support
Housekeeping and meal preparation
Transportation
Financial support
Personal care (help with washing, dressing, and so forth)
Home repair
Companionship
Spiritual support
Protection, safety
Bureaucratic mediation—helping the older person navigate through government or other bureaucracy

brother calls me too much. Every time I fall asleep, the telephone rings. But you're sweet to think of me. Just come whenever you feel like it."

"Is there anything else you need?" asked Isabel. "Would you like me to stop by your apartment to pick up your mail or water your plants?" Mary replied, "My neighbor is taking care of everything. But I'm worried about Toby, my Schnauzer. My neighbor has three children and they tease him a lot."

"Oh, I'd love to watch Toby!" exclaimed Isabel. "Can I bring him to my house until you come home? I'd enjoy taking care of him."

"Isabel, that would be wonderful! I've been really concerned about Toby. Now I can stop worrying and concentrate on getting better. The doctor said I should be home in three weeks if I work really hard at my physical therapy."

Isabel assumed that Mary was lonely and wanted company. In reality, Mary was worried about failing to meet one of her responsibilities while she was in the hospital. When Isabel asked Mary what she needed, Mary explained her situation and Isabel was able to provide the help that Mary truly needed.

Let's look at some of the most common challenges in caregiving—problems and issues that arise when the older adult in your life needs care. These problems and issues include balancing obligations and entitlements, deciding how much help is needed, deciding if the older person should live with you, dealing with your own guilt and anger, dealing with the care receiver's stubbornness and refusal, confronting the older adult's resistance to care, handling your loved one's increasing dependence, and that ever-difficult subject, handling money.

BALANCING OBLIGATIONS AND ENTITLEMENTS

Family therapists use different approaches to analyze the feelings, events, and relationships—both past and present—that affect family members' responses to one another. One approach that's particularly helpful in thinking about caregiving relationships is the idea that a balance must be struck between obligations and entitlements. In other words, this is the very important idea that give and take occurs, or should occur, between family members and that, in general, people want to feel that they're both giving and taking something of value in their relationships.

In healthy relationships, balance or reciprocity (the give and take that's essential in a healthy relationship) exists to some degree. Each person in the relationship has certain obligations that he or she is expected to honor. The other person (or people, in the case of a family) also has certain obligations that he or she is expected to honor in return. The obligations of one person are, in effect, what the other is entitled to in the relationship. If one person continually fails to honor his or her obligations—always takes without giving—the relationship eventually breaks down. Consider the following example: Judy expects love, respect, and intimacy from her husband Jim. He, in turn, expects the same from her. If both Judy and Jim reciprocate these feelings and attitudes, then their affection for each other will deepen, their trust in each other will increase, and the relationship will flourish. But if Jim feels that he gives Judy love, respect, and intimacy and doesn't receive the same in return, he's likely to be disappointed at the unfairness of the situation. If neither Jim nor Judy give or receive love, respect, or intimacy, then their "relationship ledger" is bankrupt, and, therefore, the relationship is unhealthy.

In intergenerational relationships (relationships across generations; for example, father and adult daughter) the reciprocity of the relationship ledger isn't always so evenly balanced, and the expectations of each person in the relationship aren't always the same. Parents and their infant children are an example of an unbalanced intergenerational relationship. Parents give an infant a great deal: nourishment, shelter, clothing, protection, love, comfort, and personal care, among other things. In return, they're satisfied to receive evidence that the infant responds to their efforts. As the infant grows and matures, reciprocity evens out, and perhaps achieves balance when the infant eventually becomes an adult.

At some point in any family's life cycle, the balance between obligations and entitlements may shift abruptly. For example, an adult son may be badly injured in a car accident, leaving him needing to be cared for by either his wife or his parents. In most family life cycles, however, it's the older adult who needs help from spouse or children. Perhaps an older woman has a stroke that leaves her unable to speak clearly or walk without using a cane. If she is married, she'll probably be cared for by her husband. If he's unable to provide care—perhaps because of his own health problems—he may turn to his adult children for help.

Although society wholeheartedly supports, even demands, the all-encompassing care that parents give an infant, it's ambivalent about the amount of help an older person can or should expect from his or her family. If the person's relationships with family members have been mostly good and there has been some level of reciprocity, help or care usually is given freely and without resentment. If family relationships have not been well-balanced, and help is provided anyway, it's likely to be given in an atmosphere of conflict and stress. Bitterness, anger, guilt, resentment, anxiety, or depression can develop in either or both caregiver and care receiver.

AVOIDING BECOMING OVERWHELMED

Luisa and John

Luisa and John, both in their mid-80s, live in a retirement community located 150 miles from their oldest daughter, Anna. Their youngest daughter, Linda, lives closer to her parents, but because Anna is a registered nurse and older, they felt that she was the logical person to go to in a crisis. They turned to Anna after Luisa was involved in a minor automobile accident. Although Luisa sustained only minor bruises and the other driver was unhurt, she became more and more nervous in the days following the crash. She had difficulty sleeping and ate little. John responded to Luisa's psychological distress by becoming agitated and irritable, often losing his temper when Luisa wouldn't eat.

When her father called her to help, Anna put aside her other responsibilities to visit her parents. On arriving at her parents' home, Anna found them greatly altered, not so much in their physical states as in their emotional states and their ability to make decisions. The nervousness and anxiety they both experienced as a result of the accident left them unable to cope with the everyday demands of living, although they had done so successfully in the past. During the following 2 weeks, Anna drove every day from her parents' home to her job and to her own home and back again. No sooner would she return from her parents' house than she would get a telephone call from either Linda or, most often, her parents to respond to another "crisis." Anna found it easier to say that she would come back than to find a solution from a distance.

Anna quickly began to feel trapped in an increasingly stressful cycle of long-distance travel, caregiving, and responsibilities at work and at home. Because she lived so far away from her parents, she was unable to add the time demands of caregiving easily to her existing roles. She felt guilty, realizing that she was neglecting her work and family because of the constant traveling to help her parents, and she was frustrated by her inability to juggle these conflicting demands. Because she was under increasing emotional and physical stress, Anna was unable to evaluate the situation objectively or to identify options that might resolve her dilemma.

If you were in Anna's situation, what would you do to minimize the stress associated with taking on the role of primary caregiver and to prevent potential problems? When you assume the responsibilities of caregiving, you need to ask yourself the following questions:

- What are my responsibilities and obligations to the care receiver(s)? to other people (my spouse, my children, other members of my family)? to my friends? to my job? to my employer?
- Does the person for whom I have assumed the caregiving role live far away from me? Will I need to make long-distance arrangements for care or a change in the person's living arrangements?
- What impact will a change in my loved one's living arrangements have on everyone?
- If the living arrangements aren't changed, what impact will that have on me (the primary caregiver)?
- Do I feel guilty or angry because of the change in this relationship and the addition of the caregiving role to my other responsibilities?
- Is my guilt or anger making me impatient? Do my feelings occasionally lead me to neglect the person I'm caring for, myself, or other people? Am I afraid that I'm going to strike out, physically or verbally, at my loved one?
- Am I feeling financial pressures and changes that are related to the addition of caregiving to my life?

The answers to these questions can help you identify whether you need additional support or alternative strategies to help you cope with the demands of caregiving.

When you make caregiving a priority, the sudden, intense involvement can take over your life, placing personal and professional commitments on the back burner, as it did in Anna's life. Caregivers sometimes allow their sense of responsibility regarding the older adult in their life to grow out of proportion, and they focus on what they can't do rather than on what they're able to accomplish. Some caregivers even believe that an injury or other crisis will happen to their loved one(s) if they aren't physically present. This exaggerated sense of responsibility and overprotectiveness—thinking, feeling, or acting for the older adult—can interfere with your other responsibilities. Not only can overprotecting the care receiver emotionally or physically take over your life, but it can make the person feel helpless rather than helped. You must give care in such a way that your loved one's sense of autonomy and individuality aren't diminished.

Luisa and John had been doing fine on their own before the car accident. They were temporarily unnerved by the accident and needed some support until they recovered. Anna was in danger of making them far more dependent than they needed to be. Anna did come to realize that she was doing too much and began to turn over the responsibility for decision making to her parents. She began limiting her visits; soon her parents were advising Anna that she needed to spend more time with her own family! They assured her that they were doing just fine on their own.

MOVING IN TOGETHER

When the older adult in your life is no longer able to live independently, you may have to decide whether to move him or her into your home or that of another family member. You'll need some guidance to make that decision, so let's look at some hypothetical pros and cons.

Pros
Mom's health and safety are at risk, so having her live with us will help her and lessen my concerns. I can keep an eye on her and spend more time with her, too.

If Dad comes to live with us, we'll have more opportunities to reminisce, to have the kind of friendly talk that we've never seemed to have enough time for.

If Mom comes to live with us, the kids will have a chance to really get to know their grandmother. If Mom takes over in the kitchen or watches the 10- and 13-year-olds after school, I won't have to rush home to make dinner or struggle so hard to balance the demands of my job and home. (WARNING: *Although this scenario seems ideal, it may not be so easy to adjust to the changes in living arrangements, and the older person may not be willing or able to assume some of your responsibilities.)*

Cons

Dad and I have lived independently for a long time, since I was a teenager. His habits, routines, and experiences are probably very different from my family's. Whose routine will have to change?

I'm not sure we have enough room for all of Mom's furniture, pictures, china, and other mementos. I don't want the girls to have to give up their play space in the attic or share a bedroom, but Mom shouldn't have to give up anything either.

Dad's ideas about disciplining the kids aren't a problem during a short visit, but they are different, which could become a serious issue if he comes here to live.

Questions you may want to ask yourself if you are considering asking a parent or older family member to move into your home include the following:

- Does he want to move in with us? Is this a good move for him? Is it really necessary? What are the alternatives?
- Have I consulted my spouse and children about making this change, or am I making the decision without their input, not seeing the effect this decision could have on our relationship and our living arrangements? Is this an opportunity for everyone to establish a closer relationship with each other?
- How do I feel about the loss of freedom or privacy that will come with moving her into our house? Will we still feel comfortable here? Will we need to close doors just to have private time?

Issues such as what is the meaning of privacy and personal space to each person living in the house and how individual privacy and personal space can be achieved and maintained in the new arrangement must be considered before making a final decision. Ask each family member directly about his or her concerns regarding privacy and personal space. When all of the members of a family are involved in the decision-making process and knowledge of the full extent of their own and others' responsibilities and commitments is available, the transition period that comes with integrating another family member into the household is easier. Family members who are prepared will be less resentful about giving up some of their privacy and/or personal space and will more likely view the change as an opportunity for greater closeness and for sharing life experiences with the older adult.

FEELING AND HANDLING GUILT AND ANGER

Guilt and anger, which often occur together, are common to both caregivers and the people they care for. This position of dependence is not what the older adult expected; up to this point, he or she had been able to handle the various responsibilities and problems of adulthood. The older adult may feel that parents are supposed to care for their children, not the other way around, or that this situation is in some way self-induced: Perhaps choices or mistakes made earlier in the older adult's life have resulted in a progressive debilitating health problem or in financial dependence. Guilt can stem from the individual's feeling that he or she didn't eat the right foods, exercise enough, stop smoking, or save enough money for retirement.

An older adult may feel anger with him- or herself, with a spouse who promised "to love and to cherish" but who died instead, or with God because God deserted him or her in a time of need. You (the caregiver) might be angry because you'd looked forward to having fewer responsibilities at this time of life: Your children may be grown or increasingly independent, your finances may be somewhat more stable, and your lifestyle may be more relaxed. Your anger may grow from the feeling that the choice wasn't entirely voluntary but was based on the obligations of child to parent or of one family member to another. Guilt can grow out of anger. (Chapter 3 examines how to deal with these feelings and with other family members.)

Family members can create feelings of guilt in one another. They also may attempt to control one another's actions by engaging in manipulative behavior:

Bill's older brother, Frank, who has a chronic heart condition, has come to live with him. Whenever Bill starts toward the front door, Frank pleads with him not to leave, exclaiming, "I'll have a heart attack if you leave." Even though Bill has made arrangements for necessary care to be performed in his absence and has explained these arrangements to Frank repeatedly, he still feels guilty when he leaves. Bill is becoming increasingly short-tempered with Frank and is curtailing his outside activities to avoid feeling guilty or, as Bill says, "God forbid I should give him a heart attack. I could never live with myself!"

Bill needs to recognize that Frank's behavior is manipulative before he can stop reacting to it. Keep in mind that the use of manipulative behaviors isn't always deliberate or conscious. Frank may be feeling extremely anxious about being left alone. In this instance, discussing his concerns may help Bill identify a solution that meets both of their needs.

Family members' uncertainty about what is the "right thing to do" can generate a lot of different feelings at once, fear being only one of them:

Ginny eats only a small portion at each meal, telling her son, David, that she isn't hungry and doesn't want to eat. David is scared and angry with his mother but isn't sure whether he should let her have her way or force her to eat. Is he being neglectful or respectful of Ginny's independence if he accedes to her wishes? Is it guilt that makes David angry?

David needs to determine whether his mother's behavior is unhealthy or unsafe or her nutritional needs are being met. If not, David is neglectful if he doesn't take action to remedy a potentially harmful situation. Maybe Ginny is depressed. Perhaps changes in taste and smell associated with normal aging are affecting Ginny's desire for particular foods. Awareness of these normal changes of aging (described in detail in Chapter 6) can give David the knowledge to explore food preferences with Ginny, which may result in her eating more food at each meal.

You need to analyze every situation before you can make any decisions or take action: Why are you feeling guilty or angry? Is your loved one really at risk, or is something else going on?

DEALING WITH YOUR LOVED ONE'S STUBBORNESS/REFUSAL

Older adults who refuse to eat, go out, go to the doctor, get a hearing aid, or who you feel are just being stubborn about everything can be very frustrating. Frustration aside, they do have the right to refuse. What's needed in such situations is a full understanding of your loved one's reasons for his or her stubbornness/refusal.

If your loved one refuses to eat, you need to ask yourself whether this action has to do with his or her feeling lonely, especially if the older person lives alone. Food and eating are vehicles for communication and socialization. When a person who lives alone eats alone, he or she misses out on the social aspect that's associated with eating (for example, reminiscing about "the good old days," sharing a sumptuous dessert). The lonely person may lack the desire to prepare and eat food and this can lead to malnutrition, which then leads to apathy and listlessness.

You may feel at a loss about what to do when the older person in your life, whether living with you or living alone, refuses to leave the house. Your mother may say that she prefers to be alone to watch television, or to be by herself with her thoughts. Don't jump to the conclusion that she's depressed; she may simply be actively engaged in reminiscing about her life. The best that you can do in such a situation is to compromise—let her have her reminiscing sessions but ask her to promise to go out with you once a week for lunch.

Some older people stubbornly refuse to go to the doctor. This situation can be difficult to handle without your seeming autocratic or overbearing to your loved one. Most doctor visits are for preventive treatment services—a mammogram, a Pap test, an examination for testicular cancer, a test for blood in the stool, a follow-up evaluation of the prescribed treatment for a chronic medical condition. In responding to their refusal, you should ask yourself some questions. These questions focus on the possible personal discomfort and embarrassment that the older person may associate with examinations such as Pap tests and colorectal testing. It's important to understand and try to accept generational differences about health care practices as you measure the benefits against the mostly psychological risks of the tests. If you believe that the benefits are advantageous, you might explain the examination in as much detail as possible to the person to decrease the stress of the experience.

Some older adults who refuse to get a hearing aid, new glasses, or a new winter coat do so because they feel guilty about the cost of these services/aids. Many older people feel that at this stage of their life, they would rather "make do" with what they already have. They may have "rainy day" or emergency funds set aside, but in many cases they want the money to go to their children and grandchildren after they die. It's a way for them to feel that they achieved something in life and are still able to give to others. Take the example of Mary, who at age 83 was fairly alert and oriented and still had a very strong sense of pride. All through her life she'd found it very difficult to accept help from others; she believed that she had to be the giver, even if giving involved sacrifice on her part. When Mary found herself becoming physically dependent on others because of her increasing frailty, she couldn't cope with the change in role. After watching her bump into furniture repeatedly, her daughter suggested, "Mother, I think you need new glasses." Mary dismissed her claim: "No, dear, my glasses are just fine. Don't worry about me." But her daughter had reason to worry; in reality, Mary's doctor told her that she needed cataract surgery, but Mary hadn't informed her daughter. Because of the cost of the surgery and because she didn't want to worry her daughter, Mary decided that she could "make do" by using her other senses to compensate for her vision loss.

Caregivers need to understand and accept the losses that have occurred in the older person's life, such as a spouse's death, illness, or relocation to a nursing facility. They need to make time to talk with their frail loved one, to express their admiration and thanks for all that he or she has done for them. And they need to say, gently, that the person must understand that the way they need to show their appreciation is to give to the older person. Many times the older, dependent person doesn't know how to respond to such an offer. Caregivers need to understand, accept, and be patient.

CONFRONTING RESISTANCE TO CARE

Older people's resistance to care is another behavior that can be frustrating to caregivers. Sometimes resistance is focused on an individual who's helping the family caregiver. What's important to consider in this case is the type of care that's being resisted; ask yourself whether the way care is provided is necessary to the older person's well-being. For example, before he broke his hip, Sam liked to take a bath before bedtime. He said that it helped him relax after a long day. After he returned home from hip surgery, his youngest sister hired someone to help her with his activities of daily living (ADLs). The home health care worker's set schedule included giving a bath after breakfast. This had not been a part of Sam's routine before, and he couldn't see any reason to change now, so he strenuously resisted this care. The best solution in this case would've been for Sam's sister to negotiate a compromise. She could've said, "Since I can't help out much during the week because I have to work, and I would much rather spend time relaxing and talking with you at night, maybe you could take your bath in the morning. Then, on the weekend, I could help you bathe right before bed, just like you're used to. What do you think?"

Another consideration in handling a person's resistance to outside caregiving is the need for the primary caregiver to make sure that the reason for the resistance is not inappropriate care. Ask whether the older person is being cared for with loving care. Spend some time with the older adult and the caregiver. Observe their interactions and how care is provided. Is the caregiver being rough with the older person? Be careful how "rough" is interpreted, however. Because of the normal changes associated with aging, skin is thinner and more fragile than it was when the person was young, bones are more brittle and sometimes painful to move, especially if the person also has arthritis. Simple motions that are used in dressing, moving, and bathing the older person can result in discomfort, which observers can interpret as the caregiver's handling the person roughly. Many older people don't want to complain but tend to "voice" their discomfort by resisting care. Again, the best solution is open communication among the primary caregiver, the outside caregiver, and the older person, along with a full assessment of the situation.

Suppose you're the primary caregiver and your loved one is resisting your care. Your approach shouldn't be different from that used with outside caregivers. You still need to take into account the normal changes associated with aging and how they may affect your caregiving procedures. Also ask yourself whether you need to do that particular task every day. Let's take the example of bathing. Is your loved one participating in activities that necessitate daily bathing? If so, maybe you can reach a compromise with the person. Maybe she could give herself a sponge bath, which lets her feel clean and independent, and that she's not a burden on you. Be aware, however, that most older people should not bathe every day. Older skin has decreased fat stores and lubrication, so daily bathing can deplete the skin's oils and make it susceptible to injury from simple handling. Open communication also is important in this situation. Try to talk with the older person about what you feel is his resistance to care. Don't make accusations or speak in an angry tone of voice; just share your feelings and express to him that you hope he will share his.

Some people's resistance to personal care is because they're embarrassed about exposing their bodies to you. Their embarrassment may be based on cultural and/or religious beliefs and practices. You may hear, "In my day, this just wasn't done." In such cases, providing them with privacy during caregiving is a priority. Again, using bathing as an example, give the older person the opportunity to wash her own genitals or breasts if she is physically able to do so. When you help her to go to the bathroom, provide privacy and sufficient time, even if she is using a bedpan or bedside commode (or, in the case of an older gentleman, a urinal). Put yourself in her shoes—think about what you would need to attend effectively to your bodily functions.

HANDLING YOUR LOVED ONE'S INCREASING DEPENDENCE

As people age and become frail, they become increasingly dependent on others to care for them. They need help to dress, eat, urinate/defecate, move about the house, shop, and so forth. Their decreased ability or complete inability to manage may cause them to lose confidence, experience shame and diminished self-esteem, and feel incompetent. Some become angry and fear for their future; others do nothing (become immobilized) to seek help in a passive-aggressive way by becoming helpless or manipulative. These behaviors are certainly challenging to caregivers, but you can handle them.

The first step in dealing with these behaviors is to "walk a mile in their shoes." Think about how you'd feel if your ability to care for yourself was taken away, and you became dependent on others for everything. What do you think you would do to hold on to a small piece of independence, of yourself? You'd probably appreciate your caregiver's letting you do everything you were still capable of doing. That's your goal as primary caregiver—to give back some control to the older person, within his remaining capabilities, to allow him to preserve his self-esteem and dignity. If he is unable to make any decisions about his care, he can still participate in the process, even if in a small way. For example, ask him to help you with his bath or at mealtime: You soap up the washcloth (requires dexterity), but let him wash his face; you cut up his food, butter the bread, and pour the coffee, but let him feed himself with the proper utensils. It's not important that the act of bathing or eating be tidy or efficient or be done your way; what is important is that the older person in your life be allowed to keep his dignity and independence. Just be there for him and with him; give him the time, patience, and support he needs to maintain some measure of independence in ADLs. He could be a happier, more content person as a result.

HANDLING MONEY

Money—who has it and how it's used or misused—is an emotionally charged issue. Whose responsibility is it to make decisions regarding the use of the older adult's money? Is a dependent older person obligated to turn over her money to her children or grandchildren? Is it acceptable to save the money for a "rainy day" or to spend it in a way that brings her pleasure in later years? Should you go into debt to care for your parents or older sibling or spouse? To what extent? Should you give up your job in order to become a full-time caregiver? If you do so, will you be able to manage despite the loss of income? These are difficult questions and the right answers for you and your family will depend on your situation.

Family members need to discuss the financial obligations of caregiving before one or more members assume the responsibility. They should identify how these obligations will be handled and who'll be responsible in a particular situation. Whenever possible, family members should share financial responsibility for caregiving. If this approach fails, then a third party (for example, a trusted friend or religious counselor) can be brought in to mediate and resolve the situation.

Some older adults, especially those with cognitive impairment, are unable to manage their finances without assistance and don't know how to negotiate the system to obtain help. The interests of both care receiver and caregiver usually are best served in these cases if the caregiver takes control of the older adult's finances. Many older people are eligible for government assistance (food stamps or welfare, for example), which could lessen their caregiver's financial burden, but they refuse to even consider it because, "I'd rather starve than go on welfare." Your first response might be anger. This is a normal response, but step back from the situation and think about why they might refuse government assistance. Perhaps they're worried about what the neighbors will think if they find out. Maybe it signals a loss of "face" for them. It may remind them of their childhood during the Great Depression. Exploring the reasons behind their refusal helps you to reach a fuller understanding of and resolution to this issue. One solution may be to remind your loved one that he or she worked hard and contributed to these assistance programs through taxes and therefore earned the right to them; this may change your parent's perception of these services as a demeaning "handout."

Often, family members view an older adult's financial status from dramatically different perspectives. Younger family members who are caring for Uncle Willie may feel that they should get his money now, while caregiving is consuming their own money, rather than be forced to wait until he dies. Uncle Willie, in contrast, may view his life savings as his "security blanket" and not want to give it up. Many older adults were children or young adults in the 1930s and remember the hard times of the Great Depression, when they or their parents didn't have money for food, clothing, or medical care. These experiences still resonate strongly with them, and cause many people to be very cautious and conservative in money matters. Younger people may not understand the effects that a profound experience like the Depression can have on their older relatives, and anger and resentment may result.

3   Understanding Family Relationships

"My husband's aunt died last week," a friend told me, sorrowfully. "She was the last of the older generation. Over the past 30 years he was always helping one or the other of his older relatives with something. He won't be doing that anymore. He's going to miss that." Although profound sadness was evident in what she said, her words also conveyed the deep satisfaction and the love that her husband had gained from helping his older relatives. My friend described the events of the previous week as she and her husband sorted through his aunt's possessions. "All the treasures of the family wound up at her house. It was a wonderful way to mourn."

These activities, although painful, provided an opportunity for a friend and her husband to connect with their past, to be reminded of both the continuity and the change that occur through time, and how the past relates to who we are in the present.

Another friend has taken up genealogy. In her kitchen she has mounted what looks like a huge sunburst; it's actually a very detailed genealogical chart. She and her husband are at the center, their respective parents form the first circle around them, each of their parents form the next circle out, and so forth. While researching the chart, she uncovered information about many family members, some long-dead, that brings the lives of these individuals into sharper focus and provides stories that fascinate both family members and friends.

The power of family to affect our lives deeply is evident in both situations.

THE SIGNIFICANCE OF FAMILY

Families are significant influences on our lives—sometimes helpful, sometimes hurtful. At times, our families place extraordinary demands on us; at other times they're heroic in the ways that they come to our rescue. For some of us, the word *family* primarily represents pleasure, for others, it denotes mostly pain. Family relationships seem to have the dual power to hurt us more deeply and satisfy us more fully than most other relationships. In fact, when a relationship with another person becomes close or intimate, the person often is described as being "just like family."

Our relationships with family members generate love, joy, concern, grief, sadness, anger, and, sometimes, even hatred. J. L. Framo, a well-known family therapist, describes the enormous impact of family:

> Families can provide the deepest satisfaction of living: unreserved and unconditional love; gratifying bonding; measureless sacrifice; enduring dependability; compassionate belonging; the joys of warmth and family holidays, dinners and vacations; the fun and the play; the give and the take; and knowing your family is always there when needed. Still, the hurts and damage that family members can inflict upon one another are infinite: scapegoating; humiliation and shaming; parentification; crazy-making; physical, sexual and psychological abuse; cruel rejections, lies and deceit, and the manifold outrages against the human spirit.

Why are family relationships different from other relationships? Why, for example, do family members seem to matter so much to us, even when we're distant from them? First, they're not entirely voluntary relationships. Each of us is born into a certain family often called "the family of origin"; we're related to a given set of people by definition, not by choice. Most of our other relationships have at least some element of choice about them, but our relationships with our families of origin don't.

Second, by the time we reach middle or old age, our family relationships have endured, for better or worse, for decades. Whether these relationships are pleasant or unpleasant (usually in combination), we share memories with other family members. Even more than the memories themselves, many of us share our interpretations of these events as well.

Third, families develop traditions—the proper way to cele-brate a particular holiday, for example. Families also develop their own styles—how to relax, how to have fun, how to respond to a crisis, how to handle a problem. When a problem arises, some families talk about it continuously, others bury it under a shroud of silence, and still other families try to work out a solution to-gether. Unless we stop to think about it, most of us are unaware of how deeply ingrained those traditions and styles are, the extent to which we use the same approaches that our parents or grandpar-ents used.

MYTHS ABOUT AMERICAN FAMILIES

There are numerous myths about the way American families in-teract with their older family members. These myths are so em-bedded in our national psyche that they are like punching bag

clowns: Every time you knock them down, they spring right back up. Let's consider three of the most stubborn myths.

We Used to Live Together in Big Extended Families

Prior to the post–World War II move to the suburbs, many Americans lived in a nuclear family unit—mother, father, sister(s), brother(s). The average life expectancy was much shorter than it is now. Because most people did not live to their 80s and 90s, few families included among their members someone of that age.

Americans Today Have Less Contact with Older Members of Their Families

More than 30 years of research has disproved this myth, but we still believe it even after we read the research results. The research shows that most older Americans live near at least one of their adult children and that they hear from their children several times a week, if not daily. This certainly does not constitute a nation-wide abandonment of our elders.

Most Older Adults Are Dependent on the Younger Generation

Most older people are relatively healthy and independent and are quite capable of taking care of themselves. At any one time, only about 5% of people older than 65 live in a nursing facility or other long-term care facility. In addition, most older adults who are still married give more help than they get. Furthermore, the help that family members provide to one another usually is reciprocal (each family member gives some kind of help as well as receives it). Any imbalance that exists usually occurs when older people become ill and unable to care for themselves.

LIFE CYCLE OF THE FAMILY

The life cycle of the family is similar to an individual's life cycle. The cycle begins with a newly married couple and then progresses through the stages of childbearing, raising children, the empty nest (it doesn't remain empty in all cases, as adult children move in and out of the home), the retirement years, and death. This cycle has many variations. Whatever the scenario, most families experience cycles of expansion and contraction.

The importance of the life cycle of the family to caregiving is especially evident in middle age. This is the time when adults are confronted with not only their own concerns but also those of their nearly grown or grown children and their aging parents.

The problems faced by young adults are widely known, including divorce, single parenting, unemployment or underemployment, and drug and alcohol abuse. Some young adults, even adult children who are well into their 30s and early 40s, continue to depend on their parents for help. Help may range from moral support and advice to childcare and financial support; help may even include providing a home to return to and help with the care of grandchildren.

Middle-age couples who are still raising their children may be called on to provide assistance to their parents, who are now in their 70s and 80s. This situation can create a set of stresses that, in some families, stretch the limits of their caregiving abilities. The term "the sandwich generation" has been applied to these middle-age couples, caught in the middle between two generations that need help.

LINGERING EFFECTS OF LONG-AGO EVENTS

Family relationships are complex, and family patterns of behavior and attitudes run deep and are remarkably persistent. A son who was considered irresponsible and a "free spirit" in youth by his parents may continue to be viewed as undependable in adulthood, despite taking on and managing the significant obligations of job, home, and family. When a family member does change, other members of the family may find it hard to adjust their view of the individual, maintaining an image of the person that is 20, 30, or more years out of date.

Past events and long-standing perceptions can greatly influence family members' willingness to provide care to an older adult. Some adults refer to the past to explain why they can or can't assume the responsibility of primary caregiver for an older family member. Consider the following statements:

"Dad saved every penny he could to put us through college. Now he needs some financial help, and I'll do my best to come through for him."

"My aunt was always there for us. She took care of us and now we'll take care of her."

"I know my wife would do this for me if she could."

"My mother was always a good sport. She never complained about anything when we were children. Just because she's lost some of her spirit doesn't mean we're going to abandon her now."

"My mother was always so critical of everything I did. Why should I give her the chance to criticize me again?"

"Father was never available to me. Why should I be available to him?"

"My husband never helped me with the children. Now he expects me to help him. Why should I?"

"My wife was always so demanding. This stroke will make her worse. I don't think I can stand it."

Do any of these statements sound familiar? Perhaps you've said or thought something similar on occasion. Some people have a hard time letting go of things that happened in the past, particularly negative events. They haven't accepted and resolved their feelings for certain individuals and the events surrounding them. They may feel, as noted in a few of the negative statements above, like acting out, exacting revenge on someone who hurt them long ago. Understandable, but not a healthy reaction.

Relinquishing Images of the Past

Some images of the past are so deeply etched in our minds that we can't see other family members as they are today. Relinquishing the images of the past isn't always easy, but a "new look" at the members of our families may be in order.

When we, as adults, take a new look at our parents, these all-powerful influences of our childhood are revealed as ordinary people with strengths and weaknesses, just like everyone else. As adults, we can more easily see them as people who, in most cases, did their best as they perceived "their best" at the time. Although it's often difficult for us to imagine, our parents may have been inexperienced, immature, or troubled themselves while they were raising us. If we can imagine this, we can at least understand, maybe even forgive, our parents' actions and mistakes. Sometimes this is easier to do after we become parents ourselves because we recognize what a difficult job parenting is. Relationships with brothers and sisters, too, can benefit from a new look.

Spouses may need to step back and look at each other with new eyes. A husband or wife who refused to take responsibility in a situation years ago, for example, may have changed or matured or may be ready to change if given some encouragement.

Resentment and bitterness about the past can be reduced or dissipated entirely by talking with those involved. Framo contended that too many people tell "Dear Abby" or their friends about their feelings rather than telling the people involved (see Chapter 4 for an explanation of why people behave this way). He said that most people can work out these problems if they talk openly with their families. Some family therapists are more pessimistic than Framo. They advise people to avoid "toxic" family members and to get on with their lives without them. The problem isn't solved by eliminating someone from our lives, however. Whether or not we speak to them, these family members are still in our hearts and minds; they are part of our memories and of our present thoughts and feelings. The more a person tries to suppress his or her feelings, the stronger the feelings become, and these feelings may be released suddenly, perhaps unexpectedly.

Recognizing that you belong to a family and that this bond cannot be denied may make it possible for you to feel free, both to belong to that family and to be an individual who's separate from that family. Although admittedly this idea is complex and somewhat paradoxical, it may be worth considering if you're struggling with your family relationships and your role as caregiver for an older family member.

BUILDING HEALTHIER FAMILY RELATIONSHIPS

The ingredients of a healthy intergenerational relationship are open communication, flexibility, treating one another as adults, involvement without interference, a steady flow of give-and-take, and, of course, affection. In a healthy relationship help is expected and given freely. Given these ingredients, a family will find it easier to fulfill the needs of its members. Difficulties still will be encountered, but the family will be better prepared to handle them if these ingredients are present. Each ingredient, along with approaches that can be used to develop a more satisfying relationship between caregiver and care receiver, is discussed in Chapter 4.

Father Time

The furnace in my parents' home was not working properly. Each time it was called upon for heat, it coughed up a miserable sound, then rumbled. After my mother phoned and explained the problem, I drove the 30 minutes to the house where I grew up. My father had, once again, forgotten to drain the furnace.

My father is 82.

The trees in the yard seemed to droop. The house looked old and worn out. As I entered the foyer, I heard the television blaring in the living room. My father sat in his chair reading the closed captions on the bottom of the TV screen. His hearing aid sat on the table. My mother explained that their cat, Misha, was dying, and that the vet thought it best that it be put to sleep the next day. The cat was 17 years old.

I walked down to the basement. It was cold and damp. As I reached for the string that was attached to the single light bulb, I looked around the dim room: work-bench, tool board, discarded wood. This was the basement where my father built a 12-foot sailboat, a fort for my plastic soldiers, and a weaving loom for my sister.

My father was a lawyer.

The tools in the basement were rusted; the workbench was covered with thick dust. I heard the loud television's muffled squawk through the floor above me.

After I opened a valve at the bottom of the furnace, I watched the brown sludge drain into a dry, empty bucket. Then I closed the first valve and opened the second, which filled the proper chamber with new water. The water level, which hadn't been checked in months, was precariously low.

My father was a college professor.
I turned out the basement light, walked up the creaking stairs, stepped into the kitchen, and helped myself to several grapes from the bowl of fruit that always seemed full. When I was a child, my father held my hand in the fruit market and asked me to help him select the best grapes. My father tells the story about the day he was released from the prisoner-of-war camp in Belgium during World War II. "I had a bit of money in my pocket, and the first thing I bought was a small bag of grapes, so cold and sweet."

My father was an editor.
I walked into the living room with the grapes in my hand. My father leaned out of his chair and tried to adjust his reading glasses. My mother sat on the couch petting the thin, dying cat.

Just as I sat down beside her, my father turned and said, "Christopher, your mother and I took a walk yesterday afternoon through the park, around by the old swamp, and we saw the biggest turtle. Bring the children this weekend and we'll see if we can't find that turtle again." Then he turned to the television and adjusted the color quality.

My father was a writer.
After I kissed my mother goodbye, I left the house, slid into my car and drove off.

That following weekend my father led my wife, our three children, and me on a grand turtle hunt. We walked single file between dried bulrushes, jumped over streams, startled geese, and climbed the park observation deck.

We returned to the house two hours later with pussy willows, apple blossoms, three types of wild violets and three smiling grandchildren.

We didn't see a turtle that weekend. But for a few hours I forgot that my father was an old man. For a few hours I stepped along the outer edges of the swamp and tried to hear the turtle's laugh as I stood upon the spring afternoon with my father, expecting nothing more than our togetherness, and that was good.

Christopher de Vinck

4   Resolving Family Caregiving Issues

Chapter 3 talks about the ingredients of a healthy family relationship as being flexibility in roles and relationships, open communication, noninterfering involvement, and genuine expressions of affection. Some families achieve these easily, whereas others never achieve them. All families run into problems at some time, and all can find themselves involved to a greater or lesser degree in struggles over caregiving issues when an older family member needs care. The lack of one or all of the ingredients listed can become a problem when families are engaged in these struggles. This chapter expands on the discussion in Chapter 3 by suggesting strategies for resolving the family issues that were described. These strategies can make caregiving constructive rather than destructive for all concerned.

LOOKING AT FLEXIBILITY IN ROLES AND RELATIONSHIPS

It's amazing how long-established family roles "stick" to people. Once a person takes on a particular role within a family, it can be difficult to shed it, even if it no longer fits.

Claude

It was a familiar breakfast routine. Claude's grandfather stopped by Claude's house at 8 every weekday morning to say good morning, drop off the newspaper, and pick up letters to mail. His grandfather was a very energetic man who rose early and finished reading the daily newspaper before Claude's own parents opened their eyes. He also was an affectionate man who gave all of the grandchildren a big bear hug every morning, asked them a few questions about their day, and shared a story about someone in town before he left their house.

Most of the time, Claude just hugged his grandfather back and continued with his breakfast, but one morning, he noticed that his mother and grandfather were engaged in more than the usual early-morning banter. This conversation was serious, and Claude began to pay attention. Claude's parents were planning to buy a bigger house, but Claude's grandfather thought that this was an unnecessary expense. He believed that they should save their money and made it clear that he disapproved of their plans. To Claude's surprise, his parents backed down, assuring his grandfather that they would rethink their decision to buy a new house. "Good," his grandfather said, "You won't be sorry that you took my advice." And with that, he put on his hat and waved goodbye as he left the house.

Claude was astonished. Like most children, he thought of his parents as powerful beings who made their own decisions and answered to no one. All of a sudden, he realized that his grandfather had been speaking to his mother as if she were still his young, inexperienced daughter. To his grandfather, this adult woman was still a child and still in need of his guidance. More surprising, Claude's mother and father seemed to accept this assessment. In fact, they actually waited 5 years before buying a bigger house!

Whether Claude's grandfather's advice was good isn't as important as the manner in which it was given and received. His grandfather played the role of the "wise old man," who knows what's best for other family members. Claude's mother assumed the role of the "good girl," who does as she's told. She seems to have adopted the role of the "baby of the family," for whom decisions are made, problems are solved, and messes are cleaned up, no matter how old the "baby."

Inflexibility of Roles

It's natural for family members to assume different roles on different occasions, but problems arise when the roles aren't suitable—the "baby of the family" tag for a 50-year-old man, for example—or when they are too rigid, and people become stuck in and stereotyped by them. The "good boy" can do nothing wrong no matter what awful things he does, whereas the "bad boy" can do nothing right, no matter how hard he tries. The "bad boy" may make genuine attempts to be good, but members of an inflexible family can't see them as such. For example, a gift may be interpreted by other family members as a "bribe to get on dad's good side for a change."

A compliment from the "bad boy" may be interpreted as an attempt to ingratiate himself with other family members. For the "bad boy," the situation seems hopeless. After several incidents, the "bad boy" may say, "Why bother? No matter what I do, it's wrong in this family."

Inflexible roles can be hurtful, even though they may seem harmless. In an inflexible family the "good boy," isn't allowed to be mad at anyone, to be too upset to listen to someone else's problems, or to be too tired to help another family member with a chore. When inflexible families trap their members inside roles, escape isn't easy.

Kinkeeper Role

A family role of special interest is that of kinkeeper. It isn't unusual for one or two family members to be designated the provider(s) of all types of care to the whole family. Often, the oldest daughter is assigned this role, but the oldest son or another family member may find him- or herself in this role. The kinkeeping assignment becomes a problem when the designated individual isn't the appropriate choice because she or he doesn't have the time, energy, or ability to provide the kind of care that's needed. The problem deepens when it absolves other family members of any responsibility for providing care. This leaves the kinkeeper with all of the responsibility for caregiving, which can be overwhelming. Inflexibility in assigning the kinkeeping role can hurt both the kinkeeper and the care receiver. The following is an example:

Jonetta

Jonetta is the oldest of five children. Her brothers and sisters are married with school-age children. Jonetta is a single attorney who commutes 90 minutes each way to work during the week, and usually she brings work home with her. Jonetta's mother, Barbara, took care of her husband from the time that he developed throat cancer to the day he died. Barbara lived alone for 5 years until she had a severe stroke. Afterward, she was unable to care for herself or to communicate clearly what she wanted.

The five adult children met to discuss their mother's situation. To Jonetta's dismay, her brothers and sisters expected her to take care of their mother. "But I live in a one-bedroom apartment," said Jonetta. "And I come home only to eat and sleep. How can I take care of Mother?" "You can hire help," they responded. "You have more money and less responsibility than any of the rest of us." "I have a very responsible job," Jonetta protested, "and no one to fill in for me like all of you have." "You don't have any children, so you can take care of Mother," they responded and refused to discuss the matter further. Despite increasingly frantic protests to the contrary, Jonetta couldn't convince her siblings that she was the wrong person for the job.

Feeling that she had no choice, Jonetta agreed to move her mother into her small apartment. She hired round-the-clock aides and arranged for their supervision by a home health nurse. She also arranged for occupational therapy and physical therapy for her mother. Slowly but steadily, her mother began to show signs of improvement. Despite this, Jonetta couldn't concentrate on her paperwork at home, couldn't sleep well, knowing that the home health aide was in the next room, had no place to entertain friends because her mother slept in the living room, and began to show signs of high blood pressure. She decided that she could no longer manage this arrangement. She moved her mother to a nearby retirement home, where she could continue to receive therapy and help with personal care.

Although Jonetta and her mother were quite satisfied with the arrangement, her brothers and sisters were furious with her because she had "institutionalized" their mother. After a series of angry telephone calls in which they tried to persuade Jonetta to let their mother move back into her apartment, they stopped talking to Jonetta altogether.

This situation could have been resolved differently were Jonetta's brothers and sisters able to discuss alternatives and accept a reassignment of the kinkeeper role to another person, perhaps to all of them:

When Jonetta's brothers and sisters suggested that she take their mother in, Jonetta said, "I wish I could, but my hours are long and my apartment is too small for two people. If one of you has room in your house, I'd be happy to help with the expenses. I could take Mother on weekends so you would have a break." Jonetta's oldest sister offered, "I could alternate weekends with you." Her oldest brother added, "Toni [his wife] and I have room now that Robert is in college. We can't afford to pay for round-the-clock aides, but with your help on that, we could take care of Mother. I think that she'd enjoy visiting you two on alternate weekends after she gets a little better." Her younger brother and sister added that they would share the cost with Jonetta.

After some discussion, the siblings decided to go ahead with their plan. They also agreed that as soon as their mother was well enough to make her wishes known, they could revise the plan to suit her better. In the meantime,

Jonetta's younger brother and sister said that they would take care of Barbara's house so that it would be ready for her when she was able to return home. They concluded that they were fortunate to have five siblings among whom they could divide the kinkeeping responsibilities.

The outcome of the second scenario was positive because Jonetta made her own concerns clear to her siblings. At the same time, she expressed a desire to be helpful and made a concrete offer of financial help, which made it easier for her brother to let their mother move into his house. Jonetta's offer also set the standard for the rest of the adult children to help. Instead of the pattern of resistance and counterresistance of the first scenario, the pattern of the second scenario was that of give and take, in which no one felt pressure to give more than he or she could. Each brother and sister volunteered what they felt they were comfortable giving. The result was a feeling of cooperation and good will. They discovered that together they could do what they couldn't do separately—provide care for their mother until she could care for herself again. They were much more flexible about role assignments in the second scenario. In fact, they decided to share the kinkeeping role, something that they had refused even to consider in the first scenario.

SEEKING OPEN COMMUNICATION

The words you choose can be either helpful or harmful, depending on the way that they're used. In this section, we consider ways to make your words as helpful as possible.

Basics of Family Communication

In a conversation, a person is either a receiver or a sender of a message. Not all of the message is found in the words that are used, however. Tone of voice, facial expression, and body language are as important as the words. For example, a simple question such as "What are you doing?" can be asked in a neutral tone of voice, with a friendly facial expression and relaxed body posture that indicates mild interest or curiosity about what the person is doing at the moment. In contrast, the same question can be asked by a person who is screaming, "What are you doing?!" has an angry facial expression, and is waving his arms wildly. Clearly, the person who is screaming is upset by whatever's being done, whereas the person in the first example wasn't upset.

Receiving Messages

The most helpful type of communication among family members promotes mutual understanding and positive feelings. Practicing active listening is the first step in having open, positive communication. When you are on the receiving end of a message from another family member, you can do several things to make the person speaking feel understood and loved, even when you don't agree with what he or she is saying. (Of course, it's much easier to do this if you agree with your relative, but that isn't always possible.) First, try to understand how he or she feels about the situation, in other words, "walk a mile in the other person's shoes." This reminds us that all of us are different and will vary in our reactions to the same situation. Instead of immediately agreeing or disagreeing with your family member (which is the automatic response), try asking some questions that will encourage the person to explain his or her position. For example,

> *Is it just Dad's driving or is it his safety in general that you're talking about?*
>
> *Do you think that Mom really wants to live alone or that she's afraid she'll be a burden if she moves in with us?*

Once you believe that you have understood the other person's feelings or opinions, try to restate them in your own words to find out whether you're right:

> *You're worried that Dad can't manage alone any more, that he could hurt himself if he's left alone, right?*
>
> *You think that Mom wants to be independent as long as she can?*

Second, the truly understanding receiver of a communication from another family member validates what the other person has said. Having actively listened and asked questions for amplification and clarification, you can then say, "I see how you feel," or "I can understand your position," even if you don't agree with that position.

The don'ts of receiving messages are just as important as the do's. Don't cut the person off prematurely because doing so reduces the opportunities for him or her to clarify what she or he meant and for you to develop a better understanding of the other person's feelings and opinions. (This can be difficult to do when the conversation is upsetting.) Don't evade the issue, either. Again, this is difficult when a highly emotional subject is being discussed, as many caregiving issues are. Evading the issue not only makes you seem uncaring but allows the problem to grow, perhaps worsen. Problems avoided often are problems that worsen and are more difficult to resolve later.

Don't give advice unless asked. The older person may only want you to listen and understand. Giving advice also can seem condescending, especially to the person who didn't ask for it. When you offer unsolicited advice you may be saying, without meaning to, "I know better than you do." Such a perception probably will put an end to your open communication.

Don't hide your lack of agreement in an agreeable-sounding response. A common example is the "yes, but . . ." response as in, "Yes, Dad is a little more careless than he used to be, but that's just old age. I wouldn't worry about it." Instead, validate the other person's concern: "You're worried about Dad's driving, aren't you?" and then add your own observation: "I think he's still a safe driver. He just passed his driving test and he's very careful."

Sending Messages

Sending messages that promote understanding and positive feelings requires just as much care as receiving them. First, it is important to state your opinion clearly or describe your feelings firmly and directly rather than indirectly. If you say something as important as how you feel about your parent's need for care indirectly, other family members may not hear or understand you because they, too, are likely to be highly emotional. Sending direct, clear messages doesn't mean that you need to speak loudly, angrily, or even forcefully. It does mean that you need to be clear, firm, and direct.

Second, you should use "I" messages when talking about your own feelings or opinions. Consider the difference between these "I" and "you" messages and their potential effect on the receiver:

"You" message (not effective)	"I" message (better)
You're making me lose sleep over this.	I'm having trouble sleeping at night because of this.
You left me out of these decisions.	I really wanted to be included in these decisions.

"I" messages clearly convey the sender's position without implying that someone is at fault. "You" messages imply fault and almost certainly will provoke a defensive answer or counterattack from the other person (for example, "That's not my fault!" or "You've left me out of things plenty of times!").

Third, ask the message receiver what he or she thinks about what you've said. Just remember that if you ask for feedback, you must be able to accept it in as nondefensive a manner as possible. If you can't lower your guard, the conversation may deteriorate into the attack-counterattack or resistance-counterresistance pattern that was illustrated in the example about Jonetta and her family. This pattern tends to raise emotional temperatures to the boiling point and provoke people into saying things in ways that hurt rather than help relationships.

Many of the don'ts for the sender are similar to those for the receiver: Don't be sarcastic or critical of others; don't put down the other person or his or her feelings; don't overgeneralize (be specific); don't hide your feelings; and don't talk through or about a third person. For example, if Jonetta (from the earlier scenario) was upset because her youngest brother hadn't offered any kind of help to the family, then she could speak either directly to her youngest brother or to her other brothers and sisters about the situation. Most likely, speaking directly will lead to a resolution of the problem. The second option is an example of talking to a third party rather than speaking directly to the person about whom you're concerned. Although it's easier to do, talking to a third party is much less likely to lead to a resolution. In fact, if the other person finds out that you've been talking about him or her, especially if you've been complaining, he or she is likely to become upset.

People talk to others instead of going directly to the person involved for several reasons:

1. It's easier to complain than to take action.
2. Many people feel that they don't have to be as careful when complaining about someone to a third party as they do when confronting the person him- or herself.
3. They avoid the possibility of a confrontation with the person (for example, "Well, you didn't help me when my son was sick, so why should I help you now?").
4. They don't want to hurt or upset the person. (Of course, if the person finds out that you're complaining to a third party, then he or she probably will be more upset or hurt than if you'd spoken directly to the person in the first place.)

It's important to remember that problems are rarely resolved by complaining to a third party. The problems may even get worse.

Intergenerational Communication

One of the biggest problems that family members encounter when they try to discuss important issues with members of their own or other generations is broaching a taboo subject. In many families certain topics or past events are so emotionally charged that they're never spoken about, particularly by older people ("it just isn't done"). Anyone who brings up the forbidden subject (for example, Aunt Ellen's messy divorce, Uncle John's long-ago-but-never-forgotten time in prison, dad's alcoholism) is immediately, even forcefully, ordered to drop the subject. If the family member or members persist in discussing the taboo topic, they could be cut off, even shunned. Other families tolerate or even appreciate being confronted, acknowledging that they'd been avoiding it and needed to face it. Before you decide to confront your family on these taboo subjects, you need to weigh the potential risks and rewards.

As with inflexible family roles that seem to perpetuate themselves through constant use, families also may adopt inflexible communication patterns. Attack-counterattack is one of these patterns. The first step in changing them is to become aware of them. It may be necessary to step back for awhile and be a detached observer (for example, at a family gathering) to identify these patterns. Refusing to engage in these embedded patterns helps break them.

Couples Communication

Some communication experts believe that men and women communicate in fundamentally different ways. These differences can create misunderstandings because each assumes that the other uses the same approach to communication. The opportunities for misunderstandings are increased when one member of the couple is a caregiver and the other is a care receiver.

All messages have two aspects: the information conveyed by the words spoken and the metamessage (subtle information about the relationship between the sender and the receiver) that accompanies it. Communication research conducted in the United States indicates that most American men concentrate their attention on the words spoken, the direct information that is communicated. American women concentrate their attention on the metamessage, the relationship aspects of the communication, which often is ignored or overlooked by men. When neither party realizes that each has a different way of communicating, misunderstanding piles on top of misunderstanding until a simple conversation spirals into a major conflict, leaving both people feeling frustrated and misunderstood. The following is an example from the work of Deborah Tannen, a linguist who has written a great deal on the subject of miscommunication:

Maureen: *The only weekend we seem to have free is October 10th.*
Philip: *That's the opening of hunting season.*

Maureen: *Well, let's do it Saturday or Sunday evening.*

Philip: *Okay, make it Saturday.*

Maureen: *Wouldn't you want to be able to hunt later on the first day of hunting?*

Philip: [Annoyed] *I said Saturday, so obviously that's the day I prefer.*

Maureen: [Now also annoyed] *I was just trying to be considerate of you. You didn't give a reason for choosing Saturday.*

Philip: *I'm taking off Thursday and Friday to hunt, so I figure I'll have had enough by Saturday night.*

Maureen: *Well, why didn't you say that?*

Philip: *I didn't see why I had to. And I found your question very intrusive.*

Maureen: *I found your response very offensive!*

Maureen expected Philip to explain why he chose Saturday, but Philip assumed that it was sufficient simply to say that Saturday was okay. When Maureen tested his suggestion to make sure he wasn't just being accommodating, Philip thought that she was questioning his choice. Although Maureen was trying to be thoughtful, Philip believed that she had been intrusive.

Consideration and intrusiveness also are important issues in a family caregiving situation. The developing argument between Maureen and Philip is a scenario that can occur in a male–female caregiver–care receiver pair, particularly when neither is aware of the differences in the ways they communicate. Let's look at an example from a caregiving situation: Monty is caring for his wife Becca, who has been receiving chemotherapy. Becca has been feeling weak and has had very little appetite since she began the chemotherapy:

Monty: *Would you like something to drink?*

Becca: *Oh, no, don't bother to get up.*

Monty: *Are you sure? Do you want something or not?*

Becca: *Maybe I could keep down a little ginger ale.*

Monty: [Getting annoyed] *Why didn't you say so in the first place?*

Becca: [Feeling hurt] *I didn't want to disturb you.*

Monty: [Shouting] *Well, you did disturb me! Why can't you just say yes if you're thirsty. Why do I have to drag it out of you all the time?*

> Becca: *[Tearfully] I know I'm such a bother to you. I just didn't want to make you get up when you looked so comfortable sitting there.*
>
> Monty: *I have to get up anyway, so that doesn't help at all. It just irritates me so much when you say no but mean yes.*

Monty's conversational focus was on completing a task while Becca's focus was on how Monty felt about doing the task. She was trying to communicate her appreciation for him and his efforts, and he was trying to be helpful and get his "job" done. Each was trying to be considerate of the other, but both failed to communicate that attempt clearly. Instead, both Monty and Becca ended up feeling thoroughly misunderstood, even though each person was motivated by love and goodwill.

These misunderstandings can be avoided with effort from both parties. Gottman and Carrere made some suggestions that they called their "prescription" for resolving gender differences in communication styles:

1. State your complaint or concern clearly and directly. Most men withdraw rather than voice their relationship concerns, whereas most women want to discuss them. Many husbands feel "flooded" by their wives' expressions of negative emotions. They fear negative emotions and their expression, particularly by women. According to Gottman and Carrere, men should try to not become overwhelmed by these expressions of emotion. Women should try to avoid expressing themselves on minor issues using strong emotions. Men and women should feel free to voice their concerns, fears, anger, and disagreement to each other, but neither person should criticize the other or express contempt or disgust.

2. Respond to voiced concerns. Men need to work on listening to the metamessage of a communication as well as to the information contained in it. They also need to try to avoid withdrawing or criticizing a woman's expression of emotion. Women need to learn to recognize when men are responding only to the information and not to the metamessage. When they do, they can restate the metamessage more directly so that men understand it from the perspective of women.

NONINTERFERING INVOLVEMENT

The need to be both separate and connected to others, to be independent and yet be able to depend on people, is a fundamental paradox of the human condition. In fact, many therapists make an even more paradoxical statement: Only by being emotionally separate from one another can we become truly close to one another. Some families do very well at fostering independence, whereas others are better at developing connectedness. However, some families go too far in their favored direction. If they go too far in the direction of separateness, then they can cause family members to feel isolated and adrift. If they go too far in the direction of connectedness, family members may find themselves completely entangled and imprisoned within the family.

Achieving a comfortable balance between individuality and togetherness within and across generations is a delicate task. Arthur Schopenhauer, the 19th century German philosopher, suggested an image for the paradox of closeness and separateness. Imagine two porcupines trying to keep each other warm on a dark winter's night. When they come close to get warm, their quills hurt each other. But when they pull away from each other, they feel cold again. Somehow they have to figure out how to get close enough to keep warm without being so close that they get stuck by the other's quills. Many people have the same problem as the porcupines. If they become too separate, they feel cold and lonely, but if they get too close, they get stuck by each other's emotional quills. In the same way, caregivers need to get close but not too close, both physically and emotionally, to understand and care for their older adult family member. If they get too close, they will suffer the same pain as the care receiver, leaving them less objective and less able to provide care.

The paradox of closeness and separateness may contribute to a caregiving problem within a family. It may be difficult to recruit caregivers in a family whose members are too separate and independent of one another. However, in a family that's too close, the needs of caregivers themselves may be ignored, sometimes even by the caregivers themselves.

CREATING AFFECTIONAL BONDS

Bonds that are based on affection (affectional bonds) that connect family members begin in infancy and remain important throughout life. Although some people say that they don't need these bonds, no one outgrows his or her need for love, understanding, and acceptance. Of course, families aren't the only source of affection, but they are the central source for most people. Two aspects of the quality of a family's affectional bonds are examined in this section: congruence in communication of affection and unconditional love and acceptance.

Congruence in Communication of Affection

Love and affection can be communicated to family members directly or indirectly, through words or actions, or both. How love, understanding, and acceptance are expressed has a profound impact on us. Caregiving is an indirect, action-oriented way to express affection. The term *congruence* refers to consistency or agreement between one's words and actions. For example, saying, "I love you" is a lot more convincing when said in a warm tone, accompanied by a hug or kiss than when it's expressed in a cold, distant voice. The caregiver who says to a care recipient, "I care about you" but handles the person roughly when giving him or her a bath isn't being congruent and may cause the care receiver to feel unloved or at least resented. If our actions don't support our words, our words won't be believed.

Unconditional Love and Acceptance

Many people believe that they are providing unconditional love and acceptance when, in fact, they aren't. Parents in particular fall into this trap when they praise their children for good behavior, doing well in school, excelling in sports, and so forth. As the children grow up, praise is given for success in a career, being a devoted son or daughter, or producing delightful grandchildren. The unstated message (intended or not) behind the praise is that the child, youngster or adult, is valued and loved for his or her accomplishments rather than for just being. The fear of the child is that if he or she fails to continue to please his or her parents, they will withdraw their love.

Once in the habit of providing conditional messages of affection, it can be difficult to change to unconditional ones. Unconditional messages of love and acceptance say "I love you" without adding "because . . ." Indirect messages of unconditional acceptance say "I enjoy your company," "I care about you," "I'm here for you," and the like. Actions also can convey unconditional acceptance and love: hugging, kissing, looking affectionately at each other, sharing experiences, giving gifts, freely giving time and attention, and doing things together communicate affection indirectly and strengthen these affectional bonds.

HOLDING FAMILY MEETINGS

When a caregiving crisis arises such as the one faced by Jonetta and her family, families often call a meeting to discuss the problem. This section offers suggestions for making a family meeting as helpful and positive as possible.

1. Try to bring everyone together in the same place at the same time for the family meeting. The reason is to try to minimize any tendency to talk to or through a third party rather than directly to the person involved. If family members live too far apart to do this, then try to arrange a conference call. The extra cost will be worth it.

2. Try to engage others in solving problems. Once everyone has had a chance to express his or her feelings and opinions and hear others' feelings and opinions, all should be ready to work on finding a solution. This work requires a willingness to be flexible, to keep an open mind, and continue to listen to others' opinions.

3. Try to include the care receiver in solving the problem. Leaving the care receiver out of the family meeting would be like putting him or her in the role of the "baby" of the family for whom decisions are made, problems are solved, and so forth. Put yourself in this person's place: Would you want your children or your spouse making decisions about your life without consulting you?

4. Try not to overreact. It's so easy to be caught in an upwardly spiraling torrent of emotion. Once this happens, almost everyone finds it hard to return to a nondefensive, nonattacking, calm discussion of the situation.

5. Try to step back to analyze what's really happening. Look for those inflexible family roles and communication patterns that have been described thus far in this book. In addition, try to look at the situation from other family members' perspectives.

6. Try to remember that the issue wouldn't be as emotionally charged if you didn't care about one another. One of the down sides of closeness is that, like Schopenhauer's porcupines, we feel one another's pain more acutely when we're emotionally close. Unless the closeness is stifling, this is a small price to pay for the warmth and caring of one's family.

7. Try to remember that outside help is available. This doesn't mean only the possibility of counseling if your family is in crisis but also the consideration of a range of options. Your family doesn't have to solve the problem or provide the help alone. Some information and guidance from a physician, social worker, nurse, counselor, religious leader, support group, self-help group, or wise friend may be just what your family needs to work out a solution that's acceptable to everyone involved. Friends, neighbors, churches, community centers, and social and health care organizations and agencies are available to help. See Chapters 15–17 and the appendix at the end of the book for a listing of organizations.

5   Protecting Your Own Health

The notion of protecting your own health or meeting your own needs may seem out of the question to you right now. The needs of the older adult in your life may seem to take up most of the minutes and hours of each day, with little or no time left for you. But it's critical that you give thought and attention to you. This chapter reviews ways that'll enable you not only to protect your own health but also to enhance your physical and mental strength in your role as caregiver.

BECOMING AWARE OF YOUR NEEDS

To achieve wellness, you need to develop the same awareness about yourself as you have about the person for whom you're caring. If you reflect on some of the later chapters, it's clear that the tasks involved in caring for your loved one take into account essential areas such as nutrition, exercise, and rest and relaxation. As a caregiver, you have the same needs, especially if the person becomes more dependent on you. Your needs *must* be met for you to have the energy that'll be required to care for a dependent older adult.

Nutrition

Caregiving is consuming a large part of your life: Are you thinking about what you're consuming? How are you nourishing yourself? Is your daily nutritional intake similar to that recommended in the USDA Food Guide Pyramid (Figure 1), or are you eating on the run or eating mostly fast food because it's easy and gives you an instantaneous feeling of being full? Do you sometimes grab some

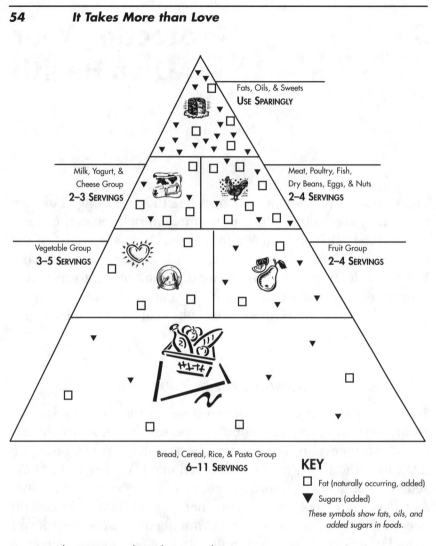

FIGURE 1. *The USDA Food Guide Pyramid.*

candy to give you a quick burst of energy, especially at the end of the day?

Your body needs the proper fuel for the physical and mental activities you put it through every day. Eating a balanced diet helps build muscle and gives you energy. The Food Guide Pyramid can be used as a guideline to help you eat a balanced diet. You may look at the pyramid and think, "How will I be able to eat and drink all that every day?" Most people are confused or misinformed about how much a serving is; it's not as big as you might think. For instance, one slice of bread is one serving, so if you eat a sandwich, you've already eaten one third of the minimum daily grains recommendation of six servings; a 1-inch cube of hard cheese weighs about ½ ounce, which is one serving; and one egg is one serving.

You can incorporate what you now know about servings and a balanced diet and create new eating habits. This suggestion may seem like a lot to ask, but the benefits to you will more than make up for the energy you put in at the beginning of the week. First, think about the foods that you like and make a list of them. As you make the list, try to group them according to the recommendations from the pyramid. Second, make up a week's menu, incorporating the foods you like from your list, and making sure that you include the appropriate number of servings. Third, write a shopping list of all of the foods on the week's menu. Fourth, purchase the groceries on the list. Fifth, dedicate some time to food preparation. You may say you can't spare the time, but to have a better-nourished body, you need to find the time. Be creative, and try to make it fun for you. Perhaps a friend or neighbor can help out with the older adult in your life by sitting with the person, or maybe you can run his or her favorite movie on the VCR while you cook. Maybe you can cook while the person is napping or sleeping. Use disposable pans that you can throw away when you're done, which makes clean up easy. When you're done cooking, separate the food into individual portions, place them in microwaveable containers, and freeze them (some frozen foods keep for months).

Just as you would do for your loved one, make eating a pleasant, relaxing time for you. Treat yourself like an honored guest: Don't eat standing up. Set a special place at the table. Put on your favorite music. If you're sharing the meal with another person, talk about anything but your responsibilities as a caregiver.

You need to know and believe that you won't be taking anything away from your loved one if you pay a little attention to your nutritional needs. In fact, you'll add to the person's life by having more energy and being in a good mood.

Exercise

Whether you know it or not, you need a regular, appropriate-for-you exercise program. The muscles and bones of your body are stressed by the demands of caregiving. The benefits that exercise brings to your body and mind will provide you with the stamina and well-being you need to be an effective caregiver. Again, you're not taking anything away from the person for whom you're caring by giving something to yourself—you're actually adding to his or her quality of life by being the best you that you can be.

As with nutrition, you may wonder, "Where am I going to find the time to exercise?" You can't afford not to find the time. You'll need to be creative; maybe you'll need to call on your family, friends, or others to help you find the time to re-energize yourself. You need to be engaged in a program of regular exercise that includes a series of stretches before and after you do the exercises. Walking, bicycling, swimming, even gardening are exercises that increase, improve, and maintain your heart's function as well as provide relaxation and calm.

As you would do with the older adult in your life, check with your health care provider before beginning any activity to make sure that it's appropriate for you and the condition you're in right now. Select an activity or activities that give you pleasure, otherwise you won't stick with your exercise program. Listen to music as you exercise because it provides a calming effect. Start slowly, gradually increasing the time that you spend in each activity. Experts say that you should exercise for at least 30 minutes 3 or more times a week.

Rest and Relaxation

Another personal need is adequate rest and relaxation. If you're constantly on the go and never rest or relax, your body will break down, just like a car that runs and runs but none of its needs for repair are attended to. When you rest or relax, you allow your body to slow down and repair itself. That is what sleep is all about—during sleep, the body's functions slow down, and repair and rebuilding take place.

What kind of activities you engage in to rest and relax depend on your individual likes and needs. Listening to music, reading a book, or just closing your eyes in a quiet place in your home may be your way of healing yourself. You can do deep breathing exercises or meditate to relax. Whatever you do, the important thing is that you must permit yourself the time and the space to rest. It's not the amount of time (it could be only 15 minutes) but the regular scheduling and continuity of this personal time that's important. How you manage to schedule this time for yourself is another exercise in creativity. Calling on others to help you may be appropriate for you or thinking back to when your children's nap time was your personal rest/relaxation time and applying it to your caregiving tasks may work best.

If you're not sleeping well at night or your sleep is interrupted, you can do several things to get the sleep you need:

Drink a glass of warm milk before bedtime.
Take a warm bath before bedtime.
Read a relaxing book before bedtime.
Listen to classical, new age, or any relaxing music close to bedtime.

If you're really concerned about your sleep patterns, try the following experiment: Keep a copy of the sleep diary in Figure 2 by your bed and chart your sleep patterns for a week. Charting can help you get a handle on how and when you're sleeping and can help you change things about the way you're sleeping—maybe you need a set bedtime or a before-bed routine or fewer (or more) naps during the weekend.

ACHIEVING BALANCE

Achieving a balance between your needs in your own life and your role as a caregiver obviously is easier said than done, but it *can* be done. Striking a healthy balance doesn't mean that you won't feel guilty about saying "no," "not today," or "maybe later" to your loved one. You may have to work from a "delayed rewards" point of view—sometimes you have to disappoint the person today so that

SLEEP DIARY

Day	Time fell asleep	Nighttime waking (time/how long)	Describe nighttime waking	Time awoke	Describe any naps
Sun					
Mon					
Tue					
Wed					
Thu					
Fri					
Sat					

FIGURE 2. Sleep diary. (Adapted from Durand, V.M. [1998]. Sleep better! [p. 236]. Baltimore: Paul H. Brookes Publishing Co.)

you have the energy to give to him or her later. You won't be taking anything away from the older adult in your life; you're just making sure that your needs are met on an equal basis as his or hers.

There are several steps you can take to achieve balance. First, try to free your mind of guilt, including any that family or friends place on you—if you don't take care of yourself, you may not be well enough or, at the extreme, be around at all to take care of the older adult in your life. Second, make a list of your caregiving tasks. Third, put those tasks into two categories: I Must Do and I Need to Do; in other words, assess what truly must be done and what needs to be done but isn't vital to the person's moment-to-moment survival. Ask yourself honestly: Does my loved one need a bath every day because he or she is incontinent or has a physical condition that warrants one or because I think that everyone should bathe every day? Do I have to be with the person at all times or would it be okay to leave the person on his or her own for a few hours so I can do something for myself? Do I need to prepare and serve full meals every day, or could someone else prepare one of my loved one's meals? Is it possible that he or she could get adequate nutrition from a less-than-complete meal? Take a really honest look at the capabilities of the older adult in your life.

SETTING LIMITS

Unfortunately, even when you try to achieve balance, you may feel unbalanced. You may find yourself in the position of trying to please the person you are caring for to such an extent that you may become frustrated and angry. What's important to understand and accept is that sometimes no matter what you do or say, the older adult in your life won't be happy. In fact, the person may get angry with you for what he or she perceives as your apparent inability to satisfy his or her needs. The person may even accuse you of not caring about or neglecting him or her.

What may work is to offer the person a choice within a limited number of choices—you set the number or type and stand firmly by those choices. Don't allow yourself to fall into the trap of offering so many choices to please the person that choosing becomes an unpleasant activity—or worse—for you both.

You also may need to set limits concerning the amount of time that your loved one wants you to spend with him or her. Strike up a verbal contract with the person and set specific times of the day or evening or the specific days or evenings when you'll be with him or her. If the person has memory impairments, you may need to remind the person of these times. You can use a large-print calendar that can be hung in the bedroom or elsewhere in his or her home. Write in large print the day(s) and time(s) that you'll be there. Plan special activities that you can enjoy together, such as sharing a meal as you commemorate a special event in your lives, going to the movies, or taking a walk. Include the person in the planning if possible. The outcome of this special time together just might be a more complete understanding of one another.

GETTING THE SUPPORT YOU NEED

It's not always easy to acknowledge that you need help caring for the older adult in your life. You may feel that asking for help is backing away from your responsibility as a child, a spouse, a sibling, or a significant other. You may let pride get in the way—you don't want to let go of the role; no one else can do it the way you do it; the person won't be happy if someone else cares for him or her. Instead of putting so much pressure on yourself, let others help, even if you can only allow them to do a small thing at first. Caregiving is an ongoing, long-term commitment, whether the person lives at home or in a nursing facility. It's not likely that you'll be available for everything that the person needs.

Your Family

Look to other family members for help with caregiving tasks. Have a family meeting either in person or, if you live in different parts of the country or world, by conference call. Detail all of the responsibilities and tasks that are involved in caring for your dependent loved one. Discuss and designate specific areas that each individual can be responsible for. You may be surprised to hear,

"I've been waiting for you to ask me to help. I didn't want to hurt your pride or make you think you couldn't handle it."

Some families' dynamics aren't positive. Some relatives may resist helping. This may be because they're afraid and/or uncomfortable with the task(s) they're asked to perform, such as preparing meals, doing some of the shopping, taking the person out for a little while, or just spending a few hours alone with the older person. It may be helpful to identify the areas that they do feel comfortable handling. They also may resist because they have issues with the older person or someone else in the family. You may just have to accept their reluctance to help and move on to another person.

However the process goes, it's important for you to understand and accept that it's okay to accept caregiving help from other family members. It doesn't mean you're not doing a good job. It does mean that you'll be able to continue in that role.

Outside Your Family

What can you do if family isn't available or the help that family members offer isn't enough? There are many agencies in the community that provide home health care, meal, chore, and companion services and support groups. Many offer free services. The final section of the book ("Getting Help") and the resource list at the back of the book can get you started.

II

Knowing What's Normal, What's Not

6   Understanding the Physical Changes of Aging

Our understanding of how people age has changed. It used to be considered normal for people to lose all of their teeth, develop hardening of the arteries, and become senile as they aged. But these changes are no longer considered a part of the typical changes that accompany aging. There are ways for you to tell whether the changes that you observe in a family member are those associated with normal aging or are signs of illness. You need to learn what happens to different organ and body systems as a person ages—what's normal and what's not normal.

The following tells the story of a person who has experienced normal healthy aging and has rarely been ill:

Sam

Sam is 89 years old and has been married for more than 60 years. He considers himself healthy and doesn't take any medication except aspirin for his arthritis, which he says doesn't interfere with any of his daily activities. He needs glasses to read the newspaper and, when asked, admits that it sometimes takes him a little longer to do things than it used to. He notes that he keeps up his strength by taking a nap every afternoon.

Sam goes bowling every week with his friends. Usually he's the designated driver because he drives very well, although he limits his driving to the daytime hours and tries to avoid rush-hour traffic because it makes him nervous. He offers his services frequently to "older" neighbors, enjoying his reputation as someone who helps out and is able to fix things. A high point is the trip he and his wife take to Greece every 2 years to visit relatives.

Sam is an example of a person who has aged successfully. He's healthy but has experienced the changes that accompany normal aging. He credits his health to good genes and his healthy outlook on and involvement in life. This chapter looks at the normal changes of aging, such as those experienced by Sam, and contrasts them with the signs and symptoms that may indicate the presence of disease.

UNDERSTANDING CHANGES IN PHYSICAL ACTIVITY

Our ability to carry out various physical activities, from carrying groceries up a flight of stairs to playing a vigorous game of tennis, depends on the proper functioning of several body organs and structures, especially the lungs, heart/cardiovascular system, bones, muscles, and joints. Changes in these organs and structures as we age contribute to changes in our physical abilities.

Lungs

Changes in the lungs as we age include a loss of tissue elasticity, thickening of the pulmonary wall, and an increase in the volume of air left in the lungs after each breath is expelled. All of these changes result in a less efficient exchange of oxygen and carbon dioxide in the lungs and can cause an older person to feel fatigued when the body is stressed. A regular routine of aerobic and muscle-toning exercises can increase a person's ability to continue to perform and participate in many physical activities well into his or her 70s, 80s, and even 90s (see Chapter 8 for detailed information on exercise).

**Breathing:
What's Not Normal**

All of the following symptoms indicate that professional help should be sought in diagnosing and treating the condition:

Shortness of breath at rest or after mild exertion— Inability to walk short distances without breathing difficulties; gasping or heavy breathing after mild exertion such as a walk around the block

Having to work harder to get air in—Sensation of being aware of every breath taken

Fatigue with mild exertion— Becoming increasingly tired after activities that require only minimal effort (should be distinguished from normal tiredness that follows overexertion and overstrenuous activity.)

Heart/Cardiovascular System

As we age, the heart undergoes many normal changes that may cause us to become tired and short of breath more easily. The heart grows bigger (*hypertrophies*) as we age. As the heart's muscle cells die, they're replaced by fat and fibrous connective tissue. This transformation affects the heart's ability to pump blood through the body. As a result, the amount of blood pumped out with each heartbeat decreases slowly as we age. The efficiency of the cardiovascular system also diminishes because of the normal thickening of the walls of the arteries. In addition, after age 30, the amount of oxygen carried by the red blood cells to the tissues of the body decreases by around 1% each year.

For these reasons, during exercise older people may find it more difficult to sustain the same level of energy as they did when they were younger. Stiffening of the arterial walls decreases the body's ability to respond quickly to changes in position. As a result, older people often become lightheaded after rising quickly from a chair or bed (*postural hypotension*). Sometimes the heart doesn't beat in a regular pattern, causing the person to experience a pounding or racing heartbeat (*palpitations*), a slowed heart rate, or extra heartbeats. These symptoms may occur because of changes in the ability of different parts of the heart to send and receive the electrical signals that stimulate the pumping action of the heart. Although these changes seem to indicate the person has a disease rather than is experiencing the normal changes of aging, the most important thing to think about in evaluating these symptoms is how they affect a person's daily activities. When an older person who lives a healthful lifestyle becomes fatigued, short of breath, and lightheaded

Alert!

The normal changes of aging shouldn't interfere in any significant way with an older person's ability to carry out everyday activities, such as walking short distances, grocery shopping, or climbing stairs.

and experiences palpitations that worsen and interfere with his or her activities, it's time to seek medical attention.

Bones, Muscles, and Joints

Many changes take place in the bones, muscles, and joints as we age. One of the most obvious changes, and one of the most noticeable, is that people get shorter as they get older. This happens to people of all races and of both sexes. The padding between the bones of the spinal column becomes thinner and narrower, and the bones become compressed, resulting in a gradual decrease in height. The cartilage of the joints also wears down, which decreases the cushion between the bones, causing the joints to move slower and stiffer.

Although the size of the bones doesn't change, a decrease in the mineral content of the bone results in a reduction of bone mass. This bone loss begins earlier in women than it does in men, in part because of a decrease in the levels of estrogen that occurs at menopause. Calcium supplements or estrogen-replacement therapy may help minimize bone loss in older women (see also Chapter 9). Bone and muscle weakness is partly attributable to normal aging but more often than not it's a result of inactivity, a sedentary lifestyle, or a lack of exercise. In addition, poor posture may alter a person's center of gravity, leading to problems in walking and an increased risk of falling.

Bones may become thinner (osteoporosis; calcium in the bones is reabsorbed by the body and excreted in the urine), which occurs more frequently and at an earlier age in women than in men, making older people more prone to hip fractures or fractures of the spinal vertebra. Older people are at increased risk for falling when they have osteoporosis. Sometimes the simple act of turning in bed or getting up from a chair causes a fracture and the person falls. In other cases osteoporosis causes a person to fall and a fracture occurs. Fractures are a particular concern when an older person is inactive or confined to bed. In these individuals, maintaining muscle activity and continuing to bear weight on the bones can slow the process of calcium loss and wasting of muscles.

Many bone and muscle changes that occur with aging affect breathing. Muscles, bones, and rib cage cartilage become less flexible as we age and don't stretch as much or as easily as they once did. The chest doesn't expand and contract as easily during breathing, and the effectiveness of coughing is decreased. This is one reason that older people are at higher risk than younger people to develop pneumonia.

UNDERSTANDING CHANGES IN ELIMINATION

The organs that are involved in the elimination of wastes from the body are the kidneys, the bladder, and the bowels (intestines) (Figure 1). Normal changes of aging in these organs are, in general, quite manageable, but abnormal changes, which often are exaggerations of the normal changes, can have a profound impact on a person's health and lifestyle.

Kidneys

The kidneys perform two critical roles: They help remove chemical wastes from the blood, flushing out wastes through the urine, and they work to maintain the proper amounts of fluids and electrolytes in the body. Electrolytes, which include sodium, potassium, calcium, magnesium, and chloride, are essential for the tissues and organs of the body to function properly.

The changes in kidney function that occur as a result of aging are closely tied to cardiovascular changes. Earlier in the chapter you read that the amount of blood that's pumped with each heartbeat and the diameter of the arteries decrease as the body ages. These changes result in a diminished rate of blood flow through the kidneys and lower the kidneys' ability to filter blood effectively. The kidneys themselves also decrease in size because of a gradual loss of nephrons. Nephrons can be thought of as microscopic funnels that filter the blood passing through the kidneys and then create urine. Urination eliminates the toxic materials that are filtered out of the blood. Each kidney contains around 1.25 million nephrons. The age-related changes in kidney func-

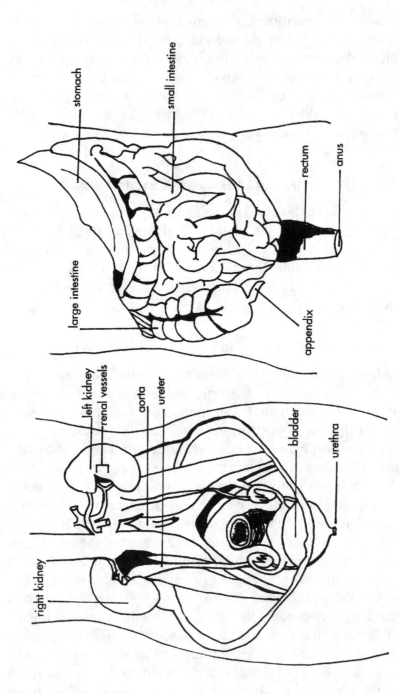

FIGURE 1. The human elimination system.

tion also affect the kidneys' ability to effectively maintain fluid balance. This makes it likely that older people will become dehydrated or, just the opposite, retain too much fluid.

Bladder

The bladder's ability to perform efficiently changes a lot as the body ages. The amount of urine that can be safely and comfortably held in the bladder until you feel the urge to urinate drops by 50% by around age 65 (Figure 2). A decrease in the muscle tone and elasticity of the structures that make up the urinary system—the ureters, bladder, and urethra—makes it more difficult for older people to "hold" their urine. In addition, changes in the five senses may have an effect on the signals that tell you when your bladder is full. Common results of these changes are urinary frequency, urinary urgency, urinary retention, and the need to urinate frequently at night (*nocturia*).

In women, a decrease in estrogen levels after menopause causes the muscles of the pelvic floor that support the bladder and the urethra to relax. These muscles

> **Alert!**
>
> Because many drugs are eliminated from the body in the urine, medication doses may need to be reduced in older people to reflect this normal reduction in kidney function. Learn more about medications and older people in Chapter 9.
>
> ---
>
> If the older adult in your life experiences a sudden change in the frequency of urination, the ability to "hold" the urine until an appropriate time for urinating, or the color of the urine, seek immediate medical assistance and treatment.

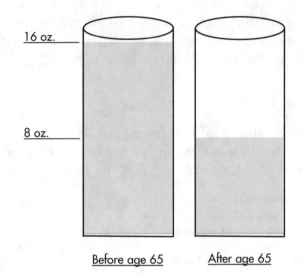

16 oz.

8 oz.

Before age 65   After age 65

FIGURE 2. *The amount of urine that the bladder can hold comfortably after age 65 drops from about 16 ounces to 8 ounces, which is equal to a regular beverage-size glass.*

help start and stop the flow of urine. This involuntary muscle re-laxation can cause small amounts of urine to leak out when increased pressure is placed on the abdomen, for example when you're coughing, bending, or laughing. This is known as stress in-continence. (Chapter 11 talks more about stress incontinence and describes several ways to manage it.)

In men, enlargement of the prostate gland (benign prostatic hypertrophy or BPH) is a normal change that comes with aging. The pressure of an enlarged prostate on the urethra makes it difficult to empty the bladder effectively. Signs of BPH include difficulty in starting the urine stream, inability to empty the bladder completely, dribbling between times of urination, and increased nocturia.

Abnormalities in bladder function also can be caused by some medications, especially diuretics (for example, Diuril, Lasix, Aldactone), which increase how much urine is excreted. Bladder infections, which irritate the urinary tract, also may make it more difficult for older people to "hold" their urine.

These changes in bladder function can cause older people to engage less often in activities that are located far from toilet facil-ities for fear of embarrassment. More dangerous to their health is that they also might limit their intake of fluids. This, of course, increases their risk of becoming dehydrated.

Bowels (Intestines)

Healthy bowel functioning is a concern for many older adults. As people age, the movement of food through the intestines slows down. Lubrication of the lining of the bowel also decreases, as does the elasticity of the abdominal muscles that help you have a bowel movement. Together these changes often lead to constipation unless the older person continues to be physically active and to consume enough fluids and fiber. Constipation that isn't due to age-related factors can occur as a result of dehydration, low-fiber diet, sedentary lifestyle, medications, depression, and diseases such as cancer. To distinguish between normal changes and changes that require further intervention, a medical evaluation is necessary.

UNDERSTANDING CHANGES IN THE NERVOUS SYSTEM

Like other body systems, the nervous system undergoes many changes with age, but it continues to carry out its many functions adequately unless disease intervenes. Disorders in other body systems ultimately can affect the brain, which controls the nervous system. For example, stiffening and narrowing of the arteries (stiffening: arteriosclerosis; narrowing: atherosclerosis) can limit the amount of oxygen that reaches the brain, affecting cognitive function; and liver disease and kidney disease hinder the removal of toxic

---

Bowel Elimination: What's Not Normal

All of the following items indicate that professional help should be sought in diagnosing and treating the condition:

Blood in the stool

Changes in elimination pattern (for example, more frequent constipation or diarrhea)

Pain on elimination

Severe or prolonged abdominal pain or cramping

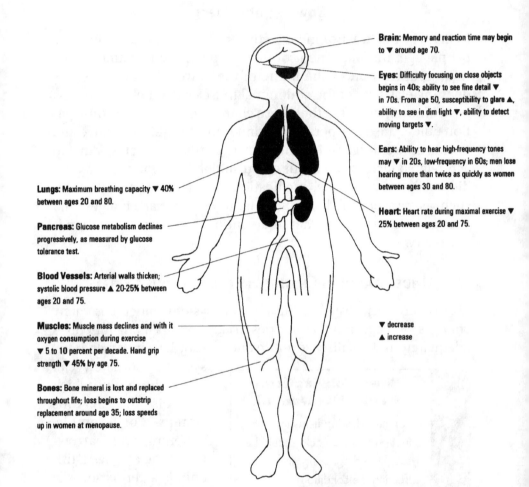

Brain: Memory and reaction time may begin to ▼ around age 70.

Eyes: Difficulty focusing on close objects begins in 40s; ability to see fine detail ▼ in 70s. From age 50, susceptibility to glare ▲, ability to see in dim light ▼, ability to detect moving targets ▼.

Ears: Ability to hear high-frequency tones may ▼ in 20s, low-frequency in 60s; men lose hearing more than twice as quickly as women between ages 30 and 80.

Heart: Heart rate during maximal exercise ▼ 25% between ages 20 and 75.

Lungs: Maximum breathing capacity ▼ 40% between ages 20 and 80.

Pancreas: Glucose metabolism declines progressively, as measured by glucose tolerance test.

Blood Vessels: Arterial walls thicken; systolic blood pressure ▲ 20-25% between ages 20 and 75.

Muscles: Muscle mass declines and with it oxygen consumption during exercise ▼ 5 to 10 percent per decade. Hand grip strength ▼ 45% by age 75.

Bones: Bone mineral is lost and replaced throughout life; loss begins to outstrip replacement around age 35; loss speeds up in women at menopause.

▼ decrease
▲ increase

How the body ages, on the average. (Illustration by Martha Blalock, NIH Medical Arts and Photography Branch. From NIA/NIH. [1993]. With the passage of time: The Baltimore Longitudinal Study of Aging, p. 53 [NIH Publication No. 93-3685]. Washington, DC: U.S. Government Printing Office.)

wastes from the body. These toxic wastes build up in the brain, affecting its functioning.

Brain

As we age, the brain loses a portion of its cells and may actually shrink in size. The number of cells that remain, however, are more than adequate to enable us to perform necessary functions, such as thinking. Chemicals in the brain (*neurotransmitters*) help to transmit information from one neuron to another. These transmitters are essential to the brain's control functions, helping to regulate body temperature, respiration, thirst, movement, mood, and memory. There also are fewer neurotransmitters as we age. The decrease in these chemicals may reduce older people's ability to respond to physical and emotional stress effectively as they did when they were younger.

Increases in the amount of a brain chemical called monoamine oxidase may be responsible for the mild feelings of depression that may appear with age. There's also a 10%–15% decrease in blood flow to the brain with aging, which may make older people's brains more vulnerable to a decrease in oxygen that results from illness or environmental changes (for example, high altitude).

Response Time

The speed with which an impulse travels from one nerve cell to another decreases with advancing age. The result is slower reaction time, which may affect an older person's ability to respond quickly in an emergency, for example while driving. In addition, the eye's ability to follow objects decreases by one third by age 80. Most people are able to adapt to these gradual changes. They can, for example, drive more slowly or keep a greater distance between themselves and the car ahead to compensate for their slower reaction time.

Thought Processes

Expert opinion about what age people's ability to learn begins to decline has changed. What was once determined to be age 25 has increased to age 50, and this statistic may change upward again. It's true that older people learn new things a bit more slowly and that their response to various cognitive demands is slower than younger people's response. Most of the changes in thought processes that occur with age are subtle, hardly noticeable to older people unless they

> ### Thought Processes: What's Not Normal
>
> All of the following possible causes indicate that professional help should be sought in diagnosing and treating the condition:
>
> | Condition | Possible causes |
> |-----------|-----------------|
> | Disoriented | Dehydration |
> | Confused | Medication interaction |
> | Paranoid | Dementia |
> | Depressed | Losses, illness |

are under pressure to complete a task in a very short time. Caregivers who avoid rushing cognitively healthy older people through a task find that their loved ones are capable of whatever mental tasks are necessary to function in everyday life.

The ability to recall recently learned information and to solve complex new problems declines somewhat with age. Visual-spatial abilities, such as recognizing faces or finding one's way around an unfamiliar town, and attention span begin to decline after age 60. It's unclear, however, whether older adults' thought processes don't function as well as younger people's because they have difficulty encoding and processing the information or whether the problem is in retrieving the information. Research has shown that distraction in the environment and lack of visual cues greatly affect this ability. Some mild problems, such as not remembering a person's name or not coming up with the right word, may occur, but these are temporary annoyances rather than serious problems.

What do all of these changes mean to older people? It may take them a little longer to understand new information such as a change in Medicare policies. It also may mean that they need to check a map twice before they figure out a new bus route. It doesn't mean that they've forgotten how to balance a checkbook or how to find their way home from the supermarket.

Caregiver Tip	Inspect an older person's glasses carefully for fit and cleanliness. More than one complaint of failing vision has been "cured" with a thorough cleaning of sticky, smudged glasses.

UNDERSTANDING CHANGES IN THE SENSES

Most of the changes in the senses (vision, hearing, taste, smell, touch, and balance) that occur with aging can be either easily adapted to or compensated for using assistive devices such as eyeglasses, hearing aids, smoke alarms, and bath thermometers.

Vision

One of the most common age-related changes in vision actually occurs in middle age. Sometime between ages 40 and 45, many people find it difficult to read the fine print of a contract or the telephone book. This is a change in accommodation; in other words, the ability of the eye to change focus on objects at various distances decreases because of the increased density and rigidity of the eye lens, which results from lost elasticity. This is a common age-related change. The term *presbyopia* is used by health care professionals to describe this change in the eye. Usually, this condition is easily corrected with reading glasses.

Other visual changes require different types of adaptation. The ability to see distant objects, perceive depth well, and tolerate glare decreases gradually with age. (You may recall that Sam, the healthy 89-year-old introduced earlier in the chapter, limited his driving to the daytime hours.) As the pupil of the eye becomes smaller and less responsive to light, older people find that it takes longer to adjust to sudden darkness. Night blindness also may make it more difficult to drive at night, especially in poorly lit areas. As the lens of the eye becomes more rigid and opaque, some older people have greater difficulty seeing clearly in dim light. Higher levels of illumination without glare can help them adjust to this change.

Reduced tear production may result in uncomfortably dry eyes. Eye drops that are made up of substances that are similar to natural tears may correct this condition. Another vision problem that sometimes worries older people is "floaters," tiny dark spots that appear to move in front of the eyes. Unless a large number appear suddenly, floaters usually are harmless, although they can be annoying.

Hearing

About one third of people older than age 75 have some degree of hearing loss. More men than women are affected. The most common change is a loss in the ability to hear higher tones. This hearing loss usually occurs in both ears (symmetrical hearing loss), progresses with advancing age, and runs in families from generation to generation. It also can be caused by prior prolonged exposure to loud noises from industrial machinery, weapons, and music.

Probably the most serious consequence of hearing loss is difficulty understanding what other people are saying. Rapid speech, poor transmission (for example, a crackly radio or poor telephone connection), background noise, or competing conversations make speech more difficult to understand, especially for the person with some degree of hearing loss. The importance of being able to hear well is underestimated. People who can't hear well may become withdrawn, socially isolated, even paranoid. They may avoid social situations and pretend not to be interested in conversations because they can't hear them and don't want to reveal their disability. Hearing loss also is a safety concern. Many

> **Caregiver Tip**
>
> Is the volume on an older person's television set really loud? The person may have a hearing impairment. Seek a medical evaluation.

danger signs come through our ears: ambulance sirens, fire alarms, and shouts of "look out!" for example. Caregivers need to be alert to the signs of hearing loss and help their loved one to seek medical attention.

Not all hearing loss results from aging, however. A relatively rapid loss of hearing may come from an accumulation of earwax (*cerumen*) blocking the ear canal. Removal of the cerumen can immediately restore some older people's hearing. If the accumulation is not too large or too hard, it can be removed after softening it with warm baby oil. Firmly impacted cerumen should be removed by a health care provider to prevent damage to the ear canal or eardrum.

Taste

Contrary to popular opinion, most healthy people don't lose their sense of taste or the ability to choose between sweet and salty tastes as they get older. In fact, these changes seem to be abnormal changes that occur in older adults with other health problems. A reduction in saliva flow due to the effects of illness or certain medications may make tasting and swallowing foods a bit more difficult.

Smell

Unlike taste, there does seem to be a well-documented decreased effectiveness in the sense of smell as people age. As many as 40%–60% of people older than age 80 have a diminished sense of smell. This not only lessens the pleasure of eating, but it's also a safety concern. An unimpaired sense of smell alerts us to such potential dangers as spoiled food, gas leaks, or smoke from food burning on the stove.

Touch

Although there's not much research on tactile changes with age, what has been found is that there's decreased sensitivity to touch and a loss in the amount of nerve endings with age. Decreased touch sensitivity is especially prevalent in the fingertips and palms and in the lower extremities (legs, feet). Some changes in touch sensitivity are related to nerve damage, circulatory impairment, and/or disease. Decreased touch sensitivity makes people less able to discriminate among levels of pain. The risk for injury from burns caused by bath water that's too hot and heating pads and ice packs that are placed directly on the body also increases with age.

Caregiver Tip

The inability to detect spoiled food is a common cause of gastrointestinal upsets in older people who are trying to stretch their limited food budgets.

Balance

To maintain balance, people rely on the sensory information they get from the skin (for example, the sole of the foot), the joints, and the eyes, as well as on the proper functioning of the inner ear structures. These structures help you keep equilibrium. Any or all of these areas can be affected by age-related changes. The ability to maintain balance may begin to decline after age 40; however, healthy older people shouldn't have any serious problems maintaining their balance.

If you observe that the older adult in your life falls frequently or limits his or her activity because of a fear of falling, then the person needs a medical exam so that vision, hearing, or possible neurological changes can be ruled out. Sometimes a problem with balance occurs because of a drop in blood pressure, which could happen for a variety of reasons, medication side effects being just one.

UNDERSTANDING CHANGES IN SLEEP AND REST

Nightly restful, restorative sleep is important at any age. As people age, normal changes in sleep patterns occur. A decrease in the

> ### Sleep Pattern Questionnaire
>
> What time do you usually go to bed at night?
>
> What time do you wake up in the morning?
>
> Do you take naps? When? How often? For how long?
>
> Do you wake up during the night? How often?
>
> What causes you to wake up?
> > The need to use the bathroom.
> >
> > Physical discomfort
> >
> > Disturbances in the environment (noise, light)
> >
> > Emotional concerns or worries

neurotransmitter serotonin may be partly responsible for these changes. Older people may awaken frequently during the night, and the length of deep sleep time may be greatly reduced. Without deep sleep, older people may feel depressed or experience general body malaise, apathy, and lethargy.

The period of rapid eye movement (REM) sleep also declines, especially in very old age (85 years and older). REM sleep is necessary for the nervous system to function properly, and people who are deprived of this sleep stage may be irritable and anxious when awake and, in some cases, may behave in ways that are out of character. The quality of sleep, not just the hours spent in bed with eyes closed, also is important. Asking the older person a few simple questions about his or her sleep pattern can help you determine whether a visit to the doctor is necessary.

Many older adults, if asked, will say that they don't sleep well, they get up pretty early, and they can't fall back to sleep once they're awake. What they don't say is that often they go to bed very early, they'd taken a nap during the day, or they'd been only minimally active the day before. All of these factors have an influence on nighttime sleep patterns.

Brief awakenings from sleep during the night, although normal, give the impression of sleeplessness, especially to worried, anxious individuals. Because of these awakenings, some older adults don't believe they're sleeping well and ask their physicians for sleep medications. Although most of these medications reduce the

Why Is My Loved One Sleeping More than Usual?

Boredom (inactivity, loneliness)

Increased number of sedating medications

Depression (illness, mourning losses)

Signs/symptoms of disease
Kidney failure
Cardiac disease

Why Is My Loved One Sleeping Less than Usual?

New environment

Stress (change in environment, illness)

Anxiety (change in environment, illness)

Depression

Pain

number of awakenings for a while, the awakenings eventually return. In addition, changes in older people's ability to eliminate these medications from the body can cause them to accumulate gradually in the body, leaving people oversedated or excessively sleepy during the day. Because withdrawal from sleep medications can cause rebound insomnia (insomnia that gets worse after medications are stopped), it's recommended that older people avoid using sleep medications unless truly necessary and then only for a short period of time.

Fluid buildup, usually the result of heart disease, causes many older adults to have difficulty sleeping. They may experience frequent nighttime urination and shortness of breath while lying down. It's important to distinguish the normal changes in a loved one's sleeping pattern from changes that suggest a disease or other abnormality.

UNDERSTANDING CHANGES IN SEXUAL FUNCTIONING

Changes in sexual functioning are related to a slowing or ceasing of processes that are necessary for reproduction. Their reproductive years may be gone, but older adults continue to be interested in and concerned about sex and sexuality.

Men

Although sperm production decreases throughout middle age and older adulthood—the sperm count for a man of 80 or 90 will be half that of a 25 year old—men in their 70s, 80s, and 90s still have sexual interest and are capable of reproduction. As they age, men experience slower arousal time and less ejaculate because of reduced testosterone levels. A man's orgasm may be less intense due to changes in the blood supply to the penis. A longer "rest" period than that experienced in a man's youth may be required after ejaculation before another erection can be stimulated. The inability to achieve or maintain an erection (impotence, erectile dysfunction) usually is caused by disease or psychological factors rather than by the normal changes of aging. Hypertension, diabetes, alcohol intoxication, and depression can also affect a man's sexual performance.

Women

The reduction in estrogen and progesterone levels after menopause in women results in diminished breast size as glandular tissue wastes away and is replaced by fat. The breasts often sag or droop because of connective tissue changes. These hormonal changes also cause the chemical composition of vaginal secretions to change, becoming less acidic. This change puts older women at greater risk for urinary and vaginal infections (for example, yeast infections are common because yeast bacteria thrive in a nonacid environment). The vulva and clitoris decrease in size and become less elastic, the lining of the vagina becomes thinner, and vaginal secretions decrease, making inter-

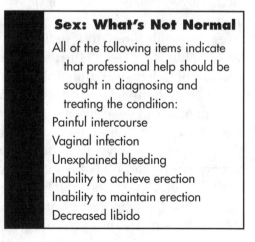

Sex: What's Not Normal

All of the following items indicate that professional help should be sought in diagnosing and treating the condition:

Painful intercourse

Vaginal infection

Unexplained bleeding

Inability to achieve erection

Inability to maintain erection

Decreased libido

course less comfortable for many women. Discomfort is easily cured through the use of water-based lubricants, such as KY Jelly, but some older women say they're too embarrassed to buy them and/or use them.

UNDERSTANDING CHANGES IN THE IMMUNE SYSTEM AND THE SKIN

Our bodies rely on the immune system and the skin to help defend against infection and disease. Both of these defense systems become a little less efficient and effective with age.

Immune System

The body responds to infection by activating the immune system whereby special blood cells circulate through the body to reach the site of the infection. These special cells mount an attack on the invader (the bacteria or virus causing the infection). A successful attack kills the invading cells and cleans up the debris of the killed cells.

Active immune responses diminish with age. The body's response to an invading microorganism may be reduced by 50%–80%. Older adults also may have a delayed or inadequate immune system response to the infection because of decreased blood flow, perhaps as a result of heart disease. In addition, very old people are less likely than younger people to develop a high fever. Not only does this reduce the body's defenses but also makes it harder to detect the first signs of serious illnesses such as pneumonia. Because the normal temperature (the baseline, which is the temperature on waking up in the morning) of many older people can be as low as 97° F, a temperature of 99° F can actually be a fever, although they wouldn't seem feverish to a caregiver. Experts believe that decreased physical and muscular activity, decreased body insulation due to an age-related loss of subcutaneous fat (the layer of fat under the top layer of skin), and thinning of the skin contribute to the decrease in the baseline temperature of many older people. These age-related changes also make it more difficult for older adults to respond to longtime exposure to low environmental temperatures (*hypothermia*) or to high environmental temperatures (*hyperthermia*).

What's important for you to understand is that the presence of frequent infections or infections that don't respond to treatment in a reasonable time isn't normal. The older adult in your life may need a health care professional's intervention to fight not only the infection but also the stress of the infection on his or her body.

Skin

The skin is an amazingly effective barrier against invasions of various kinds. It helps to protect us against bacteria and other microorganisms, cool the body, and enable us to perceive sensations. Wrinkles and dry skin are familiar signs of aging. Less familiar is the loss of subcutaneous fat, especially on the arms and legs. The loss of this cushion makes older people more vulnerable to changes in temperature and to skin breakdown.

The skin loses elasticity, leading to the decreased ability of the skin, when pinched, to return quickly to its former shape (*skin turgor*). A reduction in the size, number, and function of the sweat glands also contributes to dry skin and increased vulnerability to heat as this part of the body's cooling system becomes less efficient. Skin also heals more slowly if it's cut or injured because the cells of older people reproduce far more slowly—only 50% as fast as in younger people. The outer layers of the skin, which appear to be thinner and more translucent, may slide over the lower layer (the layer directly under the outer layer), causing bruising just under the skin (*purpura senilis*). Purpura senilis is very common in women and may be a concern until it's explained to them.

Older skin is very sensitive to the sun because of a reduction in the number of pigment cells, or melanocytes. You may see the development of liver or age spots (*lentigo senilis*), those large brown, pigmented areas on the top of the hands, arms, and face. Age spots are harmless, but they might cause older people to feel self-conscious.

Raised areas, or lesions, that appear scaly and sometimes bleed at the edges, called actinic keratoses, can show up on the exposed skin of older people. The area around a lesion may look red and inflamed. Some of these lesions could become cancerous, so they need to be examined regularly. If you or the older adult in your life notices any change in the size and/or color of the lesion(s), seek a medical assessment immediately.

• • •

Many changes take place in our bodies as we age. However, there are clear differences between age-related changes in the body and disease processes. Chapter 5 covers ways to maintain and enhance your own health and in turn the health of older family members to allow all of you to participate fully in daily activities.

7   Understanding Memory and Emotional States and Changes in Aging

Jasper was in a hurry. The "boys" would start the card game without him. He grabbed his jacket and rushed out of the house, letting the door slam behind him. Once outside, he realized that his hands were empty, and so were his pockets. He had forgotten both his keys and his wallet. They were still on the dresser where he'd left them the night before.

Instead of playing cards, Jasper spent the morning breaking into his own house and then going to the hardware store to have a duplicate set of keys made. "I'm not going to let that happen again," he told his neighbor, who promised to keep the spare set of keys in a safe place in case Jasper locked himself out again.

All of us have experienced memory lapses at one time or another; for example, we've forgotten where we left the car keys or the name of a new acquaintance. "I must be getting senile," or "I'm having 'a senior moment'" we might joke, before resuming our everyday activities. To many older adults and their caregivers, however, the possibility of developing memory loss isn't funny. It's all too real, something that lies in wait that will ruin their later years. As the media's focus on Alzheimer's disease has intensified, so have the fears among middle age and older adults that they, too, might someday experience the slow but steady mental deterioration that characterizes Alzheimer's disease.

Many people are unsure about when a minor problem remembering starts to become a major problem and may view the normal changes in memory that are associated with aging as signs of impending dementia. There's an enormous difference between minor memory lapses or even a "mental block" about something and the cognitive (mental processes of knowing, thinking, learning, judging, remembering) losses that come with Alzheimer's disease or a related dementia.

This chapter looks at memory and the changes that can occur as we age, as well as our connections with the past, loneliness, emotional states such as depression and anxiety, and the role of sexuality in old age. Like Chapter 6, this chapter points out what is an expected part of aging and what isn't. The chapter also provides information that'll help you decide whether a family member's behavior indicates a need for evaluation by a health care provider.

Understanding Memory

The English word *senility* comes from the Latin *senilis,* meaning old. Medical practitioners and laypersons alike used this term for the condition that's now known as Alzheimer's disease. As recently as 1980, any older person who was confused or forgetful was likely to be called senile, a disparaging term with little empathy for the plight of people with dementia. Often, older people whose mental condition deteriorated markedly were placed in mental institutions. There, they might be locked in a room or tied to a chair or bed. Senility was considered to be an entirely hopeless and unmanageable condition. Fortunately, our attitudes about and treatment of people who develop Alzheimer's disease and related memory problems are more enlightened now.

We all know an older adult with significant memory loss. We also know others in their 70s, 80s, and even 90s who are still "as sharp as a tack." Which of these situations represents normal aging? Is progressive memory loss an expected part of growing older? Are the people who don't experience memory loss the lucky exceptions?

Normal Changes of Aging

Most of the changes in memory and other thought processes that occur with advancing age are quite subtle and don't interfere to any extent with managing everyday tasks. As mentioned in Chapter 6, our thought processes do slow down somewhat as we age, and solving never-before-encountered problems may be a greater challenge than it was when we were younger adults.

Researchers have identified two types of thought processes, fluid and crystallized, that are affected differently by aging. Fluid abilities are the abilities that are needed to deal with new or different situations and problems. These abilities may diminish as a person gets older. Crystallized abilities draw on an older person's years of experience. Having experience with particular problems and plenty of practice solving them, the older person handles these or similar difficulties with ease.

Solving new types of problems takes longer and requires more effort from older people. The difference is most apparent when older people are rushed, tired, or anxious. These factors can interfere temporarily with clear thinking. Changes such as moving to a new town, moving into your home or a nursing facility, or going into the hospital for the first time in many years also require older adults to learn new rules, places, routines, and people. Although many older people may not process these changes as quickly or as easily as they did in the past, they certainly can learn new rules, places, routines, and people—it may take a little more time and a little more effort to do so.

Age-Associated Memory Impairments

The normal age-related changes in memory can be contrasted with the small memory lapses experienced by many older adults (for example, inability to find car keys, remember a person's name, or remember every item on a shopping list left at home). For some older people these small lapses, called age-associated memory impairment (AAMI), happen fairly often. The lapses are annoying and perhaps worrisome, but they don't mean that the person has Alzheimer's disease or a related dementia. AAMI usually doesn't get worse with time, and it interferes only minimally with everyday activities. People with AAMI may find it helpful to use memory devices (such as making lists) and memory training to reduce its effects.

Acute Confusion

Some serious problems with thought processes are temporary and can be reversed with appropriate treatment; others can't. The reduced physical reserves discussed in Chapter 6 are just as true of the brain as they are of other vital organs. The older (especially the very old) person's thought processes are extremely sensitive to the effects of fever, dehydration, medication, reduced oxygen supply to the brain, or a blood sugar level that is too high or too low. Any of these factors can create a state of acute confusion. A person in this state may appear drowsy and dazed or restless, excitable, and delirious.

Acute confusion often occurs in older people who are acutely ill or hospitalized. Two important things to know about acute confusion are that 1) usually, it can be reversed by correcting the underlying cause—reducing fever, increasing fluids, stopping the medication(s) that's responsible, controlling blood sugar, and so on; and 2) it can easily be mistaken for Alzheimer's disease. The danger is that, without proper treatment, this temporary condition can become permanent. For this reason, any sustained, major memory loss or loss of other cognitive abilities should be evaluated by a health care specialist who knows how to determine the difference between a reversible condition and an irreversible condition. Depression also can be mistaken for dementia, but depression can and should be treated vigorously (see Chapter 14 for information on treatment options).

Alzheimer's Disease

Alzheimer's disease is the result of physical changes that take place in the brain, usually affecting the parts that are responsible for memory. Although a great deal of research is being done to find the cause of and an effective treatment for the disease, the damage that's caused by Alzheimer's disease can't yet be reversed.

The early signs of Alzheimer's disease are subtle and may be missed entirely, mistaken for emotional problems, or even said to be deliberate attempts to aggravate other people. As the disease progresses, the affected individual experiences increasingly significant problems, such as getting lost in familiar places, overdrawing his or her bank account, and forgetting important appointments. Eventually the person with Alzheimer's disease can't hold a job, run a household, choose clothes, or drive a car safely. In advanced stages of the disease the person needs help with the simplest tasks, such as taking a bath, getting dressed, or eating.

It's not an overstatement that the prospect of developing Alzheimer's disease is frightening. However, the terror lessens somewhat when you understand what Alzheimer's disease is, what causes it, and how to manage it. New drugs offer hope for improving function in older adults with the disease, and an array of treatments are available to make the person with advanced Alzheimer's disease more comfortable. Many resources and support groups are available to those who are confronted with a diagnosis of Alzheimer's disease. A number of these are mentioned in later chapters and the list of resources at the back of the book.

CONNECTING TO THE PAST

It's often said that old people live in the past. Is this really true? Is it healthy to talk about the past all the time? You may be surprised that the answer to both of these questions is no.

Our concept of time changes as we get older. As years go by, the time already lived becomes greater than the time left to live. This realization changes our perspective on life. Even though the amount of time that remains to any of us is unknown, for older people there's definitely more past than future. Fewer and fewer generations lie ahead until, finally, there are none.

The older we get, the more losses we experience: first grandparents; then aunts, uncles, and parents; and, finally, brothers, sisters, friends, and spouses/partners. Although new friends and new generations fill many of the gaps that are left by those who have died, they can't fill the gap of a shared history. Caregivers who are younger relatives or new friends or neighbors don't share an older person's memories of childhood or young adulthood. They tend to think of the person as always old because they've only known him or her as old. In contrast, a member of the same or an older generation also may have known the person as a child, teenager, or young adult. Brothers and sisters, for example, can remember shared childhood adventures as well as significant events in the person's life: high school graduation, first job, birth of the first child, and so forth. Older people talk about these past events not only to review them or find purpose in them but also to remind others that they were young once and still have some of the same thoughts and feelings that they had when they were young. They may look different than they did when they were younger, but they're still the same people.

Time seems to pass more quickly as we get older. A 3-year-old child can hardly sit still for 5 minutes. For a 10-year-old, the 2 weeks before Christmas seem like an eternity. At age 80, however, 5 minutes go by in a flash and having 2 weeks until Christmas means you'd better hurry up and finish the shopping! With less time left to live and time speeding by, many older people want to take stock, to think and talk about what they have done and how they feel about it. Some may choose to engage in a serious life review. Life review can be done by writing a short autobiography (maybe two or three pages long), joining a life review group at a senior center or seniors club, or going into life review therapy with a trained counselor. Life review also provides an opportunity for older adults to think about the purpose of existence and to search for the meaning of life.

Other ways that older people can get in touch with their past are to research their family history, construct a family tree, and visit their childhood town or where their parents lived. These activities help older people answer important questions about going on with their lives and life's purpose.

UNDERSTANDING LONELINESS

You may ask, what's the big deal about old people and loneliness? Don't a lot of older people live alone? Aren't they used to it? Don't they prefer it? Being alone and feeling isolated and lonely are very different. Being alone may be welcome at times, but loneliness can be very painful emotionally. People need the company of other people to provide companionship, friendship, and affection. At any age, people need at least one confidante.

It's important to have people to care about and to have people who care about you. In surveys of older people who are ill or disabled and living at home, they often list loneliness, not finances, medical care, or transportation, as their greatest concern. Being needed is important to many people. Without it, some people lose their reason for living. If no one or nothing intervenes, loneliness and isolation can lead to depression and, sometimes, suicide (see Chapter 14 for more information on how to help someone who is feeling suicidal). Physical illness also has been linked to long-term loneliness. Researchers have found that solitary individuals are more likely to become ill after exposure to a disease than are people who are surrounded by a network of family and friends. The title of a *Time* magazine article said it well: "Loneliness can kill."

Being alone—solitude—and feeling lonely—isolation—are not the same. Solitude can be welcome. It can be time to think, to rest, to be creative without interruptions. For people with a busy lifestyle it can be a pleasure to have some moments of peace and quiet. In contrast, isolation means having no one to turn to, no one to talk with. For some people, it also means having no one who understands or appreciates you, maybe even no one who cares what happens to you. This is neither welcome nor pleasant; in fact, it may be one of the most painful experiences in life.

Isolation can result from disability as much as from the loss of loved ones. Older adults who are homebound are at greatest risk for isolation. Losing one's driver's license can contribute to isolation and loneliness, particularly for older people who live in rural areas or apartment complexes located far from the center of town or those who aren't able to use buses or trains for whatever reason.

Older people are vulnerable to loneliness for several reasons. As loved ones die, older people can find themselves alone for the first time. Imagine being married to one person and sharing a home, meals, and a bed for 60 years, and suddenly he or she dies. It's a great shock to the system, and some people never get over it. It's ironic that some older people who move in with their adult children, anticipating that this will alleviate their loneliness, discover that they're even lonelier. They're far from old friends and neighbors and may be isolated in suburban communities with no public transportation and few opportunities to socialize with people their own age. Moving too soon after a spouse dies often is regretted later; the familiar faces and caring people of the old neighborhood and the community are lost, and these losses can be very difficult to bear on top of the loss of a spouse.

Opportunities to make friends also can diminish as people age. People who developed most of their friendships at work or through their husband or wife can find themselves without a source of new friends unless they discover new associations through their church or temple, social clubs, senior and recreation centers; new or revived old hobbies; or volunteer activities.

UNDERSTANDING DEPRESSION

Depression is the most common form of mental illness among older people, and an estimated 5 million are seriously depressed. In fact, the risk of depression among people who experienced the Great Depression of the 1930s and World War II is four times greater than it is in the general population. Unfortunately, the majority of these conditions go unrecognized and untreated. Occasional periods of feeling "low," "blue," or "down" are quite normal, but when a person has the blues for more than 2 weeks, and this mood has begun to interfere with normal activities, there's cause for concern. Let's look first at some of the reasons that older adults become depressed and then at indicators of a serious, or clinical, depression.

Several factors place older adults at risk for depression:

1.   **Poor health**—When older adults become increasingly disabled or more dependent on others, they may feel hopeless and may feel like they've lost control over their lives. The way that older adults feel about the loss of control that comes with these conditions may affect how they feel about themselves and their sense of how others see them.

2.   **Insecure attachments and low self-worth**—Weak or limited attachments to others—for example, to adult children—

together with low self-esteem are strongly related to depression in older adults.

3. **Changes in financial status**—In their retirement years, many older adults don't have the same level of income as they did when they were working. Reduced financial status also may be responsible for low self-esteem, which can lead to depression. Changes in financial status can have an impact on older people's ability to feel in control of their lives.

4. **Isolation**—Losses of family, friends, and peers result in decreased social interaction and attachment to other people. The loneliness resulting from these losses has been related to depression, especially in women.

5. **Bereavement**—Older people are at high risk for psychological complications during a time of bereavement, especially following the death of a spouse or child. The effect of these losses can lead to clinical depression in some people.

6. **Other significant losses**—Losing their home, where the past was alive in a known, familiar place and in things; losing their community, where involvement and acceptance in it contributed to positive self-esteem; and losing life roles such as occupation, which made them feel important and needed

Depression can be difficult to diagnose in older adults, especially when other illnesses or medications mask its signs and symptoms. This is made more difficult by the fact that many older adults seek advice from health care professionals who don't have much education or experience in diagnosing and treating depression. The result is that depression often is overlooked or treated improperly. This is unfortunate because depression is likely to respond to the proper treatment. Without treatment depression can become chronic and disabling.

Many older people resist talking about any feelings that might suggest a mental health problem. They feel more comfortable talking to the doctor about aches and pains rather than their feelings. Some may resist counseling or therapy because they associate them with being labeled "crazy" or "weak." There also are cultural and individual differences in older people's willingness to acknowledge emotional problems and seek treatment. Some people still consider emotional distress shameful or wrong, leading them to hide their problems rather than to seek help.

People who are depressed feel a great deal of emotional pain. Being told to "get a hold of yourself," or, "you have plenty of money; what have you got to be depressed about?" isn't

Signs of Clinical Depression

Sleep disturbances (too much or too little sleep)

Significant weight loss or gain

Restlessness, agitation, or irritability

Constant complaints of feeling exhausted

Feelings of worthlessness, self-reproach, and/or excessive guilt

Difficulty thinking or concentrating

Loss of interest in other things and other people, including oneself

Suicidal thoughts or attempts

helpful. Most people who are depressed can't simply pull themselves out of it, as they're often urged to do. They require carefully selected medication and counseling with trained professionals who have experience in treating older people with depression. These professionals have a positive attitude toward aging and older people (see Chapter 14 for more information about treatments). Therapists who are condescending or pessimistic about an older person's resilience and potential for recovery should be avoided.

Earlier in the chapter, we mentioned that around 5 million older people are seriously depressed, which is also known as clinical depression. How can you tell the difference between short-term sadness and clinical depression? Be alert to the signs and symptoms that, in combination, often are clues that the older adult in your life is clinically depressed (see display above).

Seek medical attention if you notice these signs and symptoms in the older adult in your life.

UNDERSTANDING ANXIETY

Anxiety is an emotional state of apprehension, worry, uneasiness, or dread. It's sometimes overlooked because caregivers assume that older people experience these feelings less frequently than younger people do. In fact, older people may experience as much or more anxiety as younger people. They may, however, hide their feelings better or work harder to avoid anxiety-producing situations.

Some feelings of anxiety in older people are reasonable and justified. Concerns about the future are natural and understandable. People with strong religious beliefs may be better prepared to deal with an uncertain future than are people who aren't strongly religious or are agnostics or atheists. Fear about the state of their health dominates the thoughts of some older adults. One common source of mild to moderate anxiety for older adults is going to the doctor or the dentist. Consider the following scenario:

Aunt Sarah

Aunt Sarah asks you to take her to the doctor for her regular visit. Although she's worried about seeing some blood in her bowel movement, she tells you, "Otherwise I feel pretty good for an 80-year-old lady." As you help her into the car, she grabs your arm tensely. You realize that Aunt Sarah is somewhat anxious about this visit. Her voice is calm, however, and you chat easily. Once in the doctor's office, you sense a change in Aunt Sarah's mood as she waits to be called. The speed and tone of her voice change. Her eyes get wide, and you can see perspiration on her forehead as she talks about seeing the doctor.

Aunt Sarah is experiencing *anticipatory anxiety*, which means that she's nervous about the results of the doctor's examination. This is a normal feeling, given the problems that may cause rectal bleeding. Her anxiety isn't interfering with her ability to function normally, although she may need some extra time to make decisions if the doctor presents her with a difficult choice about her treatment options.

Transient anxiety is related to a specific trigger or a stressful situation. The chronic type, which is anxiety that continues to be present, eventually interferes with responding appropriately to one's own needs:

George

George is 75 and recently lost his wife. He has multiple chronic physical disorders that require frequent monitoring. By choice, he lives alone in a large house, but he's finding it difficult to care for himself and his house. He says he feels very anxious, afraid of what may happen to him and afraid that he may die alone.

Anxiety can be put in four categories: mild, moderate, severe, and panic state. Let's look at each type of anxiety and the signs and symptoms associated with each one (see also Figure 1).

Mild Anxiety

When asked to describe how they feel, people who are experiencing anxiety will say that they feel uptight, jittery, nervous, or tense. If the anxiety is mild, these feelings aren't particularly uncomfortable. In fact, mild anxiety creates a state of heightened awareness, a higher level of alertness, and a more rapid response to stimulation. People feeling mild anxiety usually are able to respond constructively.

Moderate Anxiety

When anxiety increases to a moderate level, a person's focus becomes narrower and more intent on the source of the anxiety. He or she also may feel physical symptoms such as dry mouth or sweaty palms. Many, but not all, people feeling moderate anxiety can respond constructively to these heightened feelings.

Severe Anxiety

Anxiety can increase to the point at which people hyperventilate, complain of a racing heartbeat, and appear very agitated. They're only able to focus on a single detail, they have a limited attention span, and they may feel an urge either to fight or

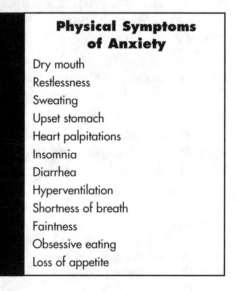

Physical Symptoms of Anxiety

Dry mouth
Restlessness
Sweating
Upset stomach
Heart palpitations
Insomnia
Diarrhea
Hyperventilation
Shortness of breath
Faintness
Obsessive eating
Loss of appetite

<u>**Mild Anxiety**</u>
Tense muscles
Calm voice
Able to function well

    <u>**Moderate Anxiety**</u>
    Increased pulse
    More rapid breathing
    Enlarged pupils
    Increased sweating
    Tense muscles (jitters)
    High-pitched voice
    Fast speech

        <u>**Severe Anxiety**</u>
        Very fast breathing
        Racing heartbeat
        Tense muscles
        Agitation
        Able to focus on only one thing at a time
        Unable to cope

            <u>**Panic State**</u>
            Dizzy
            Faint
            Pale
            Overwhelmed
            Fear of imminent death or going crazy

FIGURE 1. Some signs of anxiety.

flee the anxiety-producing situation. These are symptoms of a severe anxiety attack.

Panic State

The most serious state of anxiety is the panic state. In a panic state, people exhaust their physical and emotional resources and feel completely overwhelmed. They may feel dizzy or faint. These people have racing thoughts and may feel a sense of impending doom. They may feel that they're dying or going mad. People in a panic state need immediate intervention to relieve these fears and deal with whatever triggered them.

How to Cope

Symptoms of anxiety can escalate rapidly unless some action is taken to relieve the stress. When the anxiety is mild or moderate, people usually are able to relieve their own anxiety. If the anxiety has escalated to the severe or panic level, they may need help initiating the following coping strategies:

1. **Express your concerns.** Often, simply stating out loud that you're worried about something diminishes its enormity.
2. **Talk out your concerns.** Talking about the concerns, why they are so important, with an empathic person can lessen the feelings of anxiety.
3. **Problem solve.** Taking time to think through the reasons behind the concerns (there's always a reason!) and how the problem can be resolved is very helpful.
4. **Work off the anxiety.** Exercising, cleaning the house vigorously, or spending a few hours in the workshop helps many people reduce tension.
5. **Seek comfort from others.** The presence of a caring, supportive person—without even talking about the concern—may relieve a lot of the anxiety.
6. **Rely on your faith.** Turning to prayer and contemplation reduces anxiety in many older people, whereas others prefer to meditate or do relaxation exercises such as rhythmic deep breathing.
7. **Withdrawal.** Removing yourself from the anxiety-producing situation, even temporarily, and using some of the other strategies in this list can be very helpful.

If the person's anxiety has become so great that none of these strategies help, it may be necessary to call on a physician, religious advisor, or therapist for help. Telephone crisis lines, crisis intervention centers, and mental health centers in your community also may be able to provide immediate or short-term assistance.

UNDERSTANDING SEXUALITY

In Chapter 6 we looked at how the physical changes of aging affect reproductive ability and the sexual responses of older adults. For the caregiver, however, the approach to understanding sexuality in older adults is often more emotional than physical.

The opportunity for sexual activity decreases with age, especially if a spouse becomes very ill or dies. Unfortunately, many caregivers and health care professionals assume that sexuality is no longer an issue for older adults. "Does it really matter at that age?" is a common, if unspoken, question. In fact, it *does* matter, and very much.

There are many myths about sexuality and aging (see Figure 2). These myths convey the message that old people don't have sex or that sexual activity is unnatural, reinforcing negative stereotypes like "the dirty old man." Sexual needs don't disappear with age.

Although sexual activity may or may not continue into old age, older people don't become asexual. They continue to have a

Sex is only for young people

♦

Sexual activity by older adults is immoral

♦

Sexual desire ceases with menopause

♦

Men are impotent after removal of the prostate gland (*prostatectomy*)

♦

Masturbation is an immature activity for youngsters and adolescents and is not engaged in by older adults

♦

Elderly people are too old and frail to engage in sex

FIGURE 2. *Common myths about sexuality and aging.*

sexual identity as male or female, and they continue to have sexual needs. Older people continue to need affection and physical contact. The pleasure that comes from holding hands, hugging, or sharing a kiss isn't limited to people younger than age 50. Older people need privacy for the expression and fulfillment of sexual needs and your recognition that these needs exist. By understanding and respecting their right to express their sexuality, you can give the dependent older adult in your life a feeling of independence and control over an important aspect of his or her self-image and relationships with other people.

•••

You can't possibly fill all of the emotional needs of the dependent older person or single-handedly resolve all of his or her emotional problems. What you can do is be a caring presence in the older person's life, respect his or her feelings, help him or her to fulfill these needs through contact with other people, and recognize when mental health problems are beyond his or her ability to resolve them and require outside guidance and assistance.

8

Practicing Prevention

Our focus in this section of the book is on giving you the information you need to help keep the dependent older adult in your life as healthy as possible. Chapters 6 and 7 helped you to better understand what is normal physically and mentally as a person ages and alerted you to physical and mental changes that aren't normal. This chapter provides recommendations for promoting good health and preventing disease in the older adult in your life. It looks at exercise, nutrition, and attitudes toward health and gives suggestions for preventive health checkups and maintenance.

Because how we use our muscles and bones, what we eat, and how we feel about ourselves influence our overall health, we hope that the information will encourage you to get your loved one involved in activities that help maintain his or her highest possible level of well-being. At the same time, we ask that you take into account your loved one's health condition. Your goal as a caregiver is to maintain the current level of functioning of the body organs that aren't impaired or damaged. Doing this will slow down or delay the amount of the person's dependency on you as well as help to maintain whatever level of functioning exists in impaired systems or organs.

An increase in physical activity may help the older adult in your life maintain his or her ability to carry out daily activities such as eating, dressing, walking, bathing, and going to the bathroom without assistance (you may hear health care professionals refer to these activities as ADLs, the activities of daily living). As an additional benefit, the onset of many health-related problems associated with aging, such as osteoporosis, arthritis, and heart disease, may be slowed or delayed, which improves quality of life.

Many older adults may not know how to stay healthy. Maybe their lifestyle never included practices that we now know are important to good health—regularly scheduled exercise, a balanced diet, regular medical checkups, and immunizations. In addition, today's older adults grew up during a time when occupations and chores involved a lot of physical labor. Washing clothes, cleaning the house, and getting to and from one's home, school, or job often were done without the machines that we depend on today— washer/dryer, vacuum cleaner, automobile, and so forth. Individuals who had a physically active youth and middle age may have had little opportunity or incentive to continue to engage in regular exercise as a way of maintaining fitness and good mental health. Perhaps because they're dependent on you, they lack the motivation to engage in activities that could enhance their well-being. Feelings of low self-worth and role changes (for example, from being the giver to being the receiver of care and support) may diminish their ability to understand the benefits of these activities and engage in behaviors that could enhance their well-being.

The following describes how one man's involvement in activities and eating a healthful diet enhanced his well-being:

Stan is an older adult with hypertension that he controls with medications. He lives alone (his wife of many years died 5 years ago). His involvement in life is structured so he can get the most out of it and enhance his current level of physical and mental health.

As measured in years Stan is 80, but in physical stamina and mental well-being he considers himself much younger. Stan attributes this state of wellness to his zest for the activities that have been a part of his life for many years. Three times a week, he takes a 1-hour-long brisk walk, outside in good weather and inside the local shopping mall in inclement weather. He always takes the stairs, not the elevator, when he has to go up one or two flights. Stan doesn't make excuses to avoid what he knows will help him to maintain his physical and mental well-being.

Stan is an avid reader and is very aware of the latest research on reducing fat intake and limiting simple carbohydrate intake. He makes sure that every day he eats or drinks fruits, vegetables, a limited amount of fat, six to eight glasses of water, and a multivitamin. Sometimes, though, Stan finds it hard to stick to a healthful diet and he slips a little. Because Stan is alert to the positive consequences of healthy living, he schedules appointments for regular checkups and immunizations with his health care provider.

Stan has a lot of things going for him. Let's look at how you can encourage the older adult in your life to be more like Stan, how you can help your loved one practice prevention.

HEREDITY AND LONGEVITY

Heredity (our genetic inheritance) influences longevity (how long we live). We all have known or heard of people in their 80s and 90s whose parents and grandparents also lived to an advanced age. These elders are quick to attribute their longevity to "good genes" and a healthful lifestyle. Some researchers believe that a person's life span may have a genetically programmed limit, with organs "preset" to break down at a specified time. An individual's positive attention to diet, lifestyle, personal habits, and psychological factors can modify this preset limit.

Regardless of their genetic makeup, most older adults, especially from their mid-80s on, become more vulnerable as they age to milder and milder stressors. These stressors contribute to the decline in function of various organs that we associate with old age. Although an older adult may have one or more chronic illnesses, it's often the decline in function, not the chronic illness(es), that's the actual cause of death. Recognition of this fact can help alleviate guilty feelings in caregivers who blame themselves for the death of a dependent elder or question whether they could've done more to prevent them from "going downhill."

Caregiver Tip

A strategy for living and building yourself to last includes

- Being aware of what situations provoke stress in your life and what to do to avoid them (or if you can't avoid them, what successful methods you've used in the past to cope with them)
- Staying physically active
- Eating a healthful diet
- Maintaining the proper weight for your height
- Avoiding tobacco products
- Drinking in moderation
- Staying involved socially

CAN EXERCISE REALLY MAKE A DIFFERENCE?

Researchers have confirmed that exercise plays an important role in enhancing the quality of life of all adults, including older adults who are debilitated or frail. All parts of the body benefit from regular physical activity. The display below highlights the most significant of these benefits.

Along with the physical benefits of regular exercise come psychological benefits. Almost without exception, people who exercise regularly say that they feel better mentally—energized, upbeat, and positive about themselves. This effect is sometimes called a "runner's high." They also report sleeping better and being more rested when they wake up, which can greatly improve overall health and functioning. Enhanced well-being also can have an effect on a person's level of dependence on others. Older adults who begin exercising regularly, whatever their level of exertion, may find that they're able to participate more fully in other activities, thus increasing their self-worth and building a more positive self-image. With increased self-worth and a positive self-image, these active older adults are less dependent on others for care and support. In addition, exercise can encourage togetherness and caring, and it can be pleasurable.

Caregiver Tip

The physiological benefits of regular exercise include improved heart, lung, digestive, and musculoskeletal function.

- When the **heart** is challenged regularly, it responds by pumping a more even flow of blood to the whole body.
- **Lung** expansion increases, enabling the lungs to take in more oxygen, which nourishes body tissues more completely. As a result, older adults feel less tired and more energetic.
- The **digestive system** absorbs more nutrients and removes toxic wastes more efficiently from the body.
- The **muscles and bones** are less prone to wasting (*atrophy*) from lack of use. Limb function is improved, and there is less stiffness in the joints. Even frail older adults experience improved mobility, balance, and strength, which decreases the incidence of falls.

Reach

Forward

Reach
and
bend

Turn

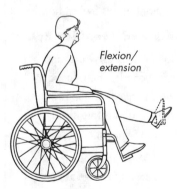

Flexion/
extension

Tilt

CREATING AN EXERCISE PROGRAM

When considering an exercise program for a dependent elder whose physical functioning is limited, choose exercises that don't go beyond the person's abilities. Exercises in which the arms and legs go through a series of simple motions can help decrease muscle wasting (*atrophy*) and increase dexterity and mobility, even in people who are bedridden. Older adults who are unable to get out of bed or who move with difficulty can perform various exercises while sitting up in bed or seated in a chair. Others whose physical function is only minimally or not at all impaired can perform stretching and dexterity exercises in conjunction with a walking program. Most important, before beginning an exercise program, even one that involves simple exercises like those in the next paragraph, check with your loved one's health care provider to make sure that the exercises are appropriate for his or her physical condition.

Four simple exercises, which can be performed by both physically active and bedridden or inactive older adults, can help improve the mobility, flexibility, and strength of key muscle groups

Four Simple Exercises

Hint: Performing slow deep-breathing exercises during these exercises helps improve lung and heart functioning.

Arm and Finger Stretches

Mime that you are putting on a pair of long gloves, pulling and stretching the glove over your fingers and hands and up each arm.

Fist Squeeze

Squeeze a soft foam ball in your dominant hand. Switch hands.

Neck and Shoulder Rolls

Bend your neck forward, and hold for 5 seconds. Then, let your head fall gently to the right shoulder, and rotate slowly around to the left side.

Arm and Leg Flexes/Extensions

Bend and then extend each arm and leg in turn.

and joints. The older adult in your life should spend about 10–15 minutes a day doing all four exercises. He or she should start slowly and work up to doing each exercise twice. If your loved one has arthritis, he or she should do the exercises in the morning, when the joints and muscles are rested and relaxed. Remember: *Never* exercise to the point of pain, and rest for 1 minute between exercises. Be aware of the limitations of the person, and be sure that an appropriate warm-up and cool-down period (about 5 minutes each) is scheduled both before and after exercise.

Warming up before exercising increases blood circulation and the pliability of muscles and helps people avoid injuries. Cooling down after exercise returns the blood to the heart from the body's extremities. Stretching slowly for several minutes the muscles that'll be used in a particular exercise decreases the tension in the muscles, which prevents injury.

For the older person who's able to get around fairly easily, short walks are beneficial (remember to use appropriate assistive devices such as a cane or walker, as needed). Your loved one can start by walking inside the house or apartment building, particularly if he or she is uncomfortable about or afraid of walking outside. Make sure that the walking path is clutter-free to prevent falls. Common obstacles are throw rugs, electrical cords, chair legs, and wet, slick, or sticky floors. Remove any objects that may present an obstacle or hazard. Also make sure that all furniture is sturdy and stable because the older person may need to lean on it. If walking outdoors, walk with the older adult on smooth, level surfaces. Model and encourage good posture. Above all, don't hurry. If the older adult in your life isn't used to walking alone, use a gait or safety belt to avoid falls and injuries. Gait belts, which

Caregiver Tip

One way to motivate or encourage older adults to participate in exercise is to play their favorite songs or Broadway show tunes. Familiar music not only stimulates people to move, but it can also put them in a good mood while they exercise.

are available from many medical supply stores, enable a companion to assist a weak or frail older adult to walk.

Before beginning any exercise program, be sure to discuss the plan with a health care provider.

The distance walked inside the house or apartment building can be increased gradually, as the older adult can tolerate, over a period of several weeks. As the older adult's energy level increases, he or she can progress to walking outside with assistance. (Remember that providing assistance means being nearby and ready to help the person if he or she feels dizzy or weak.) Often, exercising outdoors proves to be a great mood lifter. Besides the physical benefit of getting outdoors, it's well known that moderate exposure to the sun brings positive emotional benefits. The sun is also a good source of vitamin D, which is essential for keeping bones strong.

Whether indoors or out, walking requires wearing shoes that fit and support feet properly. Good shoes lessen the chances of injuring feet, and they help with balance. Walking shoes should not have slippery soles, nor should they be slippers. Refer to the section on foot care in Chapters 10 and 13 for a detailed description of what proper footwear is.

Are You Really What You Eat?

We often hear "you are what you eat," but is it really true? Certainly the food that we eat affects how our body functions and how we feel physically and mentally. Eating too much food or too much of the wrong foods (for example, high-fat, high-calorie foods like potato chips) has been linked to many health problems in older adults ranging from cardiovascular disease to cancer. As your loved one's caregiver, you can make a positive contribution to his or her physical and mental well-being by making sure that a nutritious and age-appropriate diet is consumed.

Alert!

During exercise, pay close attention to the responses of the older adult in your life. Does he or she seem tired and/or short of breath afterward? Does the person mention any discomfort or pain? Is he or she unable to talk while exercising? If so, your loved one may be overdoing the exercise or exercising beyond his or her capacity. Reassess before continuing with the program.

Look also at when the exercise session is scheduled. The time of day is an important influence on the way people respond physically to exercise. For most older people, the best time to exercise is early in the day, when the body is rested. If you're watching and listening to your loved one, the best time will become obvious to you.

Proper Nutrition

The Recommended Dietary Allowance (RDA) established by the National Academy of Science Research Council revises dietary requirements for Americans every 5 years, but the RDA doesn't address the daily requirements of people over 65. This is partly because of a lack of agreement about older people's need for increased amounts of nutrients. Studies on nutrient requirements have been carried out on younger people, and the estimations for older adults have been based largely on these results.

The Human Nutrition Research Center on Aging at Tufts University has devised a food pyramid specifically for people 70 and older (Figure 1). It depicts the amount of food that should be eaten by everyone in order of dietary importance, with the most important foods at the bottom of the pyramid.

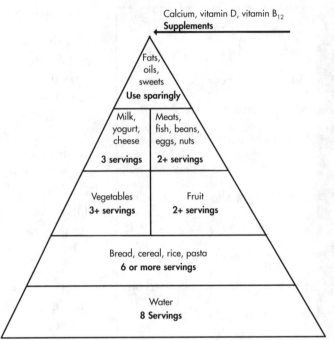

Source: Human Nutrition Research Center on Aging, Tufts University, Boston.

FIGURE 1.   *Food Guide Pyramid for older adults.*

The following eight tips can help older adults follow the dietary guidelines better:

1. **Eat a variety of foods**—Provide more servings of fruits and vegetables; frequently include dark green vegetables, beans, and starchy vegetables
2. **Maintain ideal weight**—Reduce fats, sugars, and alcohol; cut back on serving sizes; increase physical activity
3. **Avoid too much saturated fat and cholesterol**—Select lean hamburger and lean roasts, chops, and steak; trim visible fat; drain meat drippings; limit the amount of margarine or other fats used on bread and vegetables; emphasize the use of lowfat or skim milk; reduce the amount of fat in other foods when whole milk and cheese are used; reduce the amount of fat used in recipes, added to food in cooking, or added at the table; limit the

number of fried foods; use moderate amounts of organ meats (like liver) and egg yolks; use fewer creamed foods and rich desserts; limit the amount of salad dressing used

4. **Eat foods with an adequate amount of starch and fiber**—Provide more fruits and vegetables; eat more potatoes, sweet potatoes, yams, corn, peas, and dried beans; increase consumption of whole-grain cereal products and breads

5. **Avoid too much sugar**—Avoid or cut down on very sweet food; reduce the amount of sugar in recipes; rely more on fresh fruit and canned fruits packed in juice or light syrup; limit the amounts of sugar, jams, jellies, and syrups

6. **Avoid too much sodium and salt**—Use fewer salty, processed foods; use just a little salt; sparingly use commercially prepared sauces and condiments; select fresh and frozen vegetables rather than canned or seasoned frozen vegetables (high sodium content); limit salty snacks (chips, pretzels)

7. **Drink eight 8-ounce glasses of water every day**— Older adults aren't always aware that they're dehydrated; this can cause dangerously low blood pressure, poor kidney function, and chronic constipation

8. **If you drink alcohol, do so in moderation**—Provide more fruit and vegetable juices; measure your drink; eat something before you drink

There also are special nutritional considerations for older adults because often they're found to be deficient in fiber, protein, calcium, iron, zinc, folic acid, and vitamins A and B_6. Table 1 provides a quick reference guide for these substances; let's look at a few of them in-depth.

Protein

Older people need slightly more protein in their diets than younger people do because their bodies don't use it as efficiently. The protein needs of older adults are met if approximately 12%–15% of their total daily caloric intake are derived from protein. Unfortunately, many older people reduce the amount of protein they eat because one of the best sources of protein, meat, is too expensive

Table 1.   Special nutritional considerations

Nutrient	Comments	Major food sources
	Essential nutrients	
Fiber	Intakes often are inadequate. Increasing fiber in the diet may aid in preventing constipation.	Whole grain breads (whole wheat, rye, Roman Meal), Wheatena, Ry-Crisp, whole wheat crackers, cereals (Shredded Wheat, oatmeal), whole wheat pasta, brown rice, fresh fruits, fresh vegetables
Protein	Recommended level for older adults is as high as 1 gram/kilogram body weight; intakes usually are adequate (show older adult necessary portion sizes)	Dried peas, dried/canned beans, lentils, peanut butter, cheese, milk, nonfat dry milk, eggs, canned clams, salmon, sardines, tuna
Calcium	Intakes often are inadequate. Older women may need generous amounts, 1–2 grams daily, to protect against osteoporosis.	Lactose intolerant: tofu, all cheeses except cottage cheese, corn tortillas treated in lime, all greens except spinach, sardines, milk in small quantities Lactose tolerant: all foods listed above, all types of milk, yogurt, cottage cheese
Iron	Intakes often are inadequate.	Dried/canned beans, cereals, whole-wheat pastas, whole-grain breads, brown rice, liver, canned oysters
Zinc	Widespread deficiency is found in men and women.	Legumes, whole grains, meat
Folic acid	Deficiency may be linked to dementia.	Leafy green vegetables (spinach, mustard and collard greens, kale), dried beans/peas, lentils, nuts, whole-grain breads, pastas, cereals, liver
Vitamin A	Intakes often are inadequate.	Green vegetables (spinach, turnip, broccoli) yellow/orange vegetables (carrots, winter squash, sweet potato), watermelon, cantaloupe, liver
Vitamin B$_6$	Intakes sometimes are inadequate. Age has been shown to influence blood levels, which decrease markedly with age.	Liver, vegetables, nuts, seeds, dried beans/peas, bran, whole grains, bananas, raisins, cantaloupe

(continued)

Table 1. *(continued)*

Nutrient	Comments	Major food sources
	Essential nutrients	
Vitamin C	Intakes sometimes are inadequate, even in nursing-facility diets. Age influences blood levels, which decrease markedly with age. Vitamin C aids in iron absorption from vegetable sources.	Oranges, lemons, tomatoes, grapefruit, melons, strawberries, dark leafy greens (broccoli, cabbage), green peppers, fresh chili peppers, baked potato
Vitamin E	Several researchers have demonstrated that 3–4 months of treatment with vitamin E 300–400 international units (about 30 times higher than the RDA) relieves intermittent severe cramps in calf muscles during walking.	Vegetable fats, some nuts and seeds, cereal products (especially whole grains), some vegetables
	Nonestablished nutrients	
Vitamin B$_{15}$[a]	Promotional literature claims it's effective in treating a wide variety of ailments, including effects of aging	
Vitamin B$_{17}$[a]	Also known as laetrile; promotional literature claims it's effective in treating cancer.	

Adapted from Ebersole, P., & Hess, P.A. (1994). *Toward healthy aging: Human needs and nursing response* (pp. 143–144). St. Louis: Mosby–Year Book.

[a]Both have been claimed to be vitamins and wonder drugs. No research demonstrates that the body needs these compounds, and large doses of laetrile have caused death in several cases.

or too difficult to prepare, because they'd rather eat sweets, or because many protein-rich foods need to be chewed more than do other foods.

Carbohydrates

The American diet is, in general, high in fat and refined sugar and low in fiber. Having a "sweet tooth" can be a serious problem for many older people. Low cost, ease of preparation, individual preferences, and the mild psychological boost and increase in energy that some people get from eating sweets (carbohydrates) contribute to an overreliance on foods that are high in sugar. The nutritional value of these foods is limited, resulting in an intake of "empty" calories. In addition, the lack of fiber in these foods frequently is tied to constipation. Many older people need to be encouraged to eat in moderation fresh fruits and vegetables, whole-grain breads, beans, nuts, and bran to increase the amount of fiber in

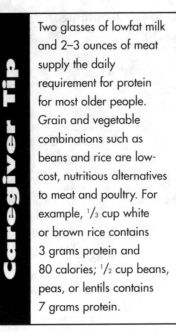

Caregiver Tip

Two glasses of lowfat milk and 2–3 ounces of meat supply the daily requirement for protein for most older people. Grain and vegetable combinations such as beans and rice are low-cost, nutritious alternatives to meat and poultry. For example, $1/3$ cup white or brown rice contains 3 grams protein and 80 calories; $1/2$ cup beans, peas, or lentils contains 7 grams protein.

their diets. The USDA recommends that older people should get about 48% of their total caloric intake from fresh fruits and vegetables and grain products, which is about double what many older people eat regularly.

Not all carbohydrates are good for you, however. Researchers have found that all the talk in the 1980s about eating more pasta because it was low in fat and healthier than eating meat was only half true. It turned out that pasta actually makes people fat (pasta is mostly carbohydrates; eating carbohydrates increases triglycerides, which are the principal lipids in the blood—lipids are fat).

Fats

There are two kinds of fat: unsaturated and saturated. Unsaturated fats are divided into monounsaturated and polyunsaturated. Monounsaturated fats are found in peanuts, peanut butter, peanut oil, and olives and olive oil. Polyunsaturated fats are found in corn, safflower, and soybean oils, and in albacore tuna and chinook salmon. Both monounsaturated and polyunsaturated fats contain HDL (high-density lipids), "the good cholesterol," which has a positive effect on the heart.

Saturated fats (for example, milk, meat, cheese, and palm and coconut oils) come mostly from animals and should be limited to less than 10% of the total daily fat intake and no more than 30% of the daily caloric intake. A person following a typical 2,000-calorie diet should average no more than 20 grams of saturated fat every day, but the typical American eats about 25–30 or more grams of saturated fat a day. And you don't have to eat much to get that amount of saturated fat in your diet:

> 1 tablespoon of butter = 8 grams saturated fat
> 1 ounce Swiss, cheddar, American, parmesan cheese = 5–6 grams saturated fat
> 1 cup whole milk = 5 grams saturated fat

Excessive intake of fats, especially saturated fats, contributes to obesity, heart disease, and breast and colon cancers.

Because, in general, fat improves the taste of some foods and gives people the sensation of being full, it's been difficult to reduce its presence in the diet. If you want to reduce fat in the diet of the older adult in your life or in your own diet, start by closely trimming fat from meats, substituting lowfat or nonfat products for high-fat foods, or using more natural flavorings/spices (for example, fresh lemon, freshly ground pepper, and fresh herbs) to enhance the taste of food. Because caring for your loved one can be time consuming, you may find that you're eating out and/or eating fast food more often (both have heavy fat content). It's difficult for some people to limit eating out or eating junk food, but try to think of it this way: Making your own lowfat food actually can be a way to care for or reward yourself for all the time and caring you're giving to others.

Vitamins

Older people need the same amounts of vitamins that younger people do, but they often don't get them in their diet. In general, adults who are consuming 2,000–3,000 calories a day are getting all the vitamins that they need. (The recommended number of calories a day for people ages 51 and older is 2,300 for men and 1,900 for women. No specific adjustments have been made for people over 65 or 75 who may be frail and/or bedridden.) Older adults may not be getting enough vitamins because of illness or decreased appetite that may be related to inactivity.

Vitamin C (ascorbic acid) helps the body absorb iron and heal damaged tissues. Vitamin C is found in fresh fruits and vegetables such as oranges, lemons, tomatoes, grapefruit, cantaloupe, strawberries,

> **Alert!**
>
> Vitamin and mineral supplements should be used with care. Excessive amounts of some vitamins (for example, fat-soluble vitamins like vitamins A and D) and minerals can be toxic, and other vitamins can interfere with the absorption of nutrients or with medications. When you or the older adult in your life can't eat a well-balanced diet, use a combination vitamin-mineral daily supplement. Individual vitamins should be prescribed or suggested by a health care provider, based on the individual's unique needs.

broccoli, green peppers, dark leafy greens and baked potatoes, and these carry an expensive price tag, particularly the seasonal items. People on a fixed or limited income are likely to have diets that are deficient in vitamin C.

People who live in long-term care facilities are likely to be deficient in vitamin D, in part because they aren't often exposed to sunlight. Sunlight is involved in the conversion of the inactive form of vitamin D to its active form.

Older adults' bodies also have been found to be deficient in vitamins B_6 and B_{12}. Vitamin B_6 is necessary for adequate immune function and is found in grains, especially wheat and corn. The low levels that are found in older adults could be related to the high number of infections they get. Vitamin B_{12} is necessary for good mental functioning, and its deficiency can cause some forms of dementia. Absorption of this vitamin depends on an acid environment in the stomach. Some older adults have a condition called atrophic gastritis, which results in low stomach acidity, and this reduces the absorption of vitamin B_{12} significantly. Both of these B vitamins are found in sufficient amounts in meat.

When your loved one's diet is deficient in vitamins and minerals, he or she may need to take a daily multivitamin supplement. Some older people rely too much on supplements, however, stocking up on a lot of expensive vitamin preparations in place of lower-cost vitamin- and mineral-rich foods. Others expect too much of their vitamin supplement—they assume that it'll make up for inadequate protein or fresh fruits and vegetables in the diet. A vitamin supplement doesn't supply the protein and fiber that is found in a well-balanced diet. Talk to your loved one's health care provider before purchasing and starting any vitamin supplements.

Minerals

Calcium   Calcium is the main component of the more than 200 bones that make up the adult skeleton. Bones store 98% of the body's calcium. Bones begin to lose calcium from age 35 onward. This process begins slowly but accelerates with age, and it accelerates specifically in women after menopause. (Premenopausal estrogen levels inhibit the breakdown and absorption of bone mass.) Estrogen replacement therapy (ERT), taken orally or applied as a patch, helps retard bone loss for menopausal women or those who have had their ovaries surgically removed. ERT, along with recommended calcium supplements and regularly scheduled weight-bearing exercise can influence the amount of bone loss.

Caucasian and Asian American women with small frames lose minerals faster than African American women do. Other factors that are associated with calcium loss include lack of exercise, smoking, and consumption of caffeine and alcohol. The following actions may help older people—especially older women—avoid osteoporosis and the increased danger of suffering fractures from falls:

> Regular walking or other weight-bearing exercise
> Taking 1,000–1,500 milligrams of calcium and 400 international units of vitamin D daily (don't take calcium and vitamin D at the same time because calcium inhibits the action of vitamin D)
> Exposing the skin to 15 minutes of sunlight daily
> Using a fluoride supplement if the water is low in fluoride
> Avoiding or minimizing intake of caffeine and alcohol
> For older women, ERT

You can find more information on osteoporosis in Chapter 6. The National Institutes of Health provides the following guidelines for calcium intake for older Americans:

> 1,000 milligrams per day for women ages 50 and older (1,500 milligrams per day if not on estrogen replacement therapy)
> 1,000 milligrams per day for men ages 51–65
> 1,500 milligrams per day for men ages 65 and older

Examples of foods that are high in calcium are the following:

> $1/2$ cup broccoli = 50 milligrams
> 1 medium orange = 60 milligrams
> 1 cup lowfat yogurt = 290 milligrams
> 8 ounces skim milk = 300 milligrams
> $1^1/2$ ounces sardines with bones = 400 milligrams

Because it's unlikely that older adults will get enough calcium in their diets, they need to take a calcium supplement. When selecting a calcium supplement, it's important to check the label for the number of milligrams of elemental calcium in each pill. Elemental calcium is readily absorbed by the body and usually doesn't cause gastrointestinal side effects. Calcium carbonate contains 40% calcium and can be found in Tums (500 mg, 5 tablets; each tablet contains 200 mg elemental calcium) and Caltrate 600

(2 tablets; each tablet contains 600 mg elemental calcium). These supplements should be taken with meals because between meals many older adult stomachs lack the right amount of acid. (Acid secretion is activated when processing food so that digestion can take place; thus, an empty stomach contains less acid.) If you have a family history of kidney stones, talk to your health care provider before using calcium supplements.

Iron   Adequate amounts of iron, folic acid, and vitamin B_{12} are necessary to prevent anemia and are necessary for red blood cells to form. Anemia is a condition that's characterized by lower-than-normal levels of red blood cells, the cells that deliver oxygen to the tissues in the body. Good sources of iron, folic acid, and vitamin B_{12} include dried or canned beans, cereals, whole-wheat pastas, whole-grain breads, brown rice, liver and other red meats, and leafy green vegetables such as spinach, collard, mustard, turnip, and kale greens. Not all anemias, however, come from dietary deficiencies. Blood loss of any kind as well as several chronic diseases can cause anemia. Anemia is fairly common but not obvious to the casual observer. Make sure that your loved one is checked periodically for anemia with a total blood count screening.

Iron absorption is enhanced by the vitamin C found in orange juice and other foods. By contrast, eggs, corn, beans, and cereal products containing phytates inhibit iron absorption.

Nutrition Facts Labeling

All food manufacturers are required by the FDA to include on product labels "Nutrition Facts," a breakdown of calories, fat, cholesterol, sodium, total carbohydrates, dietary fiber, sugars, protein, and vitamins and minerals contained in the product (Figure 2). Read this information on all food labels to help you monitor the recommended daily nutrition requirements for the older adult in your life.

Fluids

Taking in enough fluids is just as important as eating a proper diet. The human body needs water to transport nutrients to the cells, regulate temperature, and get rid of waste products. Older adults who do not drink enough water—at least six 8-ounce glasses a day—are more likely to retain sodium, get heat prostration, have difficulty coughing up secretions, or develop a bladder infection, among other complications.

Older people are at higher risk of developing dehydration than younger people for several reasons. The sensation of thirst may be diminished somewhat by age, medications, or illness. The total amount of water in the body also is reduced, and the balance of electrolytes, including sodium and potassium, is more easily disturbed, especially when older people are taking diuretics or laxatives, which increase the rate at which the body excretes fluids and solids.

Nutrition Facts	
Serving Size 1 Tablespoon (15mL)	
Servings Per Container 32	
Amount Per Serving	
Calories 35	Calories from Fat 10
	%Daily Value*
Total Fat 1.5g	2%
Saturated Fat 0g	0%
Cholesterol 0mg	0%
Sodium 5 mg	0%
Total Carbohydrate 6g	2%
Dietary Fiber 0g	0%
Sugars 5g	
Protein 0g	
Vitamin A 0%	Vitamin C 0%
Calcium 0%	Iron 0%
* Percent Daily Values are based on a 2,000 calorie diet.	

FIGURE 2.

The availability of fluids is sometimes a problem in hospitals and long-term care institutions for older people who can't get out of bed to get a drink of water and must depend on others to leave it within reach. Caregivers need to be sure that fresh water or juices are within reach of chair- or bedbound older people. Independent older adults should be encouraged to make a conscious effort to drink enough water or some other fluid every day.

Nutrition and Psychology

Keep in mind that while you're following all of this good advice about nutrition, don't completely overrule your loved one's life-long food habits or weaknesses. For example, should your 80-year-old father, who has enjoyed eating high-calorie snacks most of his life, be asked to change his diet now that he's living with you? We know that high-fat, high-calorie foods can make you feel better psychologically. Denying your father this one vice may increase his life span, but will it be at the expense of his well-being? And, at his age, is it worth it?

Weight Considerations

Strongly embedded in American culture is the image of the chubby, smiling grandmother. In fact, the majority of very old people are thin. After ages 75–80, both body fat and weight drop off slowly but steadily. Most weight charts assume a gradual increase in weight as people get old, but many experts object to this assumption (Table 2). Questions also have been raised about the common assumption that older people need only 75%–80% of the calories that young people need. Many experts believe that if older people were more active, they would need the same amount of calories that younger people do.

Being overweight is more of a problem for some older adults than for others. Estimates from U.S. nutritional surveys reveal that 25% of African American and caucasian men ages 65–74 are overweight. About 36% of caucasian women and 60% of African American women in the same age group also are overweight. Overweight peaks early in men, in their 50s, but later in women, in their 70s. Excess weight also places a lot of stress on arthritic joints.

One of the most fascinating findings to come from studies of nutrition and aging is the relationship between a low-calorie diet and long life. Researchers have found that animals that were fed a low-calorie diet lived much longer than those fed a high-calorie diet. The same seems to be true for humans. At the same time, people ages 70–80 who are moderately overweight don't have a higher mortality rate than those who aren't overweight. However, for older adults with ongoing health conditions such as hypertension or diabetes, being overweight is a risk factor.

Dental Considerations

Almost half of all Americans lose their teeth by age 65. Dentists believe that this loss is mostly avoidable given the right diet, use

Table 2.   Smooth average weights for older women and men

Height (inches)	Weight					
	55–64 yr	65–74 yr	75–79 yr	80–84 yr	85–89 yr	90–94 yr
Women						
57	138	132	125			
58	141	135	129			
59	144	138	132	118	111	110
60	149	142	136	121	116	
61	150	145	139	124	120	119
62	152	149	143	128	124	119
63	155	152	146	132	128	120
64	158	156	150	136	133	124
65	161	159	153	140	138	129
66	164	163	157	144	142	
67	167	166	160			
68	170	170	164			
Men						
62	148	144	133	135		
63	151	148	138	136	133	
64	155	151	143	138	135	
65	158	154	148	141	139	130
66	162	158	154	144	142	133
67	166	161	159	147	145	136
68	169	165	164	150	148	140
69	173	168	169	154	152	144
70	176	171	174	159	156	149
71	180	175	179	164	160	154
72	184	178	184	170	165	
73	187	182	189			
74	191	185	194			

Adapted from Ebersole, P., & Hess, P.A. (1994). *Toward healthy aging: Human needs and nursing response* (p. 157). St. Louis: Mosby–Year Book.

of proper brushing and flossing techniques, and regular visits to the dentist. Taking care of the teeth not only improves people's ability to eat but also helps them to maintain a positive self-image and to speak with ease, and thus communicate better.

As people grow older, so do their teeth: They become darker; show more stress lines, which stain easily; and may have cavities, abrasion, or erosion from grinding during sleep or other stressors. The gums and lining of the mouth become more fragile; they become damaged more easily and heal more slowly.

Daily cleaning and plaque removal are as important for older people as for younger people. Use of a soft, round-bristled toothbrush lessens the chance of injuring the gums, and it stimulates the gum tissues to remain firm and have adequate blood circulation. (*Note:* It may be easier for older people to use a child-size toothbrush rather than an adult-size one because they can get all of the teeth with the smaller bristles and because it's easier to hold.) Dental experts recommend placing the toothbrush at a 45° angle to the gumline and using short, back-and-forth strokes over one or two teeth at a time. All tooth surfaces must be brushed. Regular flossing removes plaque, which is a sticky film that attracts bacteria and causes tooth decay. If done properly, flossing only needs to be done once a day. Use a lightly waxed or unwaxed floss with an up-and-down motion between the teeth, remembering to floss under the gumline. Don't floss so hard that the gums bleed. Also remember to replace the toothbrush every 3–4 months because a worn-out brush can't clean teeth properly and it might injure the gums. The proper, step-by-step toothbrushing technique can be found in Chapter 12.

Halitosis (bad breath) is caused by gum disease that has occurred because of a buildup of plaque beneath the gumline, but it also can be caused by problems in the digestive system, such as gastroenteritis (an upset of the upper and lower digestive tracts). Sometimes simply remembering to gently brush or clean the surface of the tongue can help cut down on bad mouth odors; a lot of bacteria live on the tongue, and it's important to remove them periodically. Reusable plastic tongue scrapers are available in most drug stores.

If the older adult in your life wears dentures, it's important to care for them properly and visit the dentist regularly. Dentures must always be worn during waking hours, but if the person likes to sleep with them in (most people like to remove them at bedtime), he or she should be encouraged to remove them for at least 4 hours during the day. Removing dentures provides enough time for them and the oral tissues to be cleaned. They also should be removed and cleaned after each meal to remove soft debris. If they aren't removed, the debris could cause pressure on and shrinkage of the gums).

Dentures should be checked by a dentist once a year. The average time that the gums can support a denture is 20 years. Many people lose as much as 50% of supporting gum and bone in 5–10 years. When dentures don't fit correctly, rapid bone loss occurs; commercially available denture adhesives help only temporarily.

IMPORTANCE OF CHECKUPS IN PRACTICING PREVENTION

When you assume responsibility for the care of an older person, it's not just the daily physical care to satisfy the immediate needs of that person that's important. A goal for you as a caregiver is to ward off, when possible, a further decline in function that could leave the person even more dependent. Achieving this goal depends in part on scheduling regular medical examinations. Table 3 lists the examinations and tests that are recommended for people age 65 or older, along with their suggested frequency.

Common Issues in Preventive Screening

Marty, who is in her late 70s and lives alone, panics suddenly when she discovers during a bath "there's something hanging from my privates." Frightened and feeling a lot of discomfort, she calls her daughter, who immediately contacts her own doctor. Marty is admitted to the hospital with a diagnosis of a prolapsed uterus and is quickly scheduled for surgery. Marty experienced not only fright but also embarrassment in this situation. She hadn't sought regular health care and has never had a pelvic examination.

The doctor explains that the early symptoms Marty had been experiencing—the need to urinate more often and low back pain—were probably early indicators of a prolapsed uterus. Had she sought regular preventive health care, this emergency admission could've been avoided.

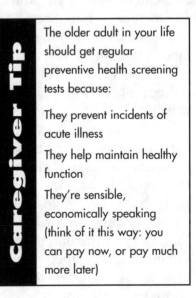

Caregiver Tip

The older adult in your life should get regular preventive health screening tests because:

They prevent incidents of acute illness

They help maintain healthy function

They're sensible, economically speaking (think of it this way: you can pay now, or pay much more later)

Table 3.   Adult preventive care timeline, ages 65 and older

	Tests	
Men/women	Complete physical	Every 1–3 years until age 75, then annually
	Blood pressure measurement	Every 2 years
	Height and weight	Periodically
	Cholesterol	Every 5 years
	Hearing	Periodically
	Stool occult blood	Annually
	Sigmoidoscopy	Every 3–5 years
	Urinalysis	Periodically
Women	Mammography	Every 1–2 years
	Pap smear	Every 1–3 years
Men	Prostate-specific antigen	Annually
	Exams	
Men/women	Dental	Annually
	Vision/glaucoma	Every 2 years
Women	Breast	Annually
Men/women	Exams for cancer	Annually
	Thyroid, mouth, skin, ovaries, testicles, lymph nodes, rectum, prostate	
	Immunizations	
Men/women	Tetanus-diphtheria	Every 10 years
	Pneumococcal	Every 6 years
	Influenza	Annually
	Health Guidance	
Men/women	Smoking, alcohol, drugs, sexual behavior, AIDS, nutrition, physical activity	Periodically

It's often difficult to convince older adults of the importance of regularly scheduled medical examinations and tests that can confirm healthy body function or identify potential problems at an early stage. Many older people respond, "I don't get colds. Why do I need to get a flu shot? It might make me sick." Furthermore, many older adults have a lot of fear and anxiety about undergoing screening tests such as Pap smears, mammograms, and prostate and rectal examinations. Although since January 1998 Medicare pays for screening mammograms every year as ordered by a physician, only

37% of older American women who were eligible for the screening in 1992–1993 took advantage of the Medicare benefit. Most older people's fears focus on the possibility of cancer. Anxiety also may stem from their lack of knowledge about the test or examination: Will there be pain? What exactly will the doctor do? Open communication about the need for and benefits of preventive health examinations, acknowledgment of the person's fears and anxieties, and what to expect during the scheduled examination can go far to answer questions, ease fears, and dispel misconceptions.

Perhaps you're saying to yourself, "My mother (father, sister, brother, aunt, uncle, neighbor, best friend) has lived a fairly long life and survived many losses. What do I do if they find cancer or some other life-threatening condition?" Keep in mind that many times the results of preventive examinations and tests are normal. These results can relieve your loved one's anxiety about his or her health and can validate for you, the caregiver, the positive impact you've had on his or her health. If an abnormal result were reported, the condition would most likely be identified at an earlier stage, and the earlier it's caught, the more responsive it is to treatment.

Vision and Hearing Screening

Because you know from reading Chapter 6 that changes in vision and hearing are common with aging, you know that screening tests of the eyes and ears are particularly important, but you might not recognize the signs of diminished vision right away. Too often, an older person stops reading, has a hard time eating, or stops watching favorite television shows because his or her vision is impaired, but you may not understand that these are clues for scheduling an eye examination. Eye exams for people ages 65 and older should be scheduled every 2–3 years, with a test for changes in vision and for glaucoma during each visit. If the older adult is diagnosed with glaucoma and medication has been prescribed, more frequent assessments by an ophthalmologist may be needed. Of course, a frequent cause of impaired sight that's more benign and often overlooked is the need for the older person to clean his or her glasses.

Difficulty hearing can cause older people to withdraw emotionally because they don't understand what's being said and they feel left out. Hearing loss is very common as people age, and it's recommended that hearing be tested every 3 years. If a doctor identifies a hearing problem, assessment should be done more often. Many times, hearing loss occurs because of a buildup of wax (cerumen) in the ear canal. It's amazing to observe the difference in older people's behavior when this condition is identified and the wax is removed. If they're using a hearing aid and their hearing is diminished, the solution may be as simple as changing the batteries. The hearing aid should be checked often, particularly if you notice they're not wearing it regularly (maybe it's not working right) or there's been a change in communication between you and your loved one.

Immunizations

Immunizations are important for the simple reason that older adults are more susceptible than are younger people to infection. Older people, especially those with chronic diseases such as hypertension, diabetes, and heart disease, have a decreased ability to resist infection and an increased risk of the disease getting worse or of death. The Immunization Practices Advisory Committee of the U.S. Centers for Disease Control and Prevention recommends that everyone ages 65 and older get a flu shot every autumn, before flu season starts. A single-dose pneumococcal vaccine is also recommended. People at high risk for pneumonia should get a pneumococcal vaccine every 6 years.

Older people who've never been immunized against common childhood diseases or who didn't receive a complete series of vaccinations for tetanus and/or diphtheria should get the complete sequence of three doses. Those who got the initial series should get combination diphtheria and tetanus boosters every 10 years. It's especially important that older people with chronic illnesses follow these recommendations. Because not many older people kept their childhood immunization records (if they're immigrants, childhood immunizations probably weren't done), they've probably never had a complete series of vaccinations for common diseases, or they don't remember exactly which shots they received. The best thing for you to do is discuss this issue with your loved one's health care provider.

INSULIN AND DIABETES

Insulin is a compound that lowers blood sugar. If the older adult in your life hasn't eaten properly prior to an injection or isn't feeling well, insulin can produce a condition called hypoglycemia, or low blood sugar. The signs and symptoms of hypoglycemia are sweating, confusion, and lightheadedness.

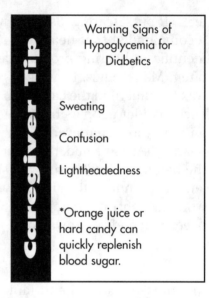

Warning Signs of Hypoglycemia for Diabetics

Sweating

Confusion

Lightheadedness

*Orange juice or hard candy can quickly replenish blood sugar.

It's critical for you to be able to recognize the signs and symptoms of low blood sugar. Write them down and post them in a visible place, like on the refrigerator or by the telephone. Always act promptly to counteract low blood sugar. Failure to respond to these symptoms could have serious results. Make sure that hard candies are always available to the person with diabetes and that he or she is taking insulin. Remember that the brain needs glucose to function. When blood glucose drops quickly, the symptoms you see are the brain's reaction to not getting its food (glucose).

Be particularly careful if the person on insulin isn't feeling well (for example, he or she has the flu). Any illness that involves vomiting and/or diarrhea can be very serious, so call your loved one's health care professional immediately. At the same time, the person should drink fluids and eat a light meal. Don't discontinue giving the insulin, however—the person's health care professional may alter the dosage during the illness.

A POSITIVE ATTITUDE IS AN ESSENTIAL PART OF PRACTICING PREVENTION

Maintaining a positive attitude about aging and about being a care receiver can have a direct, positive effect on older adults' health and on their relationship with their caregiver. The ability and the opportunity to give to others fosters a positive self-image in people, and the older adult in your life has been giving for a long time. The reversal of roles, finding that they need to be cared for by you, can be very disorienting for them, but it doesn't have to be; they don't have to become passive, withdrawn, or demoralized. Taking appropriate action can help reestablish, or establish for the first time, a positive self-image.

What can you do to enhance a dependent older adult's self-image? Emphasize what the older person can still do and contribute, and encourage him or her to participate in daily activities and decision making. For example, you can encourage your father-in-law to get involved in meal planning; it can be as simple as asking him to set the table or make sandwiches for his grandchildren. Helping you to fold laundry is another active way that an older person can contribute to family responsibilities—it's also good exercise for joints and muscles. An added benefit is that it gives both of you a time to communicate and share. Depending on your personality, you may need to make a concerted effort to avoid focusing on the negative aspects of your loved one's situation. The rewards of "accentuating the positive" can be enhanced relationships and well-being for all members of the family.

As you seek to engage the older adult in your life in daily activities, remember the interaction between the mind and body (see Chapter 6): What affects one affects the other. The older adult who participates in activities that enhance physical well-being—exercise, proper diet, regular checkups, immunizations—enhances mental well-being in return. Engaging in mentally stimulating activities has a good effect on physical well-being. For example, the immune system seems to work more effectively when a person keeps a positive outlook.

By encouraging the older adult in your life to "look on the sunny side of life," you can feel better about your role as caregiver, and you'll be able to interact more positively with your loved one. Both of you are using your energies (physical and mental) to focus on what is and can be and not on what was and is no longer. Acceptance and satisfaction replace anger and frustration. As you encourage and participate in activities that emphasize the prevention of more serious illnesses, you also experience greater peace of mind. Remember that as you balance the responsibilities and tasks that at times seem to be—and probably are—overwhelming, you're doing the best that you can.

What we wanted to share with you in this chapter is the concept of focusing on the whole person—mind, body, and spirit—in your interactions with the older adult in your life. This holistic approach to knowing, understanding, and being with a dependent older adult also has benefits for your well-being. It has to be said, too, that sometimes people get sick, no matter how hard we try to prevent it. With that in mind, the next section of the book shows you how to provide personal care.

III

Providing Personal Care

9

Managing Medications

People older than age 65 comprise the largest number of users of prescription and over-the-counter (OTC) medications in the United States. Surveys have estimated that although these people make up only 12% of the U.S. population, they take almost 32% of all prescription medications and take 2–3 times as many medications as do younger people. It is felt that this percentage is about the same for OTC medications.

The World Health Organization found that by 2000 there will be more than 600 million people worldwide who are 65 years old. The number of very old people, those ages 80 and older, also will grow; in fact, they're the fastest growing population group in the United States. Because medications act differently in older adults' bodies than they do in the bodies of younger people, it's important for older adults to understand and use their medications wisely.

Because older people tend to experience multiple long-term chronic illnesses, they take a lot of medications. An older adult may be medicated for as many as four different conditions, and the number can jump to nine in people ages 70 years and older. Most of these conditions will be chronic, for example, arthritis, diabetes, heart disease (congestive heart failure, hypertension), lung disease (chronic obstructive pulmonary disease), incontinence, and Parkinson's disease.

The focal point of this chapter is the comprehensive medications assessment, the purpose of which is to provide a complete understanding of what medications an older person is taking and why. You'll see how differently medications behave in older people's bodies and learn important information about how medications are processed and possible medication hazards (for instance, medication interactions, side effects, adverse reactions, and toxicity). It's possible to abuse and misuse medications without even realizing it. Examples of abuse/misuse include polypharmacy, self-prescribing, and noncompliance with doctor's orders, all of which could be harmful and are discussed later in the chapter.

One of the most common reasons that people seek or self-prescribe medication is to relieve pain. This chapter includes a discussion of ways you can intervene with older people who are in pain. In addition, you'll find helpful strategies for medication management that can make a sometimes-frightening area of care easier for you and safer for the older adult in your life.

Besides taking prescription medications for specific chronic diseases, older adults may begin taking medications to ease symptoms caused by age-related changes, as described in Table 1. The emergence of any of the age-related symptoms mentioned in the table can prompt an older adult to seek professional health care. It's not uncommon for a medication to be prescribed to help relieve many of the symptoms caused by physical and emotional age-related changes. Unfortunately, it's rare that alternative methods of intervention—interventions that don't involve taking medicine—are considered by health care professionals.

Before any medications are added to an older adult's regimen, consider the following questions:

- Why is my loved one feeling less able to do things for him- or herself?
- What could help my loved one be more active?
- What changes in eating habits have occurred and why?
- Is my loved one getting out less or does he or she have fewer social contacts? Why?

Alleviating the causes of the problem may require you to use some creativity in and make adaptations to your lifestyle. You may discover that one or more of the medications the older adult in your life is taking are contributing to or even causing the problem. The first step in understanding what medications a person is taking and what hazards they may present is doing a comprehensive medications assessment.

Table 1.   Age-related changes and their impact on older adults

Age-related change	Results in	Causes problems with
Physical ability	Stiff, aching muscles from reduced strength, flexibility	Self-care, such as dressing, ambulating, bathing
Eating habits	Reduced amount of fiber/fluids in diet	Constipation
Social contacts	Fewer living relatives and friends, more difficulty meeting with them	Depression and isolation

COMPREHENSIVE MEDICATIONS ASSESSMENT

It's not uncommon for older adults to talk to a number of health care providers as they look for relief of their symptoms. One doctor may prescribe a diuretic by its brand name, another doctor by its generic name. The medications will differ in appearance, and many older adults assume that they serve different purposes. Taking both medications puts them at risk for overdose. In addition, some older people take medications other than those prescribed by their physicians without asking permission or at least consulting them. These medications can be OTC or borrowed from family members or friends who believe that they're being helpful (these individuals may say, "When I felt like that, my doctor gave me some pills that helped a lot. I still have some. Why don't you take them?"). Taking another person's medications is never a good idea and should be strongly discouraged.

The comprehensive medications assessment includes general questions concerning the older adult's ability to manage his or her medications as well as specific questions related to his or her current use of both prescribed and OTC medications (Figure 1). (Be aware that many OTC medications, which many people don't equate with being medications because they can self-prescribe and take them on their own, can interact and/or interfere with the actions and effectiveness of prescription medications.)

HOW MEDICATIONS ACT IN OLDER ADULTS' BODIES

After completing a comprehensive medications assessment, a health care professional needs to correlate the information gath-

Comprehensive Medications Assessment Form

What is the older adult's cognitive level? (What or how much can he/she understand?) _____

What is his/her ability to see and read labels? _____

Does he/she have good muscle coordination? (Can he/she uncap/cap medicine bottles or pour the medicine?) _____

Can he/she swallow without difficulty? _____

Can he/she afford to pay for prescriptions? _____

List all medications the person is taking:

Prescribed by doctors and nurses _____

_____

Borrowed meds from family/friends _____

Over-the-counter meds

For pain _____

Sleeping aids _____

For constipation_____

Vitamins and minerals _____

Why is he/she taking each medication? _____

_____

When does he/she take these meds? How often? _____

_____

Has he/she experienced any adverse drug reactions? What happened? What did the person do? _____

_____

Has he/she ever taken less or more than the prescribed or recommended dosage?

_____

How and where does he/she store the medications? _____

_____

ered with what's known about the normal changes of aging. This includes considering how an assessed older person will ingest, absorb, or otherwise get the medication to the proper place in the body (known to health care professionals as distribution/transport); how it will be metabolized; and when and how the medication will be excreted from the body. You need to understand the relationship and the effect of the normal changes of aging on medication use, so review the information in Chapter 6 on what changes occur in absorption, distribution, metabolism, and excretion in the aging body (see display on p. 74). How efficiently the four organ systems function determines how quickly and effectively medications take action in the body.

Any changes that occur in these organ systems in normal aging can affect the absorption, distribution, metabolism, and excretion processes. If the person also has a chronic and/or acute disease, then the impact on these processes can be even greater. That's why it's important for health care professionals, family caregivers, and older adults to understand fully how medications are processed in older adults and what effect disease(s) can have on how medications are processed by the body.

Absorption

Absorption means the time that's required for a medication to enter the bloodstream. The small intestine absorbs most of any medication taken by mouth. Anything that interferes with the medication reaching the small intestine affects how much and when the medication is absorbed. Normal aging in the gastrointestinal system can affect both of these factors.

You've already learned, for example, that as we age the intestines move and transport (*gastric motility*) what we eat and drink more slowly, so it's more difficult to get rid of toxic products left in the body after the stomach breaks them down (*metabolism*). It's easy to understand how you can get into trouble if you take medications, either medically prescribed for specific disorders or self-prescribed OTC medications, in excessive amounts or in combinations that don't agree with each other (see display on p. 147).

Steps in the Body's Response to Medications		
Step	*Action*	*Controlled by*
Absorption	The process by which a medication enters the blood circulating in the body	Intestines
Distribution	The delivery of a medication within the body	Circulatory system, heart
Metabolism	The breakdown of a medication, typically by the liver, into substances that will be used or excreted by the body	Liver
Excretion	Elimination of the leftover medication from the body	Kidneys

On the one hand, slower gastric motility can increase the contact time (the time that a medication stays in one place and gets more of it absorbed) and the efficiency of a medication. On the other hand, gastric motility can cause adverse reactions if the dose is incorrect. Slower gastric motility can delay emptying of the stomach, which in turn slows down the time that it takes a medication to reach the small intestine. Older adults who take excessive amounts of laxatives actually speed up gastric motility, which leads to reduced medication absorption.

Another reason for altered medication absorption rates in older adults is a change in the rate of blood flow to the intestines. This is caused by a diminishment of the ability of the heart to pump blood (*cardiac output*). Slower blood flow can mean that absorption takes longer, which in turn means that the amount of the medication that's absorbed increases.

In addition, the amount of stomach acid decreases as we age. Decreased stomach acid content affects the absorption of the medications whose action depends on an acid stomach environment. Older adults often self-prescribe antacids for simple indigestion without realizing that antacids decrease the acidity of the stomach and may affect the absorption of other medications they're taking. Some antibiotics are absorbed better on an empty stomach because food in the stomach signals the secretion of more acid. Many beverages such as carbonated drinks and fruit juices that people

Myth vs. Fact

Myth:

Older adults are well-informed about the medications they take.

Fact:

Older people often use medications incorrectly, which can make them ineffective and sometimes unsafe.

use to help them swallow pills are acidic and may affect the absorption of medications such as ampicillin, erythromycin, and penicillin VK. It's important to ask a health care professional to explain to the older adult in your life all of the requirements for taking a medication, not just what the dose is, or you or your loved one could ask the following questions:

- What's the name of the drug, and what will it do?
- How often should I take it?
- How long should I take it?
- When should I take it? As needed? Before, with, after, or between meals? At bedtime?
- If I forget to take it, what should I do?
- What are the side effects? Should I report them?
- Is there any written material about this drug that I can take home with me?
- If I don't take this drug, is there anything else that would work as well?

Distribution

Distribution refers to how the medication reaches its target. Two normal changes in aging, reduced cardiac output and reduced body mass (height and weight), can affect distribution. Reduced cardiac output tends to reduce how much of the medication reaches its target site. It also can reduce excretion and in turn increase levels of the medication in the bloodstream because blood flow to the kidneys is reduced (see Chapter 6). Reduced blood flow to the kidneys reduces the ability of the kidneys to filter out impurities and cleanse the blood. See page 143 for more information on excretion.

Reduced body mass can affect how a medication reaches its target site. Older adults tend to be smaller than younger adults. As people age, the amount of water in the body and lean body mass (the amount of muscle in proportion to how much a person weighs) decrease. Moreover, the amount of body fat increases in relationship to the amount of muscle. Typically, the fat content in men ages 65 and older is twice that of younger men, and the fat content in women below age 65 is half that of older women. This increased amount of body fat improves the body's ability to store fat-soluble medications, and they accumulate in the fat. Reduced lean body mass affects the distribution of medications by decreasing the amount of fat in which the medication circulates. This can result in higher levels of the medication in the bloodstreams of older adults when it's given in doses that are more appropriate for younger adults—older people shouldn't be prescribed the same dosage of a medication that younger people receive. Commonly prescribed medications for which this can pose problems are Valium (diazepam), Thorazine (chlorpromazine), and Haldol (haloperidol), antipsychotics that are used to treat anxiety.

The transport of water-soluble medications such as Tagamet (cimetidine hydrochloride; used to inhibit gastric acid secretion) and Lanoxin (digoxin) are affected by the decrease in the amount of water in older adults' bodies. As mentioned previously, the result can be a higher-than-usual level of the medication in the bloodstream.

Metabolism

Medications are metabolized primarily in the liver. Conflicting research results have caused uncertainty about what happens to the process of metabolism during normal aging of the liver. What is certain, however, is that blood flow both to the liver and especially within it decreases with age. The result is diminished metabolism of medications, which means an increase in the half-life (the time that's required for half of the amount of medication in the body to be reduced) of a medication. Therefore, in older adults, care must be taken in prescribing a medication that is metabolized chiefly in the liver. Phenothiazines (antipsychotics such as Thorazine and Haldol) are metabolized mainly in the liver. Lab tests of an older adult's liver function should be conducted before prescribing medications that are metabolized in the liver. Table 2 gives you some examples of the effects that aging can have on liver drug metabolism.

Excretion

The excretion of most medications is handled primarily by the kidneys. Normal age-related changes in kidney function (see

Table 2.   Effect of aging on liver metabolism of medication[a]

Metabolism reduced by age	Metabolism unaffected by age
Analgesics/anti-inflammatories	
Dextropropoxyphene	Acetaminophen
Ibuprofen	
Meperidine	
Morphine	
Naproxen	
Heart medications	
Amlodipine	Labetalol
Diltiazem	
Lidocaine[b]	
Nifedipine	
Propranolol	
Quinidine	
Theophylline	
Verapamil	
Psychoactives	
Alprazolam[b]	Ethanol
Chlordiazepoxide	Oxazepam
Desipramine[b]	Lorazepam
Diazepam	Temazepam
Imipramine	Phenytoin
Nortriptyline	Valproic acid
	Trazodone
	Triazolam[b]
Others	
Levodopa	Erythromycin
	Fluorouracil
	Isoniazid
	Warfarin

Adapted from Abrams, W.B., Beers, M.H., & Berkow, R. (Eds.). (1995). *The Merck manual of geriatrics* (2nd ed., p. 262). Whitehouse Station, NJ: Merck & Co., adapted with permission.

[a]The effect of age on liver metabolism is sometimes controversial. In such cases, the effects indicated represent those reported in the majority of studies.

[b]In men but not in women.

Chapter 6) probably have the single greatest impact on changes in the levels of medication in the bloodstreams of older adults. The kidneys' ability to cleanse the blood is hampered even more by the lower level of fluids that are frequently found in older adults' bodies, which results from dehydration. Beginning at about age 40, the blood flow to the kidneys decreases steadily. When combined with a disease such as congestive heart failure, the reduction in renal (kidney) blood flow can be serious. What results is prolonged medication exposure and higher levels of the medication in the blood. With a medication such as penicillin, the effect can be helpful in completely eradicating the infection. With toxic levels of medications such as streptomycin (an antibiotic that can cause hearing loss) there can be serious consequences. (The kidneys excrete 90% of streptomycin, so any reduction in kidney function because of age or disease must be taken into account in assigning doses.) Table 3 gives you some examples of medications with decreased kidney elimination.

Interactions

A medication may interact negatively with a number of other substances, functions, or diseases in the body. When a medication produces negative results because another medication is present, it's called a *drug–drug interaction*. When certain foods decrease or

Table 3.   Medications with decreased kidney elimination

Antibiotics	*Diuretics*	*Others*
Amikacin	Amiloride	Amantadine
Gentamicin	Furosemide	Chlorpropamide
Streptomycin	Hydrochlorothiazide	Cimetidine
Tobramycin	Triamterene	Lithium
		Ranitidine
Heart medications		
Captopril	N-Acetylprocainamide	
Digoxin	Procainamide	
Enalapril	Quinapril	
Lisinopril		

Adapted from Abrams, W.B., Beers, M.H., & Berkow, R. (Eds.). (1995). *The Merck manual of geriatrics* (2nd ed., p. 263). Whitehouse Station, NJ: Merck & Co., adapted with permission.

accelerate the effects of a medication, it's called a *drug–food inter-action*. Some medications interact negatively with certain diseases, producing a *drug–disease interaction*. Finally, there are social or emotional factors that can influence the way a medication responds in the body.

Older adults are at high risk for interactions between the different medications they take and between preexisting diseases and their treatment. When acute or chronic health conditions are treated by several different health care providers, the result can be even more problematic. The combination of disease processes and the normal changes of aging can result in what often are quite different responses to medications in older adults than in younger individuals. It's not surprising that older adults report increased side effects from their medications.

Most medication interactions are the result of interference with absorption, metabolism, distribution, and excretion or some combination of these processes. The following list gives examples of how medication interactions can interfere with the four processes:

Absorption
Antidepressants (for example, Elavil) interfere with absorption of other medications by decreasing intestinal motility

Milk in combination with antibiotics can cause body to fail to respond properly to antibiotic therapy

Laxatives (for example, Dulcolax) when taken with milk disintegrate in the stomach prematurely and cause stomach irritation, nausea, and/or vomiting

Distribution
Oral hypoglycemics (for example, tolbutamide; given to lower blood sugar) taken simultaneously with or close in time to aspirin, sulfur medications for infection, or oral anticoagulants (blood thinner; for example, Coumadin) can increase lowered blood sugar response

Metabolism
Anticoagulants taken simultaneously with barbiturates (phenobarbital) decrease the therapeutic effect of anticoagulants and increase possibility of bleeding if medications are discontinued

Excretion
Diuretics without potassium supplements taken along with digoxin, can result in digitalis toxicity

Because negative medication interactions are possible, you need to make every effort to become informed about and knowledgeable in the "how to" of taking prescribed medications. It's the responsibility of both health care professionals and caregivers to consider an older adult's total response to medication therapy and its potential effect on functional capacities such as vision, hearing, memory, and mobility.

Side Effects

Side effects are the additional effects that a medication may have that aren't the primary purpose of the medication. Side effects may be desirable or undesirable and can run the gamut from being an annoyance that is tolerated so that the person can benefit from the medication to being serious and life-threatening. In assessing whether to continue or stop taking a medication, the health care provider with input from the older adult should evaluate the severity of the side effects. Side effects can be categorized into three levels of severity: hazards, adverse reactions, and toxic.

Hazards

If your loved one is given a new medication and begins complaining of other symptoms, be sure to consider the possibility of medication-induced illness before other diagnoses are made and more medications are prescribed. In older adults in particular, many side effects produced by medications can mimic other conditions. This phenomenon is called *medication-induced illness.* The display on page 148 lists some common medication-induced illnesses. The hazards of prescribing more medications to treat the symptoms of a medication-induced illness are that they not only can cloud the true reason for the symptoms but also increase the risk of medication interactions.

Adverse Reactions

Adverse reactions are the development of undesired side effects that are caused by medications. A negative reaction may occur immediately after taking the medication or it could take days to occur.

Approximately 40% of older adults living in the community experience adverse medication reactions, 80% of which occur with well-known medications given at usual doses. It's also estimated that hundreds of thousands of older adults are hospitalized each year because of adverse medication reactions, with sometimes-fatal consequences.

Adverse reactions don't always lead to hospitalization, but they can affect the quality of an older adult's life. The antacid Tagamet can cause confusion or disorientation in an older person, leading his or her family to suspect Alzheimer's disease. Inderal (lowers blood pressure) can cause fatigue or sexual difficulties in men and may affect short-term memory in both men and women. Medication-induced dizziness can lead to a fall and the complications of a broken hip. (It has been reported that almost one third of older adults ages 65 and older living in the community will experience one fall every year.)

Common Medications that Produce Adverse Reactions

Coumadin (blood thinner)

Digoxin (strengthens heartbeat; common brand names include Lanoxicaps and Lanoxin)

Prednisone (anti-inflammatory; common brand names include Deltasone, Medicorten, and Orasone)

Diuretics (flushes excess fluid from the body; common brand names include Esidrix, Hydrazide, Lasix, and Midamor)

Antihypertensives (lowers blood pressure; common brand names include Aldomet, Catapres, Hytrin, Inderal and Tenormin)

Insulin (lowers blood sugar)

Aspirin (relieves pain)

Antidepressants (treats depression; common brand names include Effexor, Elavil, Norpramin and Zoloft)

Common reactions that are produced by these medications include feeling an increased need to sleep sedation), not having the energy to do anything (lethargy), confusion, vision problems (Lasix and Inderal, in particular), and falls.

Sampling of Medication-Induced Illnesses

Illness	Medication
Forgetfulness (electrolyte imbalance)	Diuretics
Weakness (potassium depletion)	Diuretics
Confusion	Tranquilizers, Indocin (anti-inflammatory), digoxin
Blurred vision, dry mouth, retention of urine, constipation, postural hypotension (decreased blood pressure level on standing up)	Antihistamines, tricyclic antidepressants (Elavil), phenothiazines (Thorazine)
Urinary incontinence	Diuretics, sedatives
Constipation	Pain medications, especially those of codeine and narcotic composition
Restlessness	Sedatives
Motor restlessness (the need to be moving constantly)	Phenothiazines
Feeling faint, falls	Blood pressure medications
Apathy, tiredness, clinical depression	Inderal, Aldomet (blood pressure medications)

Any of these medication-related problems can reduce an older adult's level of independence, and may, as in the case of a broken hip, require invasive medical procedures such as hip-replacement surgery that can be life-threatening.

Identifying adverse reactions can be tricky (see also the section on drug holidays on p. 152). Consider, for example, someone with Alzheimer's disease who experiences sudden confusion. It's easy to attribute the confusion to the disease and even increase the medication dose rather than consider the possibility of an adverse reaction to a medication. It's also easy to perceive sudden confusion in an older adult as a symptom of a new condition for which another medication is prescribed. In either case the underlying adverse reaction isn't addressed and potential complications are introduced. Intense confusion also can be produced by analgesics prescribed for pain, antihistamines, and diuretics and by combining antidepressants; for example, an older person may be treated with several medications that were prescribed for depression and anxiety.

> **Alert!**
>
> The more medications a person takes, the greater the potential for an adverse reaction. When two medications are taken together, the probability of an adverse reaction is 6%; when five medications are taken together, the probability of an adverse reaction jumps to 50%; and when eight or more medications are taken together, the probability is 100%.

Lethargy is another common symptom of an adverse reaction, but it's often misinterpreted as a symptom that's connected to a problem in the heart, lungs, or nervous system instead of to a negative response to medication.

Not all adverse reactions are easy to observe. Studies show that thousands of people die each year because of internal bleeding or perforated ulcers brought on by arthritis medicine. On any given day, 10%–15% of Americans ages 65 and older have a prescription filled for a nonsteroidal anti-inflammatory drug (NSAID). NSAIDs often are prescribed to relieve arthritis pain, and their widespread use (some people would argue overuse) can be attributed in part to the frustration felt by both older adults and their health care providers in relieving this painful condition. Unfortunately, very little effort has gone into prescribing alternative treatments for arthritis, including exercise/weight loss regimens, which can lighten the load on affected joints. Because alternative approaches take longer and don't give instant relief, the prescription of pain medications typically is the first line of attack despite the possibility of medication-induced illness from an adverse reaction.

Toxicity

Toxicity occurs when the amount of a medication that's absorbed by the body is higher than is necessary for bringing about a positive, or therapeutic, effect. Toxicity also can be defined as the presence in the body of a medication dose that's at a level that's higher than the therapeutic level established for the medication. Normal aging can cause toxic levels of medications to build up in an older adult's body. Some examples are slowed metabolism and altered excretion by the kidneys secondary to decreased blood flow from the heart.

Other common factors also contribute to toxicity:

- Polypharmacy (when a person is taking more than one medication, doses sometimes get doubled if one generic and one brand-name version of the same medication are being taken; see chart, p. 149, for more information on polypharmacy.
- Dehydration (some older adults drink less fluids because they're afraid of losing bladder control; a lower amount of fluids in the body causes higher medication concentrations)
- Self-medication errors (for various reasons, some older people choose to increase dosages without consulting their health care provider)
- Inappropriate dosage (the prescribed dose is

What's in a Name?
Generic versus Brand-Name Medications

A generic name is the official descriptive and nonproprietary (not a brand name) name assigned to a new medication. Although all drug manufacturers license medications under their generic names, most sell formulations of it under specific proprietary names that each company trademarks. (*Quick tip:* Generic names usually aren't capitalized when referred to in written materials; brand names are. Brand names may be followed by the symbols ® or ™.)

For instance, ibuprofen is the generic name for a medication that is marketed by various companies under brand names such as Advil, Motrin, or Nuprin. The chemical composition of all three is identical. This seems simple enough, but beware! Even though generic equivalents have the same chemical composition as brand-name medications, they don't always have identical therapeutic effects. Ask the health care provider whether there's a generic equivalent to a prescribed brand-name medication and whether it can be substituted. Generic equivalents often are considerably less expensive than brand-name medications.

Myth vs. Fact

Myth:
Standard medication doses are appropriate for older people.

Fact:
Research on medication metabolism is, in general, conducted on adults in their mid-20s. The data from these studies have demonstrated that the "normal adult dose" often is inappropriate for older people. Because the aging process changes the way the body uses medications, they tend to have prolonged action before they're excreted, which places older adults at increased risk for developing side effects and adverse reactions. A lower dosage often is necessary for older people.

Introducing medications at lower initial doses is wise because many older people have one or more chronic ailments, such as arthritis, diabetes, and hypertension, for which they are being treated with combinations of medications. In addition, scientists and health care providers neither fully understand the impact of aging on the metabolism and excretion of medications nor the overall effect of a slowing circulatory system. Slowed circulation delays the distribution of medications in the body and may contribute to delays in their excretion.

The percentage of body fat increases with age. Because many medications are stored in body fat and are only slowly returned to the circulatory system, this physical change can either decrease the intensity or increase the duration of the effect of the medication. Therefore, it's important to make sure that dosages are prescribed appropriate to a person's age and physical condition.

more appropriate for a younger adult; see the "Myth vs. Fact" display on this page)

Each body system can be affected by medication toxicity. What is important to understand is that toxicity can be prevented. Most important for you as the caregiver is to have a good understanding of the medications your loved one is taking, along with knowledge of the characteristic signs and symptoms of toxicity in any medication prescribed (you may want to refer to the comprehensive medications assessment that you filled out at the beginning of this chapter).

A simple and sometimes beneficial way to identify adverse or toxic medication reactions is to schedule a drug holiday. A drug holiday is a planned omission of a specific medication(s) for one or more days or weeks. This intervention has worked really well in institutional settings.

Older adults residing in the community who are taking prescribed and OTC medications also can benefit from a drug holiday. Benefits include increased alertness and decreased cost. Activities that perhaps couldn't be scheduled because of the effects of a medication(s) may be possible during a drug holiday. For example, an older man on a diuretic normally wouldn't leave the house because he wants to be close to a bathroom, but when on a drug holiday, he feels greater freedom to leave because he's not afraid of having an accident.

Caregiver Tip

Drug holidays can be good for everyone, but they should be undertaken only on the advice of a health care provider in order to avoid negative effects. Abruptly stopping certain medications, such as hypertensive and antiseizure medications, can cause serious adverse effects.

A drug holiday can be a great idea, but many factors must be considered on an individual basis. Certain medications tend to settle in body fat and require more than 1 or 2 days to go below therapeutic levels. Eliminating a medication for the time that's necessary to go below therapeutic levels may not be recommended. An alternative to a drug holiday is to try to reduce the number of medications prescribed. Sometimes, after a careful assessment by the health care provider of all of the medications that are being taken, both drug holiday and reduction interventions can be used.

Common Offenders Four major medication groups are associated with most of the toxic effects that are seen in older adults:

- Antihypertensives—including diuretics; to lower blood pressure
- Digoxin—given to patients with heart failure
- Benzodiazepines—sedative/hypnotic medications that help a person relax and reduce anxiety
- Phenothiazines—antipsychotics given to patients with depression or anxiety disorders

Antihypertensives are medications that, either singularly or in combination with another medication, work to lower blood pressure. *Diuretics* are the most commonly prescribed first-choice medications to reduce blood pressure. Because diuretics decrease the amount of fluid in the body, they can cause older adults, especially frail older adults, to become lightheaded and perhaps fall. Older adults who are on diuretics should be advised to be careful when changing position, for example from a lying to sitting position or from a sitting to standing position. Some toxic effects of diuretics could be dehydration and decreased electrolyte level (not enough potassium or sodium in the system) as well as too low a drop in blood pressure.

Digoxin is used either alone in treating people whose heart is beating out of rhythm (arrhythmia) or with diuretics in treating people with congestive heart failure (when the heart as a pump isn't as effective). It can be very toxic to older adults. Lab tests that monitor blood levels of medications have found that the levels in 15% of older adults lie outside the accepted normal range. More alarming is that many medications, such as aspirin taken in high doses to manage arthritis, may interfere with laboratory test values and make results undependable. Test values for digoxin blood levels, for example, can't definitively identify toxic levels of the medication in blood, and they're not a substitute for direct observation of the person. Compounding the fact that blood levels in older adults can be misleading is that digoxin toxicity looks different in older adults than it does in younger people (see display on p. 154)

A toxic reaction to digoxin is more likely when the dose is too high for an older adult, not taking into account age, gender, body composition, and normal changes associated with aging. A toxic reaction often is first signaled by changes in the EKG, along with changes in mental function, such as confusion, lethargy, apathy, or listlessness. Episodes of confusion can contribute to incidences of incontinence.

Concern over digoxin toxicity should increase when a diuretic also has been prescribed. The loss of potassium caused by diuretics can result in an arrhythmia. This extreme hazard can be avoided with proper education and professional intervention. Simple instructions on the importance of taking a potassium supplement and/or increasing the intake of potassium-rich foods (for example, bananas, orange juice) can help to alleviate this problem.

The side effects of the benzodiazepine (sedatives/hypnotics) and phenothiazine (antipsychotics) medication groups are both uncomfortable and frustrating to older adults. Dry mouth, constipation, and blurred vision are side effects that have added impact in the normal changes associated with aging. For example,

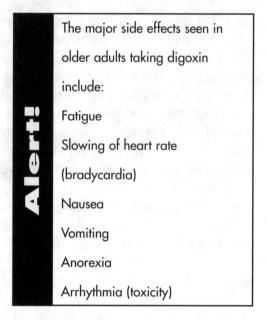

The major side effects seen in older adults taking digoxin include:

Fatigue

Slowing of heart rate (bradycardia)

Nausea

Vomiting

Anorexia

Arrhythmia (toxicity)

severe gum irritation can be caused by the combination of age-related decreases in saliva production and the dry mouth effect of antipsychotic medications, which is compounded further by wearing dentures. The byproduct can be poor nutritional intake and an increased risk for precancerous lesions of the mouth.

Constipation together with the normal slowing of intestinal motility can delay the excretion of these medications. Overuse of laxatives and enemas may result from the effort to alleviate the uncomfortable symptoms of constipation, which can lead to dehydration and electrolyte imbalance.

PATTERNS OF USE

In addition to recognizing the high levels of medication use among older adults, it's helpful to be aware of common use and misuse patterns to be sure your loved one is getting the maximum therapeutic benefit from medications with minimal risk to health.

Polypharmacy

Polypharmacy happens when a variety of medications are being prescribed by a health care professional for a number of different

The following factors expose older adults to serious risk from undesirable medication actions:

An excessive dose of a medication—because of the normal changes associated with aging that affect kidney function and the subsequent excretion of the medication

An excessive duration of use—when an older adult remains indefinitely on a medication that's intended for short-term use (for example, antidepressants, antipsychotics, and sedatives/hypnotics)

A change in the dosage form of a medication (for example, from capsules to a liquid)—which can lead to adverse effects because of how the medication is absorbed. Liquids are absorbed faster than pills and/or capsules.

symptoms or disorders and particularly when an individual also is self-prescribing OTC medications. Medication use studies report that 90% of older adults take an average of three OTC and five prescription medications daily. Medications for heart problems, infection, psychosis, depression, and excess fluid in the body are the most frequently prescribed and used medications. OTC medications to relieve pain, treat constipation, and relieve indigestion are the most-often used, with cough syrups, eye washes, vitamins, and nonsteroidal topical ointments the next most purchased and used. Complicating poly-pharmacy is that older adults tend to see more than one health care provider without sharing or even being asked about the total list of prescription and OTC medications that they're taking.

Self-Prescribing

Although Medicare provides many benefits, it doesn't reimburse individuals for their medications. Furthermore, it doesn't cover all of the costs of medical care, leaving the balance to be paid by the older adult, who may or may not be able to pay. Some older adults try to avoid spending the money on the care or medications that Medicare doesn't cover by not undergoing a prescribed treatment or not filling the prescription or taking a medication. Sometimes they self-medicate with borrowed medications from family or friends, use a medication that's already in the house, or decrease the dosage of an expensive medication to make it last longer (for example, taking it every other day instead of the daily prescribed dosage). You or the older adult in your life should make the prescribing doctor aware of the older adult's ability to pay for medications.

Some older adults self-prescribe because they have difficulty swallowing pills. Older adults who have trouble swallowing pills might borrow another person's medication or substitute the liquid form of the same medication because it's easier to swallow. The outcome, however, can be serious because liquids are absorbed faster in the body and can increase the medication level too quickly. Also, most medications come in different forms, but the dosage of the forms isn't interchangeable.

Misuse

Some older adults adjust doses, add OTC medications as they think necessary, or take a second medication to treat symptoms that are actually adverse effects of the first medication. A common drug class that's used often by older adults is salicylates (aspirin is one example). Long-term use can lead to toxicity, which is displayed as delirium, or to salicylate intoxication, with ringing in the ears (tinnitus) being a major symptom.

The use of OTC medications to alleviate symptoms of pain, constipation, insomnia, and indigestion has increased dramatically. Other overused medications include laxatives, antacids, and vitamins. All of these OTC medications contain active ingredients that in large amounts would require a prescription. Taken continually they can become dangerous substances and become potentially more dangerous given the slower processes of the aging body. Be sure that medications are being taken correctly.

Certain medications come in different forms for specific reasons. Medications with enteric coatings won't irritate the lining of the stomach. Time-release tablets allow the active part of a medication to be released slowly over a period of time. Neither kind of medication should be chewed or crushed. Chewing or crushing destroys the composition of the medication, and it could have serious consequences for the person taking it.

Out-of-Date Medications and Proper Disposal

Think of all of the medications that many older adults have taken in a year, and how many of them may not have been used up in that year. Most medications are stable for at least 3 years. Tablets are the most stable and liquids the least stable. An expiration date usually is noted somewhere on the label or package, on a separate strip, or on the foil wrap surrounding capsules. An annual inventory of all medications and their expiration dates is important. Any medication (pill, liquid, ointment) unused during the past year should be thrown away.

Usually it's impossible to detect whether a medication has lost its therapeutic benefit. Aspirin is one exception: When it decomposes it gives off a vinegar-like odor. Antibiotics shouldn't be kept around the house because the full course must be used up when it's prescribed. Taking less than the full course of an antibiotic won't kill the infection completely. Furthermore, antibiotics are made specifically for certain infections. Taking the wrong one or an inadequate dose of the right one encourages the growth of medication-resistant bacteria. In general, ointments such as antibacterial first-aid creams are resistant to damage because of their semi-liquid state and their antimicrobial nature, and most of these ointments contain preservatives to retard chemical changes.

The color of some medications and vitamins fade as they decompose. Although slight discoloration isn't necessarily a sign that a vitamin is useless, throw out any vitamins that are 2 years old or older.

Noncompliance

Seventy-five percent of older adults intentionally don't stick to the schedule of medication administration that was prescribed. Either they alter the dose because they feel that the medication isn't working or they don't like the side effects. Sometimes they simply stop taking the medication altogether, saying they feel better and don't need it anymore.

Many factors affect compliance with medication routines. Some relate to concrete issues such as

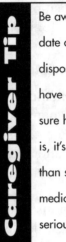

Be aware of the expiration date of all medications and dispose of the ones that have expired. If you're not sure how old a medication is, it's better to be safe than sorry: Dispose of a medication rather than risk serious consequences.

> Dealing with the high costs of medications
> Difficulty opening containers with childproof caps
> Storing medications in inappropriate areas (too hot or too moist)
> Taking medication at the wrong time
> Failing to have a prescription filled
> Ordering medications by mail or telephone, thereby missing verbal directions, information, and reinforcement, and possibly encountering delays in receipt of medications

There also are personal reasons for noncompliance:

> Misunderstanding the expected outcomes of a medication
> Mixing prescribed and OTC medications without the awareness of serious interactions
> Denying that certain OTC preparations such as vitamins and antacids are medications
> Disliking the side effects of a medication
> Believing that the doctor said it was okay to stop taking the medication
> Forgetting to take the medication

Many times noncompliance boils down to how the directions/instructions are given. If the instructions are rattled off quickly, not put in writing, and there's no opportunity for feedback as to how much the older person understands, then the probability of lack of compliance increases. Older adults typically take longer to process information, especially when information is given at a time when the person is anxious or uncomfortable. Both of

Myth vs. Fact

Myth:
Older adults take prescription medications responsibly.

Fact:
Many older adults think that OTC medications are relatively harmless. They don't hesitate to take the medication as often as needed, increasing or decreasing the recommended dose at will. Often, they stop taking the medication when they feel better. These practices can carry over to prescription medications. You may hear for example, "I feel much better now, so I'm not going to take it any more. Anyway, it upset my stomach and made my mouth dry" or "I feel real bad right now. I think I'll double the dose. I'll go back to taking the number of pills the doctor said tomorrow."

Such statements aren't unusual. Sometimes the fault lies with the health care professional, who didn't supply sufficient information about how the medication works. Sometimes the fault lies with the patient, who didn't tell the doctor about the unpleasant side effects he or she has been experiencing. The result of taking prescription drugs irresponsibly can be an ineffectual, maybe even dangerous, outcome for the patient.

these factors may come into play when health care is being sought. Also, hearing or vision impairments can affect whether older adults understand instructions. Cultural and language barriers also may be present.

Try to be aware of the potential reasons for noncompliance with a medication or treatment program. Does the schedule or the effect(s) of the medication interfere with other activities? Are the effects out of sync with the person's habits? For example, if a medication is supposed to be taken three times a day with meals, this order won't be helpful to older people who eat only two meals a day, which isn't unusual, given the decreased activity level of many dependent, chronically ill older people. Another example is a medication that makes a person tired (*lethargic*), which prevents him or her from participating in social activities. The person may respond by not taking the medication or altering its dosage, which, in general, happens without the knowledge or advice of the person's health care provider. Without good communication and understanding of the person, the symptoms under treatment may persist, causing the health care provider to increase the dosage and potentially introduce new problems.

How to Improve Compliance

Knowing that one third of all people taking medications don't comply with the treatment schedule is the first step in being able to improve compliance. The "Caregiver Tip" below describes important factors that will increase a person's compliance with a medication or therapy program. When these factors aren't addressed, the chances increase that your loved one will be part of that one third of people who don't comply with a medication regimen. The results of noncompliance might be continued discomfort and complaints and an increasing risk of developing additional problems.

PAIN

Many older adults will tell you that they're in pain. Many others will be in pain but won't tell you. When pressed for details, both types of people may be unable or unwilling to describe their pain. Part of your job as caregiver is to learn to detect and assess both the subjective (what your loved one describes) and the objective (what you observe) characteristics of someone in pain.

Caregiver Tip

Older people who have confidence in their health care providers are more likely to comply with their instructions. Older people (or their caregivers) who have an accurate understanding of a therapeutic regimen are more likely to comply with it. People who feel fully informed about what is medically wrong, what is being prescribed, how the medication is expected to help (in lay terms), the frequent side effects, and exactly how to take the medication will be more compliant. People do better with clear written instructions and an opportunity to verbalize their understanding of the instructions.

Assessing Pain

When someone says that he or she is in pain, the first step in assessing it is to ask the person to describe it and give the perceptions of it. Ask your loved one to describe the qualities of the pain. For example: Is it sharp, dull, throbbing, or achy? What makes it better— lying down, standing up, rubbing it? What makes it worse— sitting, walking, bending? Ask the person to point to the pain so that you know exactly where it hurts. Then you need to make your own observations of his or her appearance and behavior.

When pain is present over a long period of time, it's called chronic pain. Chronic pain is any kind of pain that doesn't seem to respond to traditional treatment (medications); that results in feelings of extreme fatigue, anxiety, or depression; and that affects how usual activities get done. Chronic pain is difficult to relieve. It may be helpful to look at less traditional ways of helping, a topic that we discuss later in this section.

Before starting a pain-relief treatment, it is important to find some method to tell you how intense the pain is before treatment. The method should be used again after the treatment to judge that relief, if any, has been achieved. An easy method is to use a pain scale of 1–10. Ask the older adult in your life to rate his or her pain from 1, which indicates

---

Observing Pain: Objective Qualities

A person in pain may:

Protect an area of the body, guarding where he or she feels pain

Have distorted thought processes, seeming to appear confused and disoriented, with attention directed only to self and the pain

Cry or moan and act restless, irritable, and agitated

Rub an area of his or her body (the person perceives that rubbing interferes with the transmission of pain signals to the brain)

Have a facial expression that's different from usual, with a pinched look to the face and tightly clenched jaw muscles and teeth

Have general muscle tension, sometimes accompanied by complaints of nausea

no pain, to 10, which is the worst pain imaginable. To assess how much pain has been relieved by the treatment, use a similar assessment scale, with 1 indicating no relief, and 10 indicating complete relief.

Types of Pain Relief

Two types of pain relievers are non-narcotic and narcotic medications. Non-narcotics include Tylenol, aspirin, and NSAIDs. Tylenol has very little anti-inflammatory effect and in high doses can damage a person's liver.

Aspirin has an anti-inflammatory effect, but it also has effects on the gastrointestinal system. It can upset the stomach and sometimes causes internal bleeding in the stomach or intestines. Aspirin also can affect kidney function. If your loved one has congestive heart failure or liver disease, or is on diuretics, make sure his or her health is being monitored if the person is prescribed high doses of aspirin, or even if he or she is taking moderate doses over a long period of time.

Several types of NSAIDs aren't recommended for older people, specifically Feldine, which is long lived in the body, and Indocin, which has an increasingly poor effect on the kidneys. When NSAIDs are prescribed for older people, they should be started at doses that are lower than those that are given to younger people. Ask the person's health care provider to prescribe $1/2$ to $2/3$ the recommended dose, then slowly (for example, week by week) increase the dose until the recommended dose is reached. If NSAIDs are purchased OTC, make sure that no more than the recommended dose is taken. Once the optimal dose is reached, no further pain relief occurs, only side effects. If a particular NSAID is taken for 2–3 weeks without noticeable relief, consult the person's health care provider. The NSAID may need to be changed to a different class.

There are two important cautions/hints to remember when taking NSAIDs:

1. Never take more than one NSAID at a time (this includes aspirin).
2. Take the NSAID with meals or milk to prevent stomach upset.

It's helpful to understand the following definitions when discussing pain medications:

Addiction: a habit/obsession/fixation

Physical dependence: reliance on; in need of

Tolerance: need more to get the same effect; getting used to

Narcotics usually are recommended for the relief of moderate to severe pain. Some people fear addiction, but this is rarely observed in people who are taking these medications for pain relief. The person taking narcotic medications can become physically dependent on the medication—suddenly stopping a medication can produce unpleasant withdrawal symptoms. Another drawback to taking a narcotic medication is that tolerance to it may develop, and higher doses are needed to get the same result.

Adjuvants for Pain Relief

An adjuvant is a medication that's added to a prescription to speed up or increase the action of a principal ingredient in the primary medication that's prescribed for pain. Although adjuvants aren't pain relievers, they can help relieve pain when taken either together with a pain medication or alone. They tend to relax the person, relieving some of the tension that builds up when a person is in pain. Tricyclic antidepressants are an example of an adjuvant medication for pain relief because many people become depressed when they've been in pain for a long time. Antidepressants may take 2–4 weeks to build up in the blood before any effect is felt, so your loved one needs to be patient. Also, it may help to give or take this medication 1–2 hours before bedtime because drowsiness is a side effect. Initially, a dose of 10 mg once a day is prescribed.

Alternative Methods of Pain Relief

Although medication treatment for acute pain is justified because usually it's prescribed for a short time, treatment for chronic pain can demand other interventions. Health care providers are focusing more on alternative, nonpharmaceutical ways to manage pain. Some of these alternative methods include massage, relaxation, guided imagery/visualization, meditation, application of heat or cold compresses to painful areas, therapeutic touch, hypnosis, and acupressure. These interventions give different levels of relief. For example:

- Massage uses medium to deep pressure on the painful areas to produce relaxation and, possibly, to interrupt the pain messages being sent to the brain.
- Relaxation effectively reduces pain by lessening the physical and mental stresses that come with pain. Deep breathing and focusing on a special object (guided imagery/visualization) can relieve pain by distracting the brain from sensing the pain. Using guided imagery or visualization can be helpful after pain medication is given; the person can visualize the medication working through the body to its target.
- Applications of hot or cold compresses to painful areas can help diminish the pain and/or soothe the area. Be careful, however, especially with people with peripheral vascular disease or diabetes. These conditions cause poor blood flow and decreased feeling/sensations. Thermal or ice burns can easily occur in someone with decreased sensation.
- Therapeutic touch works by transferring energy from the person doing the treatment to the one in pain. It "unclogs" areas in the body that seem to be closed, thereby easing the pain.

Caregiver Tip

Basic Principles Relating to Giving Pain Medications

1. Prevent and treat pain before it becomes severe.
2. Take pain medication on a regular schedule to achieve adequate levels of it in the blood. Take around the clock to achieve the best result.
3. The oral route is the preferred route for giving pain medications; it is less expensive and easier to use.
4. Injections are the worst way to manage pain, especially chronic pain.
5. The rectal route is recommended whenever a person cannot take the medication orally.

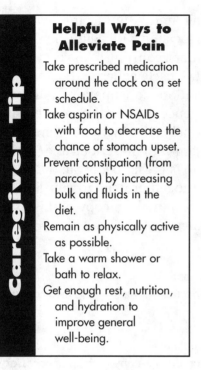

Helpful Ways to Alleviate Pain

Take prescribed medication around the clock on a set schedule.

Take aspirin or NSAIDs with food to decrease the chance of stomach upset.

Prevent constipation (from narcotics) by increasing bulk and fluids in the diet.

Remain as physically active as possible.

Take a warm shower or bath to relax.

Get enough rest, nutrition, and hydration to improve general well-being.

- Hypnosis is a method used to induce a sleeplike state during which the person is susceptible to the hypnotist's suggestions.
- Acupressure is pressure applied to specific points on the body, sometimes resulting in the reduction of pain.

Regardless of your belief in alternative methods of pain relief, it's important for you to support your loved one's use of any positive coping measures such as prayer, meditation, relaxation, or distraction. Try to understand and accept that his or her pain is real, even if a cause or site of pain can't be identified. It can be very frustrating to feel that you can't help make the pain go away, but believing what your loved one says is the first important step in providing pain relief.

ADMINISTERING MEDICATIONS

Assessing the Person

It may be self-evident, and you may already be doing it, but when it comes to taking medications, you must regularly assess the ability of the older adult in your life to be independent in taking medications. This assessment should include the person's mental status, ability to follow instructions, senses of sight, hearing, and touch, motor abilities (ability to open bottles, pour medications), and financial status (ability to purchase medications).

One of your major concerns as a caregiver is how to help the older adult in your life maintain the ability to perform activities of daily living (ADLs). These activities include dressing, eating, getting around (*ambulating*), bathing, and going to the bathroom (*toileting*). The normal changes associated with aging, often combined with common chronic disorders, conspire to make everyday activities more and more difficult. Muscle aches and pains, difficulty in eating, frequency of urination, constipation, and many more conditions create inconvenience, discomfort, and eventually a desire to seek professional help. Getting relief from these symptoms may involve treating them with prescribed and/or OTC medications. When any medication is prescribed, you, the health care provider, and the older adult together need to consider the following questions (you may want to make a copy of this list to take with you to doctor's appointments):

- Is the medication truly necessary?
- Is there an alternative form of treatment?
- What therapeutic effects can be expected from taking the medication?
- Will the discomfort go away?
- Does the older adult have other problems?
- Which problems need immediate treatment?
- What other medications is the person on? Are any of them unnecessary?
- What drug–disease interactions (see Table 4 for examples) or drug–drug interactions (see Table 5 for examples) might be expected?
- What is the person's present level of renal (kidney) and liver function?
- What amount of understanding of the therapeutic and toxic effects of medication does the older adult have?
- Have you made every effort to ensure compliance with instructions about medications?

Knowing About Medications

It's imperative that you learn everything you can about the medications that your loved one is on. Equally important is for the older adult to know something about his or her medications. Ideally, both you and the older adult in your life should know the following:

- What medications the older adult is taking (take an inventory)
- Both the generic and brand names for a medication
- The expected action of the medication

Table 4.   Important drug–disease interactions

Disease/disorder	Medications	Adverse reactions
Cardiac conduction disorders	Beta-blockers, digoxin, diltiazem, verapamil, tricyclic antidepressants	Heart block
Chronic obstructive pulmonary disease	Beta-blockers Opioids	Bronchoconstriction Respiratory depression
Chronic renal impairment	NSAIDs, radiocontrast agents, aminoglycosides	Acute renal failure
Heart failure	Beta-blockers, diltiazem, verapamil, disopyramide	Worsens heart failure
Dementia	Amantadine, antiepileptics, levodopa, psychoactives, anticholinergics	Increased confusion, delirium
Diabetes	Corticosteroids, diruretics	Hyperglycemia
Depression	Alcohol, benzodiazepines, beta-blockers, some hypertensives, corticosteroids	Brings on or makes depression worse
Glaucoma	Anticholinergics	Makes glaucoma worse
Hypertension	NSAIDs	Increase in blood pressure
Hypokalemia	Digoxin	Cardiac toxicity
Orthostatic hypotension	Antihypertensives, diuretics, neuroleptics, tricyclic antidepressants, L-dopa	Dizziness, falls, fainting
Osteopenia	Corticosteroids	Fracture
Peptic ulcer disease	NSAIDs, anticoagulants	Upper GI bleeding
Peripheral vascular disease	Beta-blockers	Periodic calf cramps
Prostatism	Anticholinergics, alpha-antagonists	Urinary retention

Adapted from Abrams, W.B., Beers, M.H., & Berkow, R. (Eds.). (1995). *The Merck manual of geriatrics* (2nd ed., p. 266–267). Whitehouse Station, NJ: Merck & Co., adapted with permission.

- The adverse side effects of the medication (which symptoms suggest toxicity)
- Common interactions between medications and foods that can have serious consequences
- How and when medications are to be taken
- What symptoms that could mean trouble that you should report to the health care provider

- When to stop taking the medication
- How to dispose of the medication correctly when treatment is finished

Once you've done a complete inventory of the medications your loved one is taking, make sure you're satisfied that, for each medication, you can answer all of the basic questions listed in this chapter. If not, be sure to seek the answers to the following questions:

- What's the name of the prescribed medication? (both generic and brand names)
- What's the disorder for which it's being prescribed?
- When should it be taken? (get very specific instructions, both verbal and written)
- How should it be taken? (with food, without food, with water)

How to Administer a Medication

Here are some commonsense but important rules to follow to get the medication as efficiently and safely as possible to the target site in the body.

1. Wash your hands thoroughly (see "Caregiver Tip" on p. 169).
2. When giving an oral medication, have the person sit upright or stand to reduce the risk of choking or sucking the medication into his or her lungs (*aspirating*; the result could be aspiration pneumonia).
3. Give the person at least 4–6 ounces of liquid with oral medications to make them easier to swallow. Liquids also ensure that the medication reaches the stomach, thus minimizing gastric irritation. Make sure that the fluid is appropriate—for example, tetracycline shouldn't be taken with milk because milk impairs absorption of this antibiotic. Read the label first.
4. After giving an oral medication, ask the person whether the pill or capsule went down or is stuck under the tongue, between the teeth/denture plate and gums, or elsewhere. (If the person is physically impaired, check his or her mouth.) Give more liquids if he or she indicates that the pill wasn't properly swallowed.

Table 5. Examples of important drug–drug interactions

	Drug	Interacting drug	Effect
Pharmacokinetic interactions			
Inhibited drug metabolism	Warfarin	Cimetidine, metronidazole	Increased anticoagulation, bleeding
	Theophylline	Cimetidine, erythromycin	Theophylline toxicity
Induced drug metabolism	Warfarin	Barbiturates, rifampin	Decreased anticoagulation
	Phenytoin	Barbiturates, rifampin	Loss of seizure control
	Theophylline	Smoking, phenytoin	Increased shortness of breath
Pharmacodynamic interactions			
Hypokalemia	Digoxin	Diuretics	Digitalis toxicity
Orthostatic hypotension	Diuretics	Tricyclic anti-depressants, alpha-blockers, vasodilators	Falls, weakness, fainting

Adapted from Abrams, W.B., Beers, M.H., & Berkow, R. (Eds.). (1995). *The Merck manual of geriatrics* (2nd ed., p. 268–269). Whitehouse Station, NJ: Merck & Co., adapted with permission.

Caregiver Tip

Proper Handwashing Technique

Of course you've been washing your hands all of your life and you've seen TV "surgeons" scrub before an operation, but you've probably never combined the two to make your hands clean enough to administer an injection. Here's how:

1. Avoid direct contact with bathroom surfaces by using a clean, dry paper towel to handle the water faucets. Make the water very warm.

2. Place a quarter-size dollop of antibacterial soap in the palm of your hand. Scrub your hands with your fingertips pointing down toward the drain (like the TV surgeons do). Make sure that you clean thoroughly between your fingers!

3. Use a fingernail brush or an orange stick to clean under your fingernails.

4. Point your hands down toward the drain and rinse your hands thoroughly, making sure all of the soap comes off (some antibacterial soaps leave a sticky film unless you rinse thoroughly). Use a clean, dry paper towel to turn off the faucet and dry your hands.

5.   If you are giving rectal suppositories, gently insert them 2 inches into the rectum and press them against the rectal tissue. Allow a little extra time for the suppository to melt and activate because an older adult's body temperature is usually lower than a younger adult's.

6.   When giving insulin injections, follow these instructions:
   •   Gather the following necessary pieces of equipment: an alcohol swab, a syringe with needle (the most common syringe for insulin injections holds 1 ml and uses a 25-gauge needle; the needle is $1/2$-inch or $5/8$-inch long), and an insulin preparation.
   •   Cleanse the injection site with an alcohol swab, and let the skin air dry.
   •   Pinch or stretch the skin in the area of the injection, and pierce the skin with a needle stab at either a 45° or 90° angle (if your loved one is thin, use a 45° angle; if the person is heavy set, use a 90° angle).
   •   Pull back on the plunger to check for blood in the syringe; if you see blood in the syringe, withdraw the needle and start again with a new syringe.
   •   Inject the person with insulin.
   •   Massage the area lightly after removing the needle.

7.   Monitor and evaluate the older person's response to the medication. Watch for possible adverse reactions, especially a change in mental status.

There are two main types of insulin preparation. One is regular insulin, with onset of action within 30–60 minutes, and the other is long-acting insulin NPH, with onset of action within 60–90 minutes. Some health care providers prescribe both types, either mixed or given at different times. Make sure that you know the particular type and instructions that relate to your loved one. Make a point to get this information in writing. Be assertive in asking questions of a health care provider if you have any doubt about the injection type, amount, and schedule.

Insulin injection sites include the upper arms, stomach, and thighs (see Figure 2). It's very important that injection sites be rotated. When you keep injecting in the same place, the tissue hardens in that area. Although your loved one will feel less discomfort from the injection, the insulin isn't absorbed as well, which may lead to an increased insulin dose. When the site is changed, the increased dosage may lower the blood glucose too much, producing the signs and symptoms of low blood sugar (*hypoglycemia*). An easy way to keep track of the injection site is to record it each time the injection is given. Adapt the chart in Figure 3 as a guide and post it in an accessible place.

Syringes usually are disposed of after use, but they can be reused. (Medicare and/or private insurance covers the cost of insulin syringes so you don't have to reuse them.) If you're reusing syringes, you must take special care to clean them thoroughly. You can wash them with alcohol or boil them in water. If you boil the syringes, the water must come to a full boil and then continue boiling for 3–5 minutes before turning off the burner.

If your loved one has difficulty swallowing, ask his or her health care provider what can be done to help in swallowing better. It may be possible to give pills with a bulky food such as a piece of banana or to crush a tablet

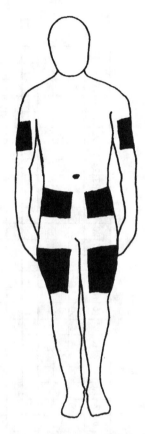

FIGURE 2. Insulin injection sites. (Redrawn from Mosby's Medical, Nursing, & Allied Health Dictionary [1994] [4th ed., p. 819]. St. Louis: Mosby.)

(nonenteric coated) into a soft food such as applesauce, jelly, or ice cream. Some people find it easier to swallow caplets—tablets that are shaped like capsules—instead of round pills.

For advice on taking medications, contact the National Institute on Aging for their publication *Medicines: Use Them Safely* (http://www.nih.gov/nia/ health/pubpub/medicine.htm).

To assist with medication use at home, be aware that many sensory or visual aids can be either purchased or built from common household materials. You can get pill-alert alarms that remind people when to take their medications and pill boxes that

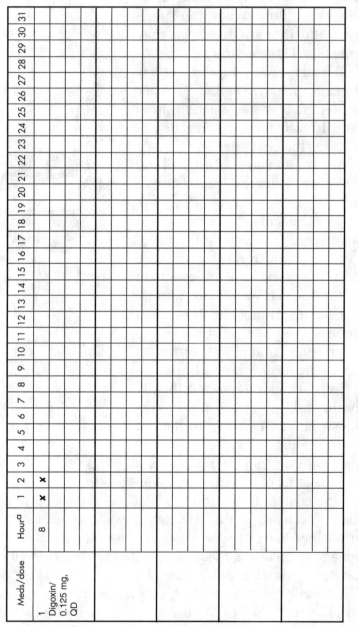

Meds/dose	Hour[a]	1	2	3	4	5	6	7	8	9	10	11	12	13	14	15	16	17	18	19	20	21	22	23	24	25	26	27	28	29	30	31
1 Digoxin/ 0.125 mg, QD	8	x	x																														

FIGURE 3. Sample medication record form.

are divided into sections for organizing pills into times of day or days of the week. You can use an ordinary egg carton to separate pills into clearly marked time/day slots. You can make a log of the schedule and names of medications and post it on the refrigerator, or use a calendar, listing the medications in bright colors. Use your creativity to come up with a system that's easy for you to use. The key to success is not to let it become a haphazard task. A system that's clearly thought out and strictly adhered to makes sure your loved one is safe and lessens your stress.

Avoiding Improper Storage

Improper storage of medications can make them either ineffective or more potent. Four factors affect the stability of medications: temperature, humidity, light, and oxygen. All medications must be kept in a cool, dry place in their original container, with labeling intact. In general, a dark closet in a cool or an air-conditioned room (during the summer) is an excellent place to store medications.

One place where medications are commonly kept but they should not be is the bathroom medicine cabinet. Because of showers and baths and inadequate ventilation, the bathroom is too humid a location. Humidity can make the gelatin in capsules absorb water, which makes the capsules stick together. It also can make tablets, which are made to absorb water in the intestines, swell up and break apart until you have nothing but bottles full of ineffective powder.

Another poor, and common, storage place is the refrigerator because it's damp. Some medications need to be refrigerated, but the label will clearly say so. Keeping medications on the kitchen windowsill also isn't appropriate. Too much light degrades medications—this is why many medications, such as nitroglycerin, come in amber-colored containers.

Being an Advocate

The importance of individualizing medication assessment, treatment, and administration when intervening on behalf and for the benefit of the older adult can't be stated emphatically enough. The uniqueness of each person in relationship to his or her need for a medication and his or her response to a medication must be part of any interaction between the older adult and the person's health care provider. As caregiver, you must take responsibility for advocating for the older person who's dependent on you for care. This role isn't always easy, but being aware of important areas of concern should help. Never hesitate to ask questions about medications, common side effects, unusual symptoms, or recommended methods for giving the medications. Strive to achieve open communication with health care providers. If communication is poor, find another professional who will listen and be caring and concerned. But be sure you're fulfilling your responsibility to share important information that needs to be heard.

10

Providing Skin, Foot, and Wound Care

The skin's job is mainly to protect the body from the environment by acting as a barrier against microorganisms, ultraviolet radiation, loss of body fluids, and environmental stresses. The skin also regulates body temperature (within a very narrow range) and is involved in activating vitamin D when the skin is exposed to sunlight. The importance of caring for the skin of the older adult in your life is magnified by the changes in the skin that take place as people age. These changes include a decrease in the number of cells in the epidermis (top layer of skin), which causes a decrease in the skin's immune response. Melanocytes, cells that are found in the epidermis, decrease in number with age, giving older adults less protection against ultraviolet radiation. In addition, decreased blood supply to the skin is a factor in delayed wound healing in aged skin.

This chapter focuses on areas of caregiving that involve intimate contact with the older person you are caring for: skin care, foot care, and wound care. The section on skin care explains why it's so necessary and what the risk factors are for developing problems. The benefits of bathing and how to maintain healthy skin are a major focus of this chapter. Specific attention also is given to assessing the feet as well to proper footwear. Foot care for diabetics and information on first aid for injuries to the feet are covered as well. The section on wound care details the importance of assessing wounds, how to cleanse them, and the importance of regular wound care.

SKIN CARE

Chapter 6 provides a lot of detail about the many changes in the skin that are caused by aging, including the loss of subcutaneous tissue (tissue that lies just below the skin), the decreased elasticity of the skin (which in turn produces decreased skin turgor, the way the skin snaps back after pinching, for instance), and the decreased amount of oil in the skin, which can result in dryness, scaliness, and itching. All of these changes make the skin more fragile and place it at high risk for problems. Taking proper care of the skin can help older people avoid or minimize potential problems.

Older adults with certain health conditions are particularly susceptible to developing skin problems. They include:

- Anyone who's confined to a bed or chair for long periods of time
- Anyone who's physically unable to move him- or herself (either in bed or a chair)
- Anyone who experiences loss of bowel or bladder control
- Anyone who's undernourished and/or not eating enough
- Anyone who has dementia or a cognitive impairment that makes him or her unaware of or unable to understand the need to change position every 1 or 2 hours

Keeping Clean

Bathing should focus on cleanliness and comfort. Because older people's skin contains fewer oils, and soap and water wash away these necessary oils, they shouldn't bathe as often as younger people do. If they aren't incontinent, they can take a complete, head-to-toe bath or shower every other day. If your loved one is frail but not incontinent, he or she can bathe once or twice a week. The face, underarms, and genitals should be bathed as often as needed. Incontinent people should bathe or be bathed every day. On nonbathing days, they can clean their faces, hands, and underarms. Mouth care—brushing teeth or cleansing dentures—should be part of daily care. If the older adult in your life can participate in his or her personal care or do the whole thing alone, it's very important to let him or her do that. Let's take bathing step by step.

Washing and Rinsing the Skin

One of the greatest caregiving challenges is to help to wash and rinse your loved one's skin with as little violation as possible of his or her privacy and self-respect. Think for a moment about when you undress for your shower or bath and then wash—you want a private environment, so you close and maybe even lock the bathroom door. Make sure that you provide the same level of privacy and respect for your loved one when he or she is bathing or being bathed. Your love and concern for the individual are demonstrated by these actions.

When preparing the bath or shower, use warm water (about 90°–100° F). Test the water temperature with a bath thermometer or use your elbow. (The skin on your elbow is thinner and more sensitive to temperature variations than your fingers are.) The water temperature should feel comfortable to the touch—it shouldn't burn. It's harder but not impossible to test the water in a shower (using a hand-held showerhead helps). Warm water not only cleans the body but also gives comfort and relaxes the bather.

Use moisturizing soaps such as Dove, Tone, and castile soap. These are the most beneficial to older adults' skin because they relieve and reduce itching and dryness. Avoid soaps that contain alcohol or perfumes and deodorant soaps such as Dial. Tempting as it may seem, avoid using bath oils because they can increase the risk of slipping and falling in the bathtub or shower.

Benefits of Bathing

Physical

Bathing cleanses the skin and stimulates the circulation of blood via the friction of washing and drying.

Bathing acts as a muscle toner and body conditioner.

The warm heat and moisture of bath water can soothe aching muscles and relieve joint discomfort.

Bathing can soothe dry or itchy skin, particularly by adding a skin-conditioning product such as Aveeno® Bath Treatment. Note, however, that the presence of oil on the skin can put your loved one at risk for falling.

Mental

Bathing refreshes the spirit and improves self-image and morale.

Bathing may improve a person's appetite and sleeping pattern.

Providing for Safety in the Bathtub/Shower

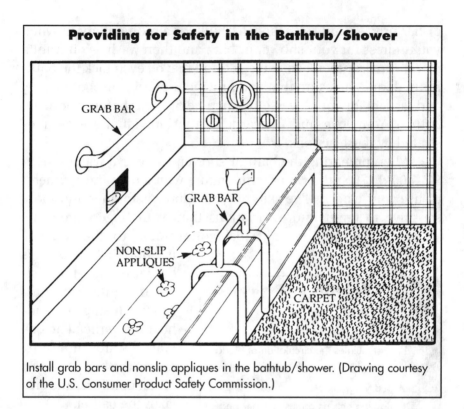

Install grab bars and nonslip appliques in the bathtub/shower. (Drawing courtesy of the U.S. Consumer Product Safety Commission.)

Use only soft terrycloth or cotton washcloths to wash the body to avoid abrading the fragile skin of older adults.

Rinsing the skin of all soap residue is a vital part of bathing because dried soap can irritate and/or dry out the skin. Flush the soap away by letting the water flow over the body. The flowing water also gives the bather a feeling of comfort and relaxation.

Drying the Skin

Before you towel off your loved one or he or she dries off, it's important to remember that older adults' skin is fragile. Rather

Caregiver Tip

If the older adult in your life is incontinent, he or she should be bathed using a shower or bath seat (available in medical supply stores). This seat also provides comfort and helps prevent falls.

than rubbing the towel over the skin as you may have done to yourself all of your life, gently pat the skin dry. Dry thoroughly between the toes and in other areas where skin meets and rubs together (for example, under the breasts and under the arms). Wet skin breaks down easily.

Lubricating the Skin

The last step in bathing/showering should be applying lotion to the skin to moisturize it. Doing this right after bathing, when the skin is still moist, is best because the pores of warm, moist skin are more receptive to moisturizing. Because you don't want to shock the skin, warm the lotion in your hands and gently massage the lotion into the skin. It's best to use emollient products containing petrolatum or mineral oil (for example, Keri, Eucerin, and Aquaphor). Avoid using products that contain alcohol, which dries the skin. During hot weather, apply a small amount of powder or cornstarch to areas of the skin that rub together.

Giving a Bed Bath

You may not be aware that it's possible to give a bath to someone who is confined to bed. Giving a bed bath isn't difficult; it just requires some ingenuity and preparation. Keep in mind that older skin is thin and at risk for injury, so unless the person is incontinent, a daily complete bed bath isn't necessary.

Make sure that the room in which you're giving the bath is warm enough and not drafty, that there's sufficient privacy to give the bath, and that you provide for safety for both you and your loved one. Before you undress your loved one, you'll want to gather the items needed for the bath:

- A wash basin
- Soap and a soap dish (Bath in a Bag is also available at medical supply stores; this is a single-use-only product containing a number of presoaked washcloths for washing the entire body)
- Two washcloths (the second cloth is for use if you're giving a shampoo)
- Two bath towels (the second towel is for use if you're giving a shampoo)
- A gown, pajamas, or clothing
- Large plastic trash bag

- A sheet or light blanket
- Toilet articles, such as deodorant, shampoo, toothbrush and toothpaste, body lotion, and hairbrush or comb

Place these items on the bedside table. If your loved one is confined to a hospital-type bed, raise the bed to a position that's high enough so you won't strain your back. Undress the person. Keep in mind that you want to protect his or her privacy and prevent the person from catching a chill. Use a sheet or light blanket to cover the areas of the body that you're not going to wash.

Fill the basin nearly full with water. The water temperature should be no higher than 115° F (you can use a bath thermometer to check). Using the washcloth, soap, and basin, gently wash one section of the person's body at a time. Wash from the cleanest to the dirtiest areas. Encourage the person to help as much as he or she can, especially in washing the genitals. Pay careful attention to the folds and creases of older skin, making sure that you thoroughly clean and rinse between the folds (collected soap can dry and crack the skin, leaving it susceptible to infection). Try to change the bath water at least once during a complete bed bath, and try not to let the soap float in the water when you're not using it.

Rinse and dry thoroughly each section of the person's body after you wash it. Pat the skin dry with the bath towel—don't rub! Rub lotion on the body to moisturize and massage the skin. Cover each section of the person's body with a light blanket or sheet after you wash, dry, and moisturize it to keep the person warm.

Shampooing the hair of a bedbound person can be challenging. Place a large plastic trash bag around the person's shoulders to prevent him or her from getting wet. Ask your loved one to place a dry washcloth over his or her eyes to prevent shampoo from getting in them. Wet the person's hair. Place a dollop of shampoo in the palm of your hand and wash the hair. Start at the hairline and work toward the back of the head. Rinse the hair thoroughly. Wrap the person's head in a bath towel to dry. As an alternative, you may be able to arrange for a hair stylist to come to the house to wash and style your loved one's hair.

Avoiding Skin Damage

Tanned skin is not healthy skin—it's a sign that skin damage has occurred. The sun's ultraviolet rays damage skin by breaking down fibers in the skin, which causes the skin to sag, stretch, bruise, and tear easily and to take longer to heal. This is especially true for older people's skin because the normal changes of aging make it more vulnerable to damage. Nothing can completely undo ultra-violet radiation damage, although the skin can repair itself to an extent.

It's never too late to protect skin from damage, even for older adults. They shouldn't sunbathe or go to tanning salons and should stay out of the sun between 10 A.M. and 3 P.M. If they have to be in the sun during those hours, they should wear protective garments—hat, long-sleeved shirt, and sunglasses—and put on sunscreen (SPF15 or higher) before going out in the sun.

Sun damage also is a cause of skin cancer. The chance of de-veloping skin cancer increases as people age, especially for people who live in the "sun belt" (the southern United States and Califor-nia). There are three types of skin cancer:

* Basal cell carcinomas are the most common skin cancers. They rarely spread (metastasize) to other organs—the skin actually is considered an organ—but the person should have these carcinomas removed as soon as they're noticed.
* Squamous cell carcinomas are more harmful than basal cell carcinomas because they can grow quickly and metastasize.
* Malignant melanomas are the most dangerous of the skin cancers be-cause they metastasize and often are fatal. Most at risk from melanoma include people with a high number of moles; with red or blonde hair, blue eyes, fair skin, and freckles; people who tan with difficulty and burn; and people with a family history of the disease. More women than men get melanomas. Although melanomas can affect any part of the body, the most common place for women to get them is on the legs, whereas men get them on the torso, in particular on their backs.

Skin should be checked often for signs of skin cancer—moles or freckles that have changed size, shape, surface quality, or color since the last time you looked at them. Call a health care provider immediately if you notice any changes. Early detection is essential because 99% of skin cancers can be cured if caught early.

Smoking also can cause skin damage, although researchers don't know exactly why. It may be because smoking interferes with normal blood flow in the skin (it constricts the blood vessels).

"Feeding" the Skin

Dry skin is common in older adults and is a byproduct of normal aging. One obvious way to keep skin from drying out is to pay attention to fluid intake because fluids lubricate skin tissues. Another way is to use humidifiers to maintain a relative humidity in the environment of between 40% and 60%. Freestanding humidifiers can be purchased in pharmacies and stores that carry health-related products. When using a freestanding humidifier, make sure that it's emptied and cleaned frequently to avoid mold buildup.

Skin needs to be "fed" certain vitamins and nutrients. Make sure that the recommended daily allowance (RDA) of vitamins A and C is included in your loved one's diet. These vitamins are essential for tissue integrity and healing and can be found in fresh fruits and vegetables. If his or her diet is lacking in these vitamins, you may need to offer nutritional supplements (vitamin pills) that contain these vitamins.

Assessing the Skin

Even when you observe proper sun care and nutrient intake, complications can still arise. To become aware of any changes in the condition of the skin, it's important for you to be actively involved in or alert the older, dependent adult in your life about assessing his or her skin. Checking the skin after showering or bathing helps avoid seri-

Caregiver Tip

When providing skin care, examine cuts and/or moles for changes in color, shape, size, and texture. Make a note of any new findings and share them with a health care provider. These changes could be warning signs of unhealthy skin conditions.

ous (or not-so-serious conditions, such as dry skin) skin conditions and enable you to identify changes and treat them at an early stage.

FOOT CARE

It's said that if your feet hurt, your whole body hurts. Sadly, proper foot care is neglected by most people. It's something that, if someone other than the older adult has to do it, is avoided as much as possible. Good foot care can help increase the person's ability to get around (ambulate), and it can be pleasurable.

Good foot care includes the following:

- Assessment and inspection
- Skin care
- Toenail care
- Consideration of appropriate footwear
- Corn, callus, and bunion care
- Prevention and care of athlete's foot
- Prevention and care of foot injuries
- Special considerations for diabetics

Let's take a look at each of these items.

Caregiver Tip

Don't prick open and drain blisters with any sharp instrument.

Don't pick at hangnails.

Immediately report any pain, discoloration, numbness, tingling, or presence of deep sores or ulcerated skin to your health care provider.

Stop smoking.

Assessment and Inspection

Assessing the possibility of a foot problem or an actual problem and initiating strategies to alleviate or lessen the problem requires that you gather information. The tools you use for assessment are physical inspection and observation. Use the list of questions on page 184 to compile the information that'll be the most helpful in determining the nature of the problem.

Assessment Questions

Feet and Legs

Is the skin clean, dry, or scaly? (Look for cracks between the toes, sores, cuts, bruises, and/or blisters, especially in diabetics.)

Is any swelling visible? (If so, note the time of day that swelling occurs. Swelling may result from too-tight shoes, immobility, or an adverse health condition.)

What color is the skin on the feet—red, blue, white, or pink—and has the color changed since the last time you observed it? (Changes in color may be an indication of infection or circulatory problems.)

Are there any cracks or discolored patches of skin between the toes? (Fungus tends to settle and grow between the toes.)

Are the toenails thick or ingrown?

Are calluses and corns visible? (The presence of corns or calluses suggests that the person's shoes may be too tight. Make sure to check the soles for both.)

Are areas of red or purple discoloration visible on the calves? (This suggests pooling of blood in the lower extremities because of poor circulation. This discoloration can travel up the leg.)

Is the temperature of the lower legs or feet warmer or cooler than expected? (Use the upper part of your hand to check the temperature, comparing both feet and both legs. Because blood flow makes our bodies warm, a feeling of coolness in the feet and/or legs suggests decreased circulation. Increased heat suggests possible infection or inflammation.)

Is hair growth on the legs normal? (Hair needs good blood circulation to grow. The absence of hair suggests decreased blood circulation.)

Foot Coverings

How appropriate are the shoes the older person is wearing? Is the toe box too narrow? Are the heels low enough to provide support for balance? (Heels that are 1 inch and lower usually are best. Pointed toes tend to pinch the foot and adversely modify the angle of the foot.)

Are the soles of the shoes made of a shock-absorbing material? (Hard soles don't cushion the foot when the shoe makes contact with the floor and therefore cause more pain when walking. The addition of innersole cushions can sometimes help. Also, shoes can be purchased with built-in cushioning.)

Is there good arch support?

What is the condition of the shoes? (Heels that are worn down can increase the risk of falls. Shoes with worn laces do not provide the tight support that is needed. Laces that are too long also increase the risk of falls.)

Do the shoes fit properly? (People's feet tend to get wider as they age.)

What is the condition of the socks or stockings?

Do the socks or stockings fit properly?

Is your loved one able to put on and remove his or her socks and shoes?

Skin Care

After assessing the problem or potential problem, wash the feet following these steps:

- Use lukewarm to warm water (wash feet daily if the person sweats a lot).
- Use a mild soap; make sure to rinse well.
- Soak the feet in warm water after washing. This softens the toenails and makes them easier to trim. Soaking also provides a soothing, pleasant atmosphere for relaxation.
- Dry the feet with a soft towel. Pat the skin of the feet gently, and be sure to dry the skin between the toes. Because it tends to be a damp area, the skin between the toes is ripe for fungal infection.
- Rub a thin coat of skin lotion over the tops and bottoms of the feet, but don't apply the lotion between the toes. This gives you an opportunity to massage your loved one's feet and toes, which most people enjoy. Gently applying foot powder after drying the feet and applying lotion may help increase comfort, especially in warm climates and if the older adult in your life has a problem with sweaty feet. Make sure that the lotion has been applied sparingly and thoroughly massaged into the skin so that the powder doesn't cake.

This tender loving care of the feet can benefit all areas of the body.

Toenail Care

Proper care of the toenails is more important than you might realize. Nails that grow improperly can cause problems, and how the nails are trimmed can affect how they grow. Follow these simple steps:

- Use nail clippers and trim the nails straight across. Don't cut nails shorter than the edge of the toe.
- Gently file sharp nail edges and corners with an emery board. Never cut nail corners to round out the nail's shape. Don't allow your loved one to cut his or her own toenails if the older adult has impaired vision or Parkinson's disease (causes hands to shake uncontrollably), or he or she can't see and/or reach the toes. Make an appointment with a podiatrist (podiatric care is covered by Medicare).
- Don't cut or treat cracked, split, and/or thick nails. Make an appointment with a podiatrist.

Consideration of Appropriate Footwear

Shoes should fit well and be comfortable when you buy them; you'll probably give up wearing the shoes before you can break them in. Some important things to consider when purchasing shoes include the following:

- Try on shoes at the end of the day, when feet are at their largest.
- Shoes should be a ¹/₂-inch longer than the longest toe and wide enough to avoid squeezing the toes.
- Leather or canvas footwear with firm soles and soft uppers give the most support and are the most comfortable to wear.
- Purchase shoes with low heels.
- Purchase shoes that cover the foot completely. Sandals and pointed-toe shoes increase the risk of injury to the feet.
- Purchase shoes with Velcro closures if your loved one has decreased dexterity with his or her fingers and hands.

New shoes shouldn't be worn all day the first time they're worn, and they should always "rest" 12–24 hours before wearing them again.

Before putting on shoes, check inside them for stones or a torn lining that could rub or bruise the feet (this is especially important for diabetics). Your loved one should wear clean, white socks (this avoids any dye sensitivity) and change them daily. Cotton or wool socks are best because these fabrics absorb sweat and breathe better than nylon or polyester. Avoid buying socks that are too tight because they restrict blood flow. Women who want to wear stockings should wear pantyhose or a garter belt—no knee-high hose or constrictive devices such as rubber garters or tying knots in the hosiery.

Your loved one should never walk barefoot either indoors or outdoors. Feet that are unprotected are more prone to injury.

Care of Corns, Calluses, and Bunions

Clearly, buying properly fitting shoes can reduce the occurrence of corns, calluses, and/or bunions. It seems simple, but too often fashion rather than comfort dictates what kind of shoes are bought. Keep in mind that it's the feet that support the whole body, so it's not surprising that when your feet hurt, your whole body hurts.

When caring for corns and calluses, remember:

- After washing the feet, gently dry them with a soft towel, being sure not to tear or peel off any skin on or around the corn or callus.
- Don't use over-the-counter or home remedies to remove the corn or callus. However, you can rub a pumice stone gently over a corn or callus in the early stages to remove it.
- Never cut a corn or callus with a razor blade, scissors, or knife.
- Visit a podiatrist if the condition continues despite providing regular foot care and wearing proper footwear.

To treat a bunion, modify the shoes to eliminate stress on the affected area. It may be necessary to purchase orthopedic shoes, wear arch supports, or have an orthotic device prescribed by an orthopedist specializing in foot problems or by a podiatrist. When a bunion can't be corrected by nonsurgical (noninvasive) methods or if the person wants the problem to be resolved quickly, surgery is performed to realign the toes. Before opting for surgery, your loved one should be aware that there'll be a lengthy recovery period.

caregiver Tip

A hand-held mirror can be used not only for checking between the toes and the soles of the feet but also can help you check other areas of the body, especially if you or the older adult in your life has difficulty moving joints because of arthritis, for example.

Prevention and Care of Athlete's Foot

Athlete's foot is a common fungal infection. This condition tends to occur in moist areas, such as between the toes or on the soles of the feet. Some simple things to remember when caring for the feet will help the older person prevent athlete's foot:

- Keeping feet clean and dry
- Applying absorbent powder that is specially formulated for feet

- Changing socks or stockings if they're moist

If you notice redness, tiny blisters, itching, or scaling between the toes or on the soles, contact a health care provider. Prescription medication(s) may be necessary. Be cautious about or even avoid use of over-the-counter medications, especially if your loved one is diabetic or has circulation problems. Self-treatment of this condition could result in further, perhaps more serious, problems.

> **First Aid for Injured Feet**
>
> Wash the injured area with soap and water and rinse well. Don't use harsh solutions such as iodine, boric acid, or Epsom salts.
>
> Cover the injured area with sterile gauze and paper tape. Paper tape is less irritating to the skin. Don't make the bandage too tight.
>
> Watch for signs of infection, such as redness, swelling, warm or hot sensation, or pus.

Prevention and Care of Foot Injuries

As noted earlier, proper foot care and footwear can help prevent injury to the feet. If you notice any signs of infection or if, after 24 hours, you haven't seen any sign of healing, call a health care professional immediately. It's better to err on the side of caution, especially in the case of a person with diabetes, who requires more vigilant care and consideration.

Special Considerations for Diabetics

People with diabetes must be especially careful about their feet because of the impact that diabetes has on blood circulation and nerve function. In diabetes, there is decreased blood flow to the legs and feet, resulting in longer healing times for wounds. Wound debris isn't cleaned up adequately by the white blood cells, so an environment is created for infection to take hold.

Alert!

Impaired blood circulation is a common symptom in people with diabetes. The following list of do's and don'ts will lessen the negative impact of this condition:

Don't allow your loved one to wear stockings with elastic tops or round garters to hold up stockings. These items tend to decrease normal circulation in the legs and feet, which often is already affected in a person with diabetes.

Encourage loved ones who still want to wear stockings to wear pantyhose instead.

Encourage your loved one to sit and prop up his or her feet several times a day to improve blood circulation.

Don't allow your loved one to cross his or her legs at the knees when sitting. This action tends to decrease blood circulation to the legs and feet.

Don't promote standing in one place without moving. Movement increases blood flow, whereas lack of it tends to decrease blood recirculation to the heart. This slows the circulation of blood throughout the body.

For nerve cells to fire properly, they need good blood circulation, and both are compromised in diabetics. The nerves can't signal the brain that an object's temperature is too hot or too cold, and the diabetic person could be burned. This condition is called diabetic neuropathy. (Diabetics should take care when using heating pads, hot water bottles, or uncovered ice packs. Unsupervised use of these aids is not recommended.)

The care of the feet of people with diabetes is the same as that of nondiabetics (see earlier material about skin and toenail care). The best thing that people with diabetes can do to take care of their feet is to make healthful lifestyle choices to keep their blood sugar as close to normal as possible. These choices include the following:

- Know how and when to test blood sugar.
- Take medications as prescribed by a health care provider.
- Eat regular meals that contain a variety of healthy, low-fat, high-fiber foods.
- Increase the amount of physical activity.
- Follow the prescribed foot care plan.
- Keep doctor's appointments, and have feet, eyes, and kidneys checked at least once a year.

Diabetics who need special shoes or shoe inserts should be aware that these assistive devices are covered by Medicare Part B (see Chapter 16 for more information on Medicare). This insurance covers one pair of depth shoes (shoes that look like athletic shoes but have more room in them for inserts or different-shaped feet) and three pairs of inserts or one pair of custom-molded shoes (including inserts) and two additional pairs of inserts. (Note: This information is subject to change; check with a health care provider or social worker for the latest guidelines.)

WOUND CARE

Wound injuries can be superficial (a scrape) or deep (lower layers of tissue and bone are exposed). They can occur anywhere on the body, but in older people, they're most prevalent in bony areas. These wounds are known as pressure sores.

Wound care depends on many factors such as the location of the wound, how it occurred, its condition, and the specific instructions for care given by a health care provider. Superficial wounds, if observed and treated early and pressure on the area is relieved, have the best chance of healing. When the wound goes unnoticed and the pressure on it isn't relieved, it becomes deeper and more difficult to heal. It can become a pressure sore.

Wounds heal best when pressure on the wound and bony areas is relieved. Specialty beds and air mattresses can relieve pressure on certain parts of the body and are especially helpful for people who are bedbound. Even if the bedbound person lies on a specialty bed or air mattress, he or she still needs to turn or be turned at frequent intervals. Skin breakdown can occur with as little as 2 hours of unrelieved pressure on a wound.

Wound care must be done at regular intervals, especially before each dressing or bandage change. Proper wound care means that you must assess the condition of the wound and clean it. Assessment dictates treatment. Follow these steps to assess a wound:

1. **Assess the size of the wound.** You can compare the size of the wound to a familiar object, such as a dime or a quarter. If you feel comfortable doing so, you can measure its length and width with a measuring tape (use this measuring tape only for this purpose). A wound that's healing gets progressively smaller, so accurate measuring helps you determine the wound's status.

2. **Assess the color of the wound.** Is the wound pink, red, yellow, green, or gray? Pink tissue is healthy tissue. Red suggests inflammation. Yellow, green, or gray tissue suggests the possibility of infection that should be brought to the attention of your loved one's health care provider.

3. **Assess the odor of the wound.** Healthy tissue doesn't have an odor. Any bad odor, especially if the color of the tissue suggests the presence of an infection, tells you to contact your loved one's health care provider immediately.

4. **Assess the discharge from the wound.** Clear, watery discharge is a normal occurrence in the wound-healing process. A sticky, yellowish, or greenish discharge accompanied by an odor likely means infection. Call your loved one's health care provider immediately.

Once you've assessed the condition of the wound, and you're able to move on to cleansing it, do so. Follow these steps:

1. **Wash your hands thoroughly.** It's essential that you wash your hands thoroughly before you care for any open wound or

body cavity. The last thing you want to do is introduce bacteria and infection to a healing wound. Equally important is that you wash your hands after you clean the wound. This protects both you and the older adult in your life. Refer to the handwashing procedure in Chapter 9. You may want to wear disposable gloves when removing the bandage and cleansing the wound.

2.   **Carefully remove and dispose of the old bandage.** If tape was used to anchor the bandage to the skin, be gentle in removing the tape to avoid hurting the skin underneath. Start at the corners, and while applying pressure to support the tissue surrounding the areas adjacent to where you are removing the tape, pull off the tape using a firm, smooth motion.

3.   **Use a detergent-free soap to clean the wound.** A good rule of thumb is to avoid cleaning a wound with any solution that's not suitable to put in the eye. Medical supply stores carry gentle-acting or saline cleaners that only minimally disrupt the surface of the wound. Avoid using soaps that contain alcohol or perfumes. Putting the soap in a pump dispenser prevents cross-contamination.

4.   **Use a shower spray or WaterPik® to rinse and thoroughly cleanse the wound.** Use a shower spray (warm water on a gentle setting) directly on the wound to force out all of the debris from the wound, which helps in the healing process. If the older adult in your life is bedbound, make sure that you place a waterproof pad (or a large plastic trash bag that's been opened up) under the area to be cleaned. This will help keep the bedlinens dry. If the person's health care provider has given specific instructions for the cleansing of the wound, you need to follow them. Also, depending on the care provider's specific instructions, you may have to apply medication to the wound. Wear disposable gloves if that makes you feel more comfortable.

5.   **Leave the wound open to the air for a period of time before you apply a fresh bandage.** (The amount of time depends on the health care provider's instructions.) Ventilating the wound helps in healing, but make sure that your loved one doesn't get chilly, especially if the wound is on the buttocks.

11   Managing Incontinence

Incontinence is the loss of physical control over the bladder and bowels. It's one of the most awkward and humiliating symptoms of illness or aging. Because of the many social and emotional consequences of incontinence, some older people rearrange their whole lives around this condition. They want to be near a bathroom at all times, they reduce their involvement in activities away from home, and they limit their intake of fluids and risk dehydration. They also may have to submit to being helped to perform these normally private functions, which can be embarrassing for them. Managing incontinence can be very frustrating for caregivers as well, who may feel uncomfortable about handling another person's urine and feces and may feel embarrassed for their loved one. Assistance with incontinence can be managed in supportive and respectful ways, however. First, you need to identify and understand the cause of the problem. Then you must take steps to reverse or manage it. Because urinary incontinence is the most common form of incontinence, we're going to concentrate on it in this chapter.

Chapter 6 describes how kidney and bladder function change as we age. For example, how much urine the bladder can hold decreases by about 50% as a person ages, and the muscle tone and elasticity of the parts that make up the urinary system—the ureters, bladder, and urethra—weaken and make it more difficult for older people to hold their urine. Older people also may experience skeletal changes and arthritis that impair their ability to get to the bathroom in time. Inconveniently located bathrooms also can compromise their ability to keep total control over their bowels and bladder. In addition, certain medications can make older people incontinent. For example, diuretics, which are usually prescribed for the treatment of high blood pressure, can increase the sensation of an urgency to go and the frequency of urination.

You may experience shame, frustration, and/or mental and physical exhaustion from being so intimately involved with your loved one's toileting. Don't keep your feelings or questions bottled up inside you. Talk to someone about what you're feeling. Get a health care professional to answer your questions.

Among older adults still living in the community (in other words, those who don't live in long-term care facilities), about 10%–15% of men and 20%–35% of women have incontinent episodes. Continuous or daily incontinence occurs in about 5% of community-dwelling older people. Incontinence is a key factor in many families' decision to place their loved ones in nursing facilities. (See the Resources list at the back of the book for a list of improving-continence programs that can help you avoid having to make this decision.) Although urinary incontinence is common in older people, fewer than 50% of incontinent people report the problem to their health care provider. Many older adults believe that incontinence is part of getting old, that nothing can be done about it, or that only surgery can cure it and they'd rather not have surgery. Health care providers may ask about incontinence while taking a general health history, but some don't.

One of the first distinctions that needs to be made before incontinence is treated is whether it's chronic (may occur frequently and is long term) or acute (develops slowly and is short term).

CHRONIC INCONTINENCE

The four most common types of chronic urinary incontinence in older adults are:

1.   Urge incontinence
2.   Overflow incontinence
3.   Stress incontinence
4.   Functional incontinence

There also are two less common types, iatrogenic and mixed incontinence, which we'll discuss later.

Urge Incontinence and Its Treatment

Urge incontinence is the most common type of incontinence for both men and women. It's a sudden need to urinate, which the person can't hold off until a bathroom is reached. This involuntary loss of moderate to large quantities of urine takes place every few hours both day and night. It happens because the signals that are sent from the bladder to the brain bypass the region of the brain that stops the bladder from contracting and releasing urine.

Several things can cause urge incontinence: irritation of the area around the urethra (for instance, in women with urethritis or atrophic vaginitis, which is degeneration of the mucous membrane that occurs after menopause), urinary tract and bladder infections, ingestion of certain beverages (for example, alcoholic beverages and coffee, tea, and colas because of their caffeine content), Parkinson's disease, stroke (cerebral hemorrhage), and dementia.

People with urge incontinence can learn to train the bladder by progressively increasing the length of time between each trip to the bathroom. Start with half-hour intervals, and aim for staying dry for 3 hours at a time. Once they're able to do this, they should train themselves to postpone going to the bathroom despite feeling that they have to go. They should be in control of this intervention if they're capable. If not, you can be in charge of scheduling bathroom visits by using points on the clock, and prompting the person to urinate.

Another way to reduce urge incontinence is to do Kegel exercises. The object of this intervention is to interrupt and inhibit the involuntary contraction of the bladder when it's ready to empty. Kegel exercises help improve the strength and coordination of the muscles surrounding the urethra. Figure 1 identifies the muscles that are involved in controlling involuntary urination. If you and the older adult in your life are comfortable doing so, use this fig-

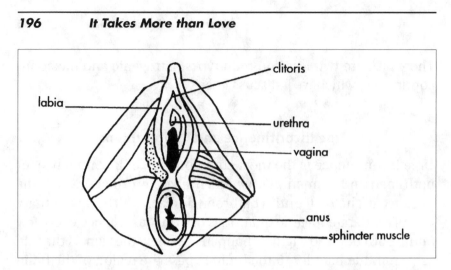

FIGURE 1.   The perineal muscles that are involved in controlling involuntary urination in women. (Adapted from Anderson, K.N., Anderson, L.E., & Glanze, W.D. [Eds.]. [1994]. Mosby's Medical, Nursing, & Allied Health Dictionary [4th ed., p. A-34]. Mosby–Year Book: St. Louis.)

ure and the following instructions to help the person find these muscles in the body:

1. Sit on the toilet (seat down) or a chair with knees apart and feet flat on floor (note that this can be done in an upright position, but it might be more difficult for a frail older adult). Tighten (contract) the anus as though holding back a bowel movement. Try not to tense the leg muscles, buttocks, or abdominal muscles while contracting the anus. This action locates the back of the pelvic floor muscles.

2. If the person is sitting on the toilet and ready to urinate, ask the person to go for a few seconds, stop the flow of urine for a few seconds by contracting the muscles surrounding the urethra, and restart the flow. This action locates the front of the pelvic floor muscles.

Kegel exercises involve using both the front and back pelvic floor muscles. The exercises can be done anytime, when sitting, standing, or lying down. The exercises are described in detail below.

1. Slowly contract the pelvic muscles, from the front to the back, and hold for a count of 4. Breathe normally during the contraction.

2. Release and relax the muscles for a count of 4. Breathe normally while the muscles are released and relaxed.

3. Repeat Steps 1 and 2 (one exercise) for 15 "reps" (repetitions) at least 3–10 times a day. Remember to breathe normally while doing the exercise.
4. Gradually increase the duration of each exercise up to a count of 10 reps for each contraction and 10 for each release/relaxation.

When trying to encourage your loved one to try Kegel exercises, be aware that any improvement in being able to control the muscles is very gradual, and the full effect may not be noticed for 3–6 months. In addition, after the highest level of control that's possible for the person is achieved, maintenance exercises have to be kept up on a daily basis.

A third intervention is to reduce the number of caffeinated beverages the older person drinks. Caffeinated beverages can irritate the bladder and increase the urge to urinate. In addition, many caffeinated beverages have a diuretic effect, increasing the frequency of urination.

The general treatment for urge incontinence caused by atrophic vaginitis or urethritis is replacement estrogen taken orally. Estrogen can help alleviate the vaginal dryness and irritation that occurs after menopause. Sometimes health care professionals will prescribe estrogen creams that are inserted in the vagina, but many older adults with atrophic vaginitis or urethritis prefer taking the oral medication.

Overflow Incontinence and Its Treatment

Overflow incontinence is the most frequently occurring form of chronic urinary incontinence in men; enlargement of the prostate gland is the most common cause of overflow incontinence. A larger-than-normal prostate along with the (age-related) reduced force of contractions of the bladder cause the bladder to not empty completely when urinating. As a result, a man doesn't feel the urge to urinate even when his bladder is full. He may say that he feels a hesitation when urinating along with feeling that he hasn't emptied his bladder. He feels wet or feels a dribbling sensation. A great amount of urine is lost, and loss occurs day and night.

Other causes of overflow incontinence and their treatment include the following:

1. *Mechanical obstruction.* An enlarged prostate gland is the most common mechanical obstruction; fecal impaction and uterine prolapse are other examples.
2. *Atonic bladder.* Atonic bladder is decreased muscle tone in the muscles of the bladder. This decreased muscle tone is caused by a disease of the sensory nerves (the nerves in the body that cause you to feel). This disease prevents the motor nerves (the nerves in the body that cause you to move in response to what you feel) from receiving the signal to urinate, which causes a greater-than-normal amount of urine to be left in the bladder after urinating (residual urine).
3. *Functional obstruction.* Functional obstruction occurs when the normal pattern of contractions of the bladder muscles and the bladder outlet (the internal and external sphincter muscles) break down. Normally, the bladder contracts first and then the sphincter muscles relax enough to allow urine to pass through the urethra. When the normal pattern isn't synchronized, the bladder and sphincter muscles relax at the same time so that the urine collects and isn't pushed out.
4. *Medications.* Many drugs can contribute to or cause overflow incontinence: muscle relaxants, antipsychotics, antidepressants, and anticholinergics. They work, in part, by relaxing the muscles, which includes the bladder muscle, thus preventing complete bladder emptying.

The primary methods for dealing with overflow incontinence are to diminish the retention of urine in the bladder and ensure complete emptying of the bladder each time a person urinates. These goals can be accomplished by the following:

• Structure a regular schedule of urinating every 2–3 hours to reduce the number or frequency of incontinence episodes.
• Teach the older person to press down on the area directly over the bladder when he or she thinks that he or she is finished urinating to push out any residual urine in the bladder.

The treatments for mechanical obstructions vary. Sometimes a medication like prazosin helps to relax the muscles that surround the urethra and the prostate gland. The obstruction is relieved enough to let urine flow more freely. Prazosin has side effects, however—fainting with a sudden loss of consciousness (especially with postural hypotension), a racing heartbeat, and dizziness. Surgery may be needed if medication isn't effective or if the gland is too enlarged. Fecal impaction, another example of a mechanical obstruction, usually is the result of an inappropriate diet, decreased fluid intake, inactivity, or all three. When a rectal examination confirms that there is fecal impaction, the obstruction must be removed, and then a bowel regimen should be created so that it doesn't happen again. The uterus falling down into the opening of the vagina (*uterine prolapse*) is another example of mechanical obstruction (for more detail, see "Stress Incontinence and Its Treatment"). Uterine prolapse can be treated with surgery or with the insertion of a pessary, which is a device that's worn inside the uterus to support it after the uterus is surgically moved back into its proper place. (*Note:* Often, a pessary is tried first in an attempt to avoid surgery.) The device's success depends on the tone of the uterine tissues. Women who have had many children tend to have diminished tissue tone and don't seem to benefit from using a pessary.

How to Avoid Fecal Impaction

Make sure that the older adult in your life:

1. Eats a daily diet that includes high-fiber foods such as fresh, uncooked fruits and vegetables, bran, or other cereal products made from whole grains

2. Drinks 8–10 glasses of water every day

3. Exercises regularly, if he or she is able

4. Avoids enemas and laxatives (note that daily bowel movements aren't the norm for everyone)

5. Takes a stool softener or bulk-forming agent (such as Metamucil) if needed (note that fluid intake must be adequate when taking these medications)

6. Responds immediately to the urge to defecate and doesn't delay or ignore the sensation

Stress Incontinence and Its Treatment

Individuals with stress incontinence involuntarily lose small amounts of urine. Most often, this loss is caused by diminished strength in the muscles that support the bladder and the urethra combined with increased pressure in the abdomen, which is caused when a person bends, coughs, lifts, laughs, or climbs stairs. Stress incontinence occurs commonly in women who have had multiple pregnancies (the weight gained during each pregnancy weakens the muscles that support

How to Care for People with Stress Incontinence

Make sure the person urinates as soon as he or she feels the urge.

Ask the person to do Kegel exercises when he or she feels the urge to urinate to reduce the chances of an accident.

Use incontinence pads or briefs during waking hours until the person achieves continence. Incontinence pads and briefs help keep urine away from the skin, thus avoiding skin irritation and breakdown.

Explain (demonstrate if necessary) proper cleansing after urinating (wiping from front to back). Proper hygiene decreases the risk of urinary tract infections.

the bladder and the urethra). This loss of urine usually occurs during the daytime hours, when a person is doing activities that can increase pressure in the abdomen. Obesity or substantial weight gain also increases abdominal pressure. In addition, estrogen deficiency after menopause thins the lining of the urethra, which in turn causes the muscles that support the urethra to weaken. This leads to episodes of stress incontinence.

Apart from avoiding obesity by maintaining a healthy weight or losing any excess weight, surgery to repair the weakened muscles can be an appropriate intervention for older adults with stress incontinence. Reconstructive surgery involves elevating or suspending the urethra, which provides support during activities that create stress or strain. The main benefit of surgery is that people are at less risk for urinary tract infections and skin breakdown.

Functional Incontinence and Its Treatment

Functional incontinence can be caused by a variety of factors and can be physically or psychologically based or a combination of both. Arthritis, muscle weakness, and sensory deficits (for example, impaired vision) may make it difficult to unzip, unbutton, or pull down clothing in time (or at all) or to sit down easily on a regular toilet seat. It can be very frustrating to finally make it to the toilet but be unable to avoid having an accident because your pants are hard to unzip! If the older adult in your life has difficulty manipulating zippers or buttons, clothing can be retrofitted with easy-open closures, such as Velcro or elastic waistbands, or purchased new. People who have difficulty getting out of bed and then getting to the bathroom in time can use a motorized bed that moves from a flat position to a sitting position. People who find it hard to rise from a chair unaided can use an automatic chair that is designed to help them get into an upright position. (A medical supply store can help you locate motorized beds and chairs.)

Sensory deficits or taking sedatives can make a person less aware of the need to urinate; the mind doesn't sense the urge to urinate, so the person doesn't make it to the bathroom in time. A sensory deficit such as that caused by impaired vision can make it extremely difficult for a person to avoid functional incontinence. Make sure that there is adequate, nonglare lighting in and near the toilet area. Placing night-lights along the pathway between the person's bedroom and bathroom enhances visibility. Because of the changes in vision caused by aging, it's helpful to use contrasting colors for the toilet seat and the tile or flooring (for example, a white toilet seat and blue floor tile). This helps people to quickly and clearly figure out where the toilet is.

Another important physical factor may be the environment itself. For example, the bathroom doorway may be too narrow for a walker or wheelchair to fit through, a problem that's found particularly in older homes; hallway and bathroom lighting may be inadequate, especially for people with vision problems; or the setting and placement of the toilet may be unfamiliar, making it difficult for people to reach the toilet in time. Retrofitting the bathroom can improve timeliness and safety. One assistive device is a toilet safety frame (see Figure 2) or appropriately placed grab bars (Figure 3). The frame or bars can help older men in maintaining their balance while standing at the toilet. Elevated toilet seats or an over-the-toilet chair helps older, frail people sit down more easily. (More information on bathroom safety and other safety issues is included in Chapters 10 and 13.)

FIGURE 2. *Toilet safety frame. (From Tideiksaar, R. [1998]. Falls in Older Persons: Prevention & Management [2nd ed., p. 121]. Baltimore: Health Professions Press; reprinted by permission.)*

If you can't modify the bathroom, you can consider other, less costly alternatives. If the doorway to the toilet can't accommodate a walker or a wheelchair, consider using a bedside commode. It can be used in a way that is not embarrassing or offputting to the older adult in your life. Placing a screen or modified curtain around the bedside commode can conceal it from view and provide privacy for your loved one.

The most frequently noted psychological factor in functional incontinence is clinical depression. Many older people who are depressed become neglectful of self-care and are passive about the need to toilet. If the cause of the person's functional incontinence is depression, then you need to become actively involved in his or her self-care. Prompted urination is one way to help your loved one get on a regular toileting schedule. Take the person to the bathroom every 2–4 hours whether or not he or she feels the need to urinate. Also, provide physical assistance, encouragement, and positive reinforcement for appropriate urinating and periods of dryness.

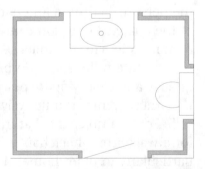

FIGURE 3. *Bathroom grab bars around perimeter. (From Tideiksaar, R. [1998]. Falls in Older Persons: Prevention & Management [2nd ed., p. 120]. Baltimore: Health Professions Press; reprinted by permission.)*

Iatrogenic Incontinence and Its Treatment

Iatrogenic incontinence is incontinence that's inadvertently caused by a health care professional or a treatment or diagnostic procedure. The side effects of some medications (for example, diuretics, antidepressants, sedatives, hypertensives) have been associated with iatrogenic incontinence. Your loved one's physician or health care provider will either decrease the dose to one that maintains the primary effect of the medication but eliminates the secondary effect of incontinence or change the medication to one that doesn't cause urinary incontinence.

Iatrogenic incontinence also can result from disease conditions such as congestive heart failure. People with congestive heart failure experience an overload of fluid in the body, so they might experience increased urination at night (*nocturia*). Many other diseases can cause iatrogenic incontinence. An open, frank discussion with your health care provider about what's going on can give you and your loved one insight into the problem.

Mixed Incontinence and Its Treatment

In some cases, incontinence is caused by a number of factors. For example, a combination of stress and urge incontinence can occur when multiple factors, including the body's structure and physiology, disease processes, or factors such as mobility, dexterity, motivation, and environment combine. To treat mixed incontinence, use the strategies and suggestions that we gave for both stress and urge incontinence. Some health care professionals include medication in their treatment plans.

Assessing Chronic Urinary Incontinence

For all types of urinary incontinence, there are specific areas of assessment that you can be—and need to be—involved in:

1. History of incontinence
2. General health history
3. Functional assessment
4. Environmental assessment

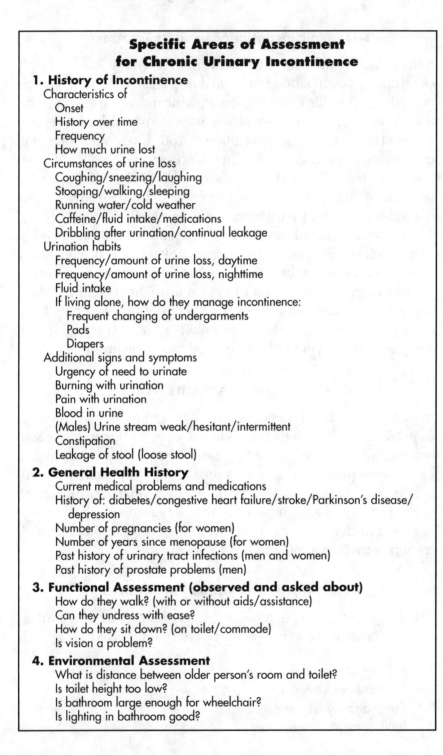

Specific Areas of Assessment
for Chronic Urinary Incontinence

1. History of Incontinence
Characteristics of
  Onset
  History over time
  Frequency
  How much urine lost
Circumstances of urine loss
  Coughing/sneezing/laughing
  Stooping/walking/sleeping
  Running water/cold weather
  Caffeine/fluid intake/medications
  Dribbling after urination/continual leakage
Urination habits
  Frequency/amount of urine loss, daytime
  Frequency/amount of urine loss, nighttime
  Fluid intake
  If living alone, how do they manage incontinence:
    Frequent changing of undergarments
    Pads
    Diapers
Additional signs and symptoms
  Urgency of need to urinate
  Burning with urination
  Pain with urination
  Blood in urine
  (Males) Urine stream weak/hesitant/intermittent
  Constipation
  Leakage of stool (loose stool)

2. General Health History
Current medical problems and medications
History of: diabetes/congestive heart failure/stroke/Parkinson's disease/
  depression
Number of pregnancies (for women)
Number of years since menopause (for women)
Past history of urinary tract infections (men and women)
Past history of prostate problems (men)

3. Functional Assessment (observed and asked about)
How do they walk? (with or without aids/assistance)
Can they undress with ease?
How do they sit down? (on toilet/commode)
Is vision a problem?

4. Environmental Assessment
What is distance between older person's room and toilet?
Is toilet height too low?
Is bathroom large enough for wheelchair?
Is lighting in bathroom good?

Sometimes the older person can supply his or her health care provider with the facts that are needed to make a proper assessment. If this isn't possible, you'll have to answer the questions. You'll have to observe what actually happens in order to gather all the information needed for your health care professional to make an accurate diagnosis of the type of urinary incontinence. The proper diagnosis tells the physician what treatment to use. The information that's required for each assessment area is listed on page 204.

Older people with urinary incontinence should have a thorough physical examination, which should include

1. Observing how they walk and keep their balance, noting any tremors
2. Examining the abdomen for distended bladder
3. Checking the rectum for evidence of impacted fecal matter
4. Doing a pelvic examination to check for prolapsed organs and for vaginal dryness; men should be examined for the size and shape of their prostate gland
5. Appropriate laboratory tests as determined by a health care professional

In addition to taking an extensive health history, various assessments, and physical examination, an important and beneficial data-gathering tool is a bladder diary (Figure 4). A bladder diary brings together in one place information about the frequency of urination and incontinent episodes, the approximate amount of urine lost in the accidents, and the circumstance(s) that triggered the involuntary loss of urine. Two weeks' worth of entries must be made in the bladder diary for a health care professional to accurately assess the type and frequency of urinary incontinence.

ACUTE INCONTINENCE

Acute urinary incontinence, which is present for a short period of time, often is reversible and usually is related to factors that are associated with an acute illness. (Don't make the mistake of accepting what's happening as part of the process of normal aging—incontinence isn't normal!) An acute illness can affect the entire body (sys-

BLADDER DIARY

(Complete diary 2 weeks before your next doctor's appt)

Name: _____

Date	Time of day	Type/amt of fluid intake	Type/amt of food eaten	Amt voided (oz.)	Amt leakage (sm, med, lg)	Activity engaged in when leakage occurred	Urge present?

FIGURE 4. A sample bladder diary.

Signs of a Urinary Tract Infection
Cloudy urine
Blood in the urine
Elevated temperature (remember that older adults usually have a lower baseline temperature)
Altered mental status (particularly confusion in someone who has never experienced it)

temic), be confined to the urinary tract itself, or occur after treatment (for example, when a person is immobilized for a period of time following hip surgery).

Medications that are commonly prescribed for older adults can cause acute urinary incontinence. Antidepressants, antipsychotics, and narcotic analgesics (for example, codeine) may inhibit or diminish bladder contractions, resulting in inadequate emptying of the bladder and overflow incontinence. Certain medications for the treatment of heart disease, such as calcium channel–blocker agents, also cause urinary retention and lead to overflow incontinence.

Older people who fear the social and emotional consequences of incontinence may limit their intake of fluids and risk dehydration. If they do become dehydrated, they're at increased risk for urinary tract infections (see also the next section on catheters). These infections can result in involuntary urinary loss.

Acute fecal impaction can change urination by either blocking urine flow or placing pressure on the bladder, initiating bladder spasms.

Acute urinary incontinence usually disappears once the acute illness heals, the medication is changed or discontinued, the fecal impaction is removed and proper diet and toilet routines are established, and the person's mobility is restored.

CATHETERS

If lifestyle and environmental interventions aren't successful or your loved one's physical condition warrants it, he or she may need to use an internal (indwelling) or external device for urine collection called a catheter. A catheter consists of a hollow, flexible tube

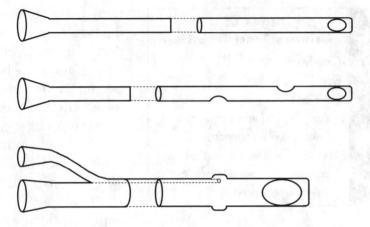

FIGURE 5. Types of catheters. From top to bottom: single-holed straight, multiple-holed straight, and Foley.

that's inserted into the bladder through the urethra and attached to a collection bag (Figure 5). The most commonly used catheter (especially for women) is the indwelling catheter. Some incontinent men use an external urine collecting system, known as a condom catheter. Constant use of condom catheters, however, isn't safe for older men because the skin under the catheter is prone to developing irritation, swelling, and fungal skin infections.

The four most important concerns for a frail older adult who uses a catheter are fluid intake, acidity of his or her urine, the possibility of urinary tract infection, and cleanliness.

Fluid Intake

Always encourage and provide a generous amount of fluids, if not advised to do otherwise by a health care professional, of 2,500–3,000 ml daily (8–10 glasses, 8 ounces each). This amount of fluid keeps urine dilute and free flowing, which prevents obstructed flow and infection. In short, there is freedom of movement of the urine from the kidneys to the bladder and into the collection bag.

Acidity of Urine

Acidic urine helps kill bacteria in the urinary tract. To promote and achieve acidic urine, your loved one should eat foods that are high in animal proteins, like meat, and drink cranberry juice.

Urinary Tract Infection

Because indwelling catheters tend to be associated with complications such as infection, it's very important for you to observe carefully and promptly report signs that are suggestive of a urinary tract infection. The box on page 207 tells you which signs to watch for.

The catheter site can be easily contaminated with germs that can travel into the body, resulting in infection, so wash your hands thoroughly before and after care (see Chapter 8 for handwashing procedure). If you feel more comfortable doing so, wear disposable gloves when cleaning the catheter site.

Catheter Care

Proper care of the catheter system and the catheter area is extremely important because serious complications can develop if you don't care for it correctly. Check to make sure that the tubing that drains into a bag is always positioned below the level of the bladder. If it isn't, urine can flow backward, possibly into the kidneys, causing a serious infection. There should be no obstruction of the free flow of urine. Make sure that there are no kinks in the tubing and that the older adult isn't sitting on it.

Watch for signs that a catheter change is needed. Roll the tubing between your thumb and forefingers. If you can feel sandy particles (uric acid crystals), it's time to change the catheter. The usual length of time between catheter changes varies from 5 days to 2 weeks.

Create a regular schedule for changing the catheter system— catheter, tubing, and collection bag: Empty the collection bag at least once every 8 hours. Date all three parts of the catheter system each time a new one is started.

Catheter care usually is done at least twice a day and especially after a bowel movement. The following suggestions for catheter care include:

1. Wipe from front to back to avoid introducing *E. coli* and other bacteria from the anus.

2. Cleanse the urethral opening (*external urethral meatus*) and the surrounding area with soap and water (you can use antiseptic soap), cleaning from the inner area to the outer area.
3. Rinse and dry the area thoroughly.
4. Apply an antimicrobial ointment at the catheter insertion site, but only if the person's health care professional recommends it.
5. Never use or apply lotion or powder near the catheter.
6. Make sure that the tubing of the catheter is secured properly to the older adult's leg to prevent movement of and pulling on the urethra.

To conserve costs, it's common to reuse collection bags (remember that one must be worn while one is being cleaned). The following measures will prolong the life of the bag and reduce the health risks to the older adult:

1. Wash the inside and outside of the bag in mild soap and water and rinse thoroughly.
2. When a bag isn't reused immediately (that is, one is used while one is cleaned), fill the bag with 1/2 cup of vinegar (vinegar kills Pseudomonas organisms and eliminates odors). Discard the contents before reuse.
3. Note the date you started using the new one.

When bathing older people who wear indwelling urinary catheters but who are still able to take showers or baths, probably with some help from you, remember that the catheter should be clamped temporarily if the collection bag is higher than the level of the bladder. With the catheter clamped, the collection bag may be hung over the side of the bathtub. If your loved one is able to shower, he or she should empty the collection bag and attach the catheter tubing to his or her leg with a leg bag. If a leg bag is used, clamping usually isn't necessary.

If the older adult in your life wears a condom type of external catheter, it shouldn't be applied too tightly. A too-tight application can prevent the blood from flowing freely, and skin breakdown can occur. The condom must be removed daily to allow the penis to be thoroughly cleaned, dried, and aired. This prevents irritation and skin breakdown.

12   Providing Oral Care and Assisting with Eating/Feeding

In some older adults, oral care is neglected or avoided altogether for various reasons. One reason could be that less value was placed on good oral hygiene by a generation of people who lived through the Great Depression than it was on later generations. Another reason could be that tooth loss is commonly believed to be "normal" in old age, so why fuss over oral care or go to the dentist? Still another reason may be that the mouth is thought to be an unpleasant area of the body to care for. Most people are taught from an early age that the mouth is full of germs, so the idea of poking around in someone else's mouth is offputting. In addition, some adult children may feel uncomfortable about giving oral care to their parents because it seems like an invasion of their privacy.

There are negative consequences to holding these beliefs. Neglecting oral care can affect a person's overall health, particularly a person's nutrition. Having few (or no) teeth or gum disease (for example, gingivitis or periodontitis) can mean that the type and consistency of food that a person can eat is limited and therefore inadequate and nutrient deficient. Jaw alignment can be changed by poor long-term oral care, and this can cause headaches and further tooth, bone, or gum loss. The development of serious problems in the mouth such as dry mouth, gingivitis, and periodontitis (see below) can put a person at risk for systemic disease, such as malnutrition and hypocalcemia, a decreased level of calcium in the body that can lead to osteoporosis.

Other negative consequences to holding to the beliefs mentioned in the first paragraph include a loss of satisfaction with life, a lack of self-esteem, and even withdrawal from friends and other social contacts. People may rarely or never smile and may cover

Table 1.   Medications that decrease saliva production

Class	Brand name	Generic name
Antidepressant	Amitriptyline Nortriptyline Chlorpromazine Haloperidol	Elavil Pamelor Thorazine Haldol
Antianxiety	Lorazepam	
Antihypertensive	Propranolol Verapamil	Inderal, Inderide
Diuretic	Amiloride Hydrochlorothiazide	Amiloride, Midamor Aldoril, Lopressor, Vaseretic
Anticholinergic/antireflux	Ranitidine Cimetidine Atropine, Scopolamine	Zantac Tagamet Donnatal, Lomotil
Antihistamine	Diphenhydramine	Benadryl, TYLENOL PM, TYLENOL Allergy Sinus, TYLENOL Flu NightTime, Actifed

Adapted from Abrams, W.B. et al. (Eds.). (1995). *The Merck Manual of Geriatrics* (2nd ed., p. 626). White-house Station, NJ: Merck & Co.

their mouth when speaking to avoid being embarrassed about their teeth or gums. Communication becomes difficult because healthy teeth and gums are essential to being able to speak clearly. Let's review some common oral problems and how you can help your loved one avoid them.

ORAL PROBLEMS COMMON IN OLDER ADULTS

Dry Mouth

Dry mouth (*xerostomia*) often is due to salivary glands that don't function properly. The most likely, but not the only, causes of this dysfunction are medications (more than 400 prescription medications can cause dry mouth; see some examples in Table 1), radiation therapy of head and neck tumors, and chemotherapeutic agents. Some byproducts of dry mouth are difficulty in swallowing dry food, difficulty in speaking at length, and a need to drink while trying to swallow.

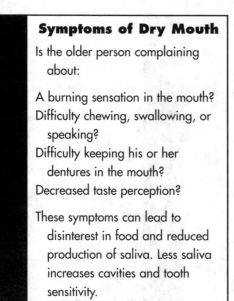

Symptoms of Dry Mouth

Is the older person complaining about:

A burning sensation in the mouth?

Difficulty chewing, swallowing, or speaking?

Difficulty keeping his or her dentures in the mouth?

Decreased taste perception?

These symptoms can lead to disinterest in food and reduced production of saliva. Less saliva increases cavities and tooth sensitivity.

If your loved one is diagnosed with dry mouth, there are ways that you can reduce its effects. Give the person an over-the-counter (OTC) or a prescription saliva substitute. Saliva substitutes, which increase oral comfort and make eating easier and more pleasurable, come in spray solutions or rinses and can be used as often as needed. Saliva substitutes contain a lubricant-sweetener such as glycerin or sorbitol, salt ions, and a flavoring agent. Other methods that you can use to help your loved one are to have him or her chew sugar-free gum, suck on sugar-free sour hard candies (both gum and candy stimulate saliva production), or drink at least 8–10 glasses of fluids during the day, if his or her physician doesn't advise against it. The person should try to avoid caffeine, alcoholic beverages, and highly acidic drinks such as orange or grapefruit juices because they can make the mouth feel even drier.

Gingivitis and Periodontitis

The characteristics of the bacterial infections gingivitis and periodontitis are inflammation of the gums and surrounding tissues. Teeth become loose and eventually fall out if the condition isn't taken care of. The signs and symptoms of gingivitis and periodontitis include the following:

- Gums bleed when the teeth are brushed.
- Gums are red, swollen, or tender.
- Teeth are loose and/or shift position, especially if there are empty spaces between teeth due to tooth loss, or if inflamed gums and tissues don't hold teeth properly in place.

- Pus oozes from the gumline when the gums are pressed on.
- Teeth detach from the gums.
- The bite pattern (the way the teeth fit together when a person bites down) changes.
- The way the dentures or partial plates fit changes.
- The person has chronic bad breath or a bad taste in the mouth.

Alert!

Any of the following symptoms may be a sign of periodontal disease. If you notice any of these symptoms, call a dentist immediately:

Sore, red, or bleeding gums

Toothache

Tooth loosening

Broken or loss of a tooth

Gums oozing pus

PROVIDING ORAL CARE

The best way to avoid gingivitis or periodontitis is to floss, brush, and rinse the teeth or dentures daily. The older adult in your life may need help managing his or her oral health or may need direct assistance with these activities of daily living. The following sections describe the basics of oral care. (We want to remind you that even if older adults do floss, brush, and rinse properly, they still need to make regular visits to the dentist for checkups and cleaning. Even if your loved one wears partial or full dentures, a dental checkup is necessary and important. Dentures should be checked periodically to ensure a snug fit and to prevent mouth tissues from becoming irritated.)

Flossing

To maintain good oral health, you have to remove the food debris, plaque, and tartar that collects on and around the teeth and soft tissues. Floss the teeth and gums every day with lightly waxed or unwaxed floss or clean them with a WaterPik. When your loved one can't floss because of a weakness in the upper torso or some other disability, you need to provide this care. Follow this procedure:

1. Break off an 18-inch long piece of floss from the dispenser.
2. Hold the floss between the middle fingers of each hand.
3. Use your thumbs to stretch the floss tight.
4. Gently move the floss up and down between each tooth and under the gumline, where possible.
5. Repeat Step 4 for both upper and lower teeth.
6. Let your loved one rinse out his or her mouth.

Brushing

Older people should brush or have their teeth brushed once a day at minimum; twice a day is even better. They should try to rinse their mouth or brush their teeth soon after eating sugary food, foods with high carbohydrate content, or candy.

Older adults should always use a soft-bristle toothbrush to avoid damaging their gums. It also may be helpful for them to use a child-size toothbrush rather than an adult-size one. A child-size toothbrush usually has soft bristles, is much smaller than the adult-size brush, and is easier to use to brush individual teeth, especially those at the back of the mouth. The toothpaste they use should be nonabrasive and contain fluoride. Arthritic older people who have a hard time holding a toothbrush handle can use adaptive devices to brush their teeth without your help. Some of these adaptive devices have round, wide handles so that they're easier to hold. A less expensive solution is to wrap the toothbrush handle with a washcloth, aluminum foil, or thin foam sheets. You can also insert a handle into a sponge ball, a sponge hair roller, or a plastic bicycle handgrip. A lightweight, rechargeable electric toothbrush with a large handgrip also can be used.

Older people have been brushing their teeth for years, but have they been doing it properly? Would you know how to brush your loved one's teeth if he or she could no longer do it? Here's step-by-step instructions and a diagram (Figure 1) to help you:

1. Wash your hands before you begin to brush the person's teeth (follow the handwashing instructions in Chapter 9).
2. Wet the toothbrush and apply toothpaste.

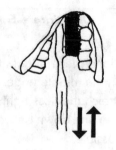

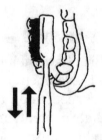

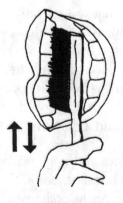

FIGURE 1. How to brush a person's teeth. (Adapted from Sorrentino, S.A., and Hogan, J. (1994). Mosby's Textbook for Long-Term Care Assistants, 2nd ed.)

3. Hold the brush horizontally, and brush the front teeth (tops and bottoms) using a gentle back-and-forth motion and short strokes.
4. Brush the inside of the front teeth by holding the brush at a 45° angle. Brush in short strokes from the gumline to the top of the tooth. Keep repositioning the brush until you've brushed all of the front teeth.
5. Brush the insides of the teeth by holding the brush horizontally and gently brushing back and forth. Remember to use short strokes. Keep repositioning the brush until you've brushed all of the inner surfaces.
6. Place the toothbrush parallel to the biting surfaces (for example, on top of the molars) and brush back and forth using short strokes.
7. The tongue also should be brushed gently to remove bacteria and substances that cause bad breath and tooth decay.
8. Let your loved one rinse his or her mouth with mouthwash or water—any substance that does not contain alcohol (see "Rinsing" below for details).
9. If your loved one wears false teeth, they should be kept in water at night and cleaned before they're placed in the mouth in the morning. Use warm water, a nonabrasive toothpaste, and a toothbrush to clean them.

Rinsing

The mouth should be rinsed only with substances that don't contain alcohol, which can be irritating and drying. Alcohol-containing mouthwashes also can stimulate alcoholic beverage intake by older people who may have a drinking problem (alcoholism is a major, "silent" problem among older adults). An antibacterial mouthwash can be used; normal saline (a teaspoon of salt added to a glass of warm water) is particularly soothing to the gums.

Because the effectiveness of the swallowing and choking mechanisms diminishes with age, the older adult in your life may have difficulty rinsing, spitting, or swallowing during brushing (see the next section for more information about swallowing problems). One way that you can squirt liquids inside your loved one's mouth without making him or her choke is to use a bulb syringe, which you can buy in any drugstore. You may need to lay the person on his or her side in bed or on the couch to minimize his or her risk of accidentally breathing liquid into the lungs (*aspiration*). To reduce the risk of choking, you may find it helpful to remove secretions (like phlegm) from the person's mouth with a tissue.

EATING/FEEDING

Chapter 8 discussed at some length nutrition and diets for older adults. There are specific considerations to keep in mind with older people and eating. Take into account that older people with dentures or without teeth can't chew as well as they did when they had a full set of permanent teeth. The foods they eat shouldn't require much chewing; they can be finely chopped or ground, semi-solid and of medium consistency (for example, mashed potatoes, casseroles, scrambled eggs, custards). These kinds of foods let them focus on swallowing instead of on chewing so that they don't need as much control to manipulate food through the mouth.

Offer them a beverage at the end of a meal rather than at the beginning or during it because liquids are difficult to control in the mouth before they swallow. In particular, avoid milk and dairy products, citrus juices, and water at the beginning of a meal because they stimulate the production of saliva. Not only is saliva overproduced but it becomes thick and ropelike, making it harder to swallow. In addition, you may need to add a commercial powder thickener to create the right consistency for swallowing water, tea, coffee, soup, or fruit juice.

As stated earlier, people's swallowing and choking mechanisms become less effective with age. Because of this, people tend to swallow larger food particles than they did when they were younger, and they can choke or aspirate. Adding to the difficulty may be the medications they're taking (see the section called "Dry Mouth" above) or

Alert! Pneumonia can develop when food or liquid enters the lungs instead of the stomach, especially if an older adult has swallowing and feeding difficulties.

contraction of a disease such as Sjögren's syndrome (an autoimmune disease that affects mostly women older than 40 that makes the salivary glands less able to produce moisture). As a loving caregiver, you'll want to observe the older adult in your life for swallowing problems. While you watch, ask yourself these questions:

- Is he or she having difficulty swallowing?
- Does he or she cough while eating or drinking?
- Does he or she appear to be choking while eating?
- After he or she finishes eating, does it look like there's still food in the mouth?
- Does he or she complain of food sticking in the throat?

If you answered yes to these questions, contact a health care provider as soon as possible. The person may have a swallowing or feeding problem that requires the intervention of a professional.

Most of the possible causes of swallowing and/or feeding difficulties are nervous system disorders resulting from Parkinson's disease, Alzheimer's disease, or stroke. Some of the other causes

Alert!

If Your Loved One Starts Choking

Don't do anything as long as he or she is coughing. If coughing doesn't help and the person's breathing is labored or he or she is turning blue, ask the person, "Are you choking?" It's extremely important to ask because a person who's choking won't be able to talk and a person who's having a heart attack is able to talk. Perform the Heimlich manuever when the older adult in your life is choking:

1. Stand behind your loved one and wrap your arms around his or her waist.
2. Make a fist and place your thumb knuckle slightly above the navel but well below the breastbone.
3. Hold your fist firmly with your other hand and, thrusting upward and inward, pull both hands sharply toward you.
4. Keep doing this until either the food or liquid is forced out or the person becomes unconscious.

Because of the force you'll have to use, perform the Heimlich manuever only in an emergency.

You may have to suction food or liquid from the mouth of a person who has a problem swallowing and is prone to choking, so suctioning equipment may be needed in the home.

are xerostomia, mechanical obstructions in the throat or esophagus, and poor eating posture.

Swallowing and feeding difficulties are manageable, as is facing the prospect of feeding the older adult in your life. Because of upper body weakness, paralysis, confusion, and other limitations, your loved one may no longer be able to feed him- or herself. Some important things to remember in feeding an older adult are the following:

- Older adults who can no longer feed themselves may be embarrassed, even angry, about being dependent on you to feed them. Let them feed themselves as much as possible. If they can hold finger foods, let them. Don't jump in right away to help—remember that you always want to support their sense of independence and dignity.
- Avoid appearing rushed or hurried when feeding them—mealtime should be a relaxing time, a time of companionship. One family caregiver told us that he solved the problem of rushing through feeding his grandmother so that he could eat—he ate from his own plate while he fed his grandmother.
- Serve manageable amounts of food with each bite. Use a teaspoon or syringe to make sure that you're serving small amounts of food.
- Serve food in the order that the person prefers, and switch between solid and liquid foods.
- Hold the person's head slightly forward when offering food, and gradually allow the head to go back to a normal position (remember to keep the head straight). When offering liquids, seat older adults in a low position and place liquids under the tongue. Eating and drinking in this position helps food and liquid to pass easily through the mouth to the stomach and prevents choking and aspiration.
- Give the person enough time to chew the food thoroughly and swallow it completely.
- Minimize distractions, and try not to ask questions until he or she is finished swallowing. <u>All of the person's attention must focus on eating, particularly if the person has swallowing or feeding problems.</u>
- After eating, your loved one should sit upright for about 30 minutes to lessen the possibility of vomiting and aspiration.

If the older adult in your life has had a stroke and has a problem with eating and swallowing, here are some additional feeding tips:

- Direct food toward the side of the mouth that isn't paralyzed. It's easier to chew and swallow food when food is placed where feeling and muscle control still exist.
- To help the person chew and swallow, tell your loved one to form a seal with the lips, if it's possible for him or her to do so.
- Teach "the voluntary swallow" by instructing the person to (1) hold the food in the mouth while he or she thinks about swallowing, and (2) actually swallow twice.
- Always check the person's mouth to make sure it's clear of food before continuing to feed him or her.

13

Promoting Safe Mobility

Being able to get up and move around (ambulate) freely and safely are goals that all older adults want to achieve. Ambulating independently is very beneficial for older people because it:

- Provides an opportunity for socializing and for interacting with the environment and getting more pleasure out of these interactions
- Makes emptying the bowels easier
- Helps improve the quality of sleep
- Reduces tension
- Improves cardiopulmonary function
- Improves muscular strength and stamina
- Maintains joint mobility
- Increases bone density

For these reasons, encourage the older adult in your life to be as active as possible, even if he or she is bedbound (see also "Helpful Hints for People Who Are Bedbound, p. 225") or in a wheelchair. At the same time that you're encouraging your loved one, remember to promote safe mobility in any activity. Reduce the possibility of falls or eliminate the incidence of falls, and help the person to move from a wheelchair to a bed (*transfer*) safely. (You'll learn how to do this later in the chapter.)

PREVENTING/REDUCING THE INCIDENCE OF FALLS

Falls are a leading source of disability and death in older people, but the consequences of falls aren't confined to older adults. Falls and their consequences also can be a burden for family members/caregivers, health care professionals, and acute and long-term care institutions. Falls happen for a lot of reasons. For example, a person may:

Before starting any activity, your loved one should get a thorough physical examination and review of his or her medication by a health care provider. This assessment should include a determination of the older adult's vision, blood pressure, range of motion, muscular strength, balance, posture, and neurological and mental status.

- Slip, slide, faint, or trip
- Fall from bed, a wheelchair, or the toilet/commode
- Experience side effects from medications (and alcohol) that cause dizziness and lightheadedness; some medications such as sedatives, antihypertensives, and diuretics cause incontinence (see also Chapter 9), which can lead to slips or urgent dashes to toilet facilities
- Become dehydrated; dehydration often causes a corresponding decrease in blood pressure, which might make the person dizzy

Neurological disorders such as brain tumors, stroke, depression, and confusion or debilitating diseases such as heart disease can contribute to falls. Neurological disorders can alter a person's ability to keep his or her balance and to avoid hazards that contribute to falls. Simple age-related changes could cause falls as well. These changes include:

- Orthostatic hypotension (for more information, see Chapter 6)
- Increased frequency in urination
- Limited or impaired vision or incorrect eyeglasses prescription
- Cataracts, which make glare more bothersome
- Impaired hearing caused by impacted wax in the ears
- An altered sense of gravity, which makes balance less certain

If any of these changes are found to be a factor in the incidence of falls, seek professional help.

The fear of falling ("fallaphobia") can seriously limit older adults' mobility, and it may actually cause falls, especially if they have fallen previously. Underlying their fear may be a problem with their gait (walking) or balance. Older adults with fallaphobia lose

Helpful Hints for People Who Are Bedbound

Temporary or permanent bed rest produces many harmful effects in the body. Any kind of activity will help counteract these effects. Try some of these:

Minimize the amount of bed rest, if possible.

Encourage your loved one to use the bathroom or a bedside commode rather than adult incontinence pads or a bedpan.

Stand the person for 30–60 seconds to restore his or her equilibrium whenever you transfer the person from bed to chair.

Encourage the person to get dressed and wear street clothes rather than a bathrobe, nightgown, or pajamas (lessens time spent in bed).

Encourage the person to eat at a table, not in bed.

Encourage the person to walk whenever possible, especially outdoors because it's a change in environment.

Encourage your loved one to use small softballs or any object that can be squeezed for range-of-motion exercises for hands and fingers.

confidence in themselves and in their ability to keep themselves from falling. They may withdraw socially or restrict their activities, or others may advise them to do so to avoid falling again. They experience loss of independence and control as well as a feeling of vulnerability and fragility. Older adults who fear falling may become depressed and focus on issues of death and dying. Other feelings may be a fear of becoming a burden to family and friends or of being institutionalized.

Many fallaphobic older people experience something called "clutch and grab." They appear fearful and anxious, clutching and grabbing at any object within sight, and then stagger, rush forward, and look like they're about to fall. If support is provided, the behavior changes, and a fairly normal pattern of stepping occurs.

External factors such as some clothing and environmental conditions also increase a person's risk of falling. Poorly fitting or improper shoes and socks (for example, slippery soles or high heels), bathrobes, or pants that are too long can cause a person to slip or trip. Room lighting that's too dim, wet or just-waxed floors, and clutter or furniture that blocks pathways in the home or in the yard are environmental hazards for older adults.

In some cases the older person is using a cane or walker improperly. For example, you may see your loved one carrying the cane rather than using it for support, which may be because the cane is too long or too short for him or her. Perhaps the person isn't using the cane as instructed by an occupational or physical therapist or nurse (for instance, he or she may be placing it too far ahead of the body). A walker that's borrowed from a friend or neighbor isn't fitted to your loved one. Each walker must be fitted to the individual body. The use of any device to help a person ambulate needs to be approached as one does the instructions for taking medications. Medications are administered in an individualized and exact way to be most effective and nonhazardous; assistive devices must be individualized and used in an exact way to achieve the same result.

Clothing Choices that Prevent Falls

The following clothing make mobility and dressing and undressing easier:

Tops with Velcro-fastened front openings, back and side openings, raglan sleeves, and cape styling

Pants with front flaps or extra room in the back

Longer, fuller skirts

In all cases, look for comfortable, durable, attractive, and easy-to-launder fabrics.

---

25 Ways to Increase Safety and Prevent Falls

1. Use side rails on the bed, if the person is bedbound and is using a hospital-style or adjustable bed, or purchase side rails that fit under the mattress (used with small children's beds). Full-length

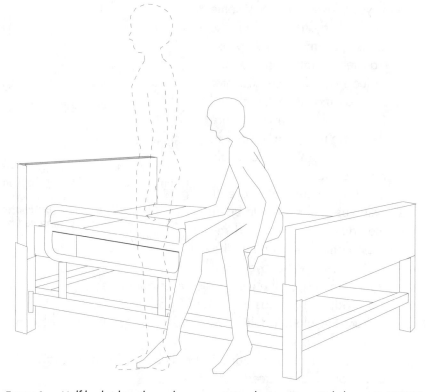

FIGURE 1.   *Half bed side rails used as an assistive device. (From Tideiksaar, R. [1998].*
Falls in Older Persons: Prevention & Management *[2nd ed., p. 102]. Baltimore: Health*
Professions Press; reprinted by permission.)

side rails (stretching the length of the bed) that are at least
14 inches above the top of the mattress can help keep your loved
one from rolling and falling out of bed. But don't use full-length
side rails on the beds of people who are able to get out of bed.
In this case it's best to use half bed side rails, which don't interfere with getting out of bed but do help keep the person from
rolling off the bed.

Side rails are good because they help build a person's confidence in his or her ability to get in and out of bed, and this reduces fallaphobia (Figure 1). Another positive aspect is that they
can support people with poor sitting and transferring balance,
such as people with Parkinson's disease or the effects of a stroke.

If your loved one has some kind of dysfunction in the arms, you may want to use transfer handles on the bed instead of side rails. Transfer handles mount to metal bed frames and are more secure than side rails, particularly in transfers from bed to chair and vice versa.

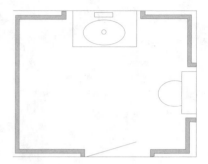

FIGURE 2. Bathroom grab bars. (From Tideiksaar, R. [1998]. Falls in Older Persons: Prevention & Management [2nd ed., p. 120]. Baltimore: Health Professions Press; reprinted by permission.)

When side rails aren't being used, they should be in the "down" position and recess completely under the bed to keep your loved one from climbing on the rails to get in or out of bed.

2. Place adjustable beds in the "low" position.
3. Instruct the older adult in your life in the proper use of canes and/or walkers.
4. Use nonskid mats or strips in bathtubs and shower stalls. Use pads or double-faced adhesive carpet tape under area rugs to secure them to flooring. Avoid using rugs that curl at the edges and replace those that do.
5. Use bathtub and shower stools and/or mount sturdy hand-rails in bathtubs or around the perimeter of bathrooms (Figure 2).
6. Install a toilet safety frame and/or elevated/adjustable toilet seat (Figure 3).
7. Wipe up spills on floors immediately.
8. Install proper lighting along the pathway from the person's bedroom to the bathroom and in hall-

FIGURE 3. Toilet safety frame. (From Tideiksaar, R. [1998]. Falls in Older Persons: Prevention & Management [2nd ed., p. 121]. Baltimore: Health Professions Press; reprinted by permission.)

ways. You can use night-lights in bathrooms and bedrooms, an easy-to-reach bed headboard light, a bedside lamp with a secure base that won't tip over, or motion-sensor lighting in the bathroom.

9. Instruct the older person to sit on the edge of the bed for a few seconds before standing up.

10. Mark the outer edge of each step on a staircase with colored tape so that your loved one can see each step more clearly.

11. Cover or secure electrical cords away from pathways in the person's home, and avoid clutter.

12. Make sure that the person is using a step stool with a handrail rather than standing on chairs, boxes, or other potentially dangerous items to reach high shelves or objects.

13. Teach the older adult in your life how to bend and reach properly. He or she should bend from the knees, not from the waist. Bending from the waist to pick up something can cause back strain or a more serious injury. The person should use an assistive device, such as an aluminum reacher or a pik stick (for people with weak hands), to reach up for objects. Some can even be outfitted with a magnet on the end to pick up coins or pins.

14. Encourage the person to purchase shoes and/or socks with non-skid treads on the soles and that fit properly. Shoes and socks shouldn't be loose or floppy.

15. Encourage the person to wear low-heeled shoes unless she always has worn high-heeled shoes—switching heel heights may cause instability rather than reduce it.

16. Avoid rushing the person through ambulating or completing a task or asking him or her to make a sudden movement. Take your time and slow down!

Caregiver Tip

How to Avoid Back Strain

Bend from your knees, not from your waist

Place feet wide apart

Use arm and leg muscles

Pull and slide rather than lift

Use a rocking motion to move a person

17. Tell your loved one's friends or other relatives that the telephone may ring 10 or more times before he or she answers it.

18. Show the older adult in your life how to get up after he or she falls. Method 1: Roll onto your stomach, get on all fours, and crawl to a nearby piece of furniture; Method 2: Shuffle on your buttocks or on your side to a nearby piece of furniture or a telephone.

> **Caregiver Tip**
>
> If an older adult falls and is unable to get up, instruct him or her to use anything that's within reach to keep warm until help arrives, such as a newspaper, a coat, an area rug, or a blanket.

19. Discuss and create an emergency exit plan with your loved one.

20. Make sure the older person is seated while he or she is eating, drinking, or taking medications.

21. Make sure that the person's eyeglasses are clean, and routinely check his or her vision.

22. Make sure that the person's ears are clean and that hearing aid batteries work properly.

23. Monitor your loved one's medication intake, especially hypertensive medications (see Chapter 9 for details).

24. Ensure proper nutrition to avoid weakness and disorientation from malnutrition.

25. Ask the person, especially if he or she lives alone, to wear a Life-Line pendant or a similar device. Pressing the Life-Line button activates the preset telephone number of a neighbor, a designated family member, and/or the 911 emergency system.

TRANSFERRING SAFELY

There may be times when the physical limitations of the older adult in your life make it necessary for you to partially (the person is able to participate physically in the transfer) or fully assist him or her in a transfer and do it safely. Some general considerations to keep in mind when assisting in a transfer include:

- Having a firm mattress or placing a bedboard under a soft mattress—a firmer surface makes transfers easier
- Knowing which side of the person's body is stronger and transferring him or her to that side; for example, when transferring, place a chair or wheelchair alongside the bed on the person's stronger side
- Making the transferring distance as short as possible

Providing Partial Assistance with Transfers

The following directions are appropriate when you're the only caregiver available to assist in a transfer.

Transferring from Bed to Chair or Wheelchair

1. Place a chair or wheelchair parallel to and near the head of the person's bed.
2. Lock the wheelchair's wheels, and make sure that the foot supports are in the "up" position.
3. If the person is using a hospital-style or adjustable bed that has short side rails, keep the side rails in the "up" position so that the person can grasp them and steady him- or herself while sitting up. If the person is using a regular bed, support his or her upper body with pillows (placed behind the upper body) to help the person sit up. Another method is to stand on the side of the bed from which he or she will be rising and, using your arms to support his or her upper body, help the person move to a sitting position.
4. Once the person is sitting up, ask him or her to sit and wait a few seconds to avoid orthostatic hypotension or fainting.
5. Pivot the person one quarter turn by supporting his or her shoulders and legs. The legs should now be dangling over the bedside. (If your loved one needs to dress at this time, assist him or her while he or she sits at the side of the bed.)
6. Place the hospital-style or adjustable bed in the "low" position, or if using a regular bed, place a stool under the person's feet so he or she can stand on it while transferring from bed.

7. Stand facing the person, and spread your feet apart about 12 inches.
8. Place your foot between the person's feet.
9. Flex your knees. This provides stability and doesn't fatigue your leg muscles.
10. Grasp the person under the arms, and ask the person to put his or her hands on your shoulders.
11. In unison, lift his or her upper body as the person lifts his or her upper body. Remember to hold the person close to your body as you lift so that you don't strain your back. Maintain a wide base of support as you pivot with the person toward the chair. His or her back should now face the chair or wheelchair.
12. Ask the person to hold onto the armrests of the chair or wheelchair as you lower him or her into it. Bend your knees slightly and keep your back straight.

If you find that your loved one always seems to be sitting too far forward in the chair or wheelchair, place a towel folded in thirds on the seat. One end of the towel should dangle from the back of the chair; make it long enough so you can grab it. Lower the person onto the chair, making sure that he or she is sitting on the folded towel. Once the person is seated, stand behind the chair or wheelchair (make sure the wheels are locked), take a wide stance and brace your feet, and pull on the piece of the towel that's hanging from the back of the chair. Pull until the person's back makes contact with the back of the chair. This technique works because it avoids friction on the person's skin and requires less of your energy than lifting him or her back into the chair.

Transferring from Chair or Wheelchair to Bed

When transferring your loved one from a chair or wheelchair to bed, reverse the technique you used in transferring him or her from bed to chair.

Providing Full Assistance with Transfers

The following directions are appropriate when you are the only caregiver available and the person isn't able to assist in a transfer.

Transferring from Bed to Chair or Wheelchair

1. Put the hospital-style or adjustable bed in the "low" position.
2. Place the chair or wheelchair parallel to and against the bed at a point near the headboard. Make sure that the wheelchair's wheels are locked.
3. If the person uses a hospital-style or adjustable bed, raise the head of the bed until the person is in an upright position. If a regular bed is used, arrange pillows so that it's easier for you to move the person into a sitting position.
4. Place your arms under the person's head and shoulders and gently slide the upper part of his or her body to the edge of the bed.
5. Move the lower part of the person's body to the edge of the bed by placing one arm under his or her waist and the other arm beneath the backside. Place one foot in front of the other, bend your knees, and begin to rock the person gently toward the edge of the bed. This rocking motion creates momentum that adds to the effort that's being exerted by your arm and leg muscles.
6. Approach your loved one from the back and place your arms under the person's arms.
7. Move to the back of the chair as you gently pull or slide the person into the chair.
8. Lean the person against the back of the chair to prevent sliding, keep the chair from moving, and provide a base for support. Rock back gently while pulling the person into the chair.

Transferring from Chair or Wheelchair to Bed

When transferring your loved one from a chair or wheelchair to bed, reverse the technique you used in transferring him or her from bed to chair.

Turning and Positioning a Person in Bed

Older adults who are confined to bed must be turned regularly and positioned properly so that the person avoids developing pressure sores. To turn the person toward you to lie on his or her left side:

1. If the person uses a hospital-style or adjustable bed, raise it to the "high" position (your waist height).

2. Stand on the right side of the bed and face it.
3. Tell the person to bend his or her knees and place the arms across the chest. This position helps prevent the person from rolling back, partially prepares him or her for lying on the side, and prevents him or her from rolling onto an arm.
4. Place one of your hands on his or her right shoulder and the other hand on his or her right hip.
5. Spread your feet apart about 12 inches, bend your knees slightly, place one foot behind the other, and, rocking gently backward, roll the person toward you until he or she is lying on the side. (Rolling requires less effort than lifting because you don't have to overcome gravity.)

To turn the person away from you to lie on his or her right side:

1. If the person uses a hospital-style or adjustable bed, raise it to the "high" position (your waist height).
2. Stand on the right side of the bed and face it.
3. Move the person to the edge of bed on your side. Place your arms under the person's shoulders, spread your feet apart about 12 inches, bend your knees slightly, and place one foot behind the other. Then slide the person's shoulders to the center of the bed. Move yourself into a position that's parallel to the person's hips and use the same actions to move his or her hips. If the person is light, you probably can move him or her in one motion; for heavier people, move their shoulders and then move their hips.
4. Roll the person away from you by pushing at his or her shoulders and hips.

Moving a Person Up in Bed

When the head of the bed is raised, it often causes your loved one to slide down to the middle or foot of the bed. He or she needs to be moved up in bed to maintain good body alignment. There are two methods for moving an older adult up in bed. You can do it with a little help from the person.

Method One

1. Make sure the bed is as flat as possible. Remove the pillows from under the person's head. Place them against the headboard. Doing this prevents the person from hitting his or her head on the headboard when being moved up in bed.
2. Ask the person to flex his or her knees. Place one of your arms under the person's shoulders; place your other arm under his or her flexed knees.
3. Spread your feet apart about 12 inches, bend your knees slightly, and slide the person toward the head of the bed while he or she pushes with the feet.

Method Two

1. Make sure the bed is as flat as possible. Remove the pillows from under the person's head. Place them against the headboard.
2. Stand facing the head of the bed on the person's right side.
3. Lock arms with your loved one: Take your right arm and grasp the person's shoulder as he or she grasps your arm near the right elbow.
4. Place your left arm under the person's shoulder, supporting his or her head and neck.
5. Place one foot in front of the other, and flex your knees.
6. Rock back and forth, putting weight on one foot and then on the other while counting "one, two, three." On the count of three, you should be rocking forward.
7. Tell the person that on the count of three, he or she should push with the legs as you pull on the locked arms. This pulls the person up in bed.

14   Providing Emotional Care

When providing personal care, you need to be aware not just of the physical health of the older adult in your life but also of his or her emotional health. This chapter describes what you should do when your loved one is depressed, anxious, and/or acting in ways that distress him or her, you, and others.

DEPRESSION

José, age 70, lost his wife Rosaria after a brief illness. They were married for 45 years and had no children. Over the years, he had become quite dependent on her for help with day-to-day activities and for companionship after he retired. After Rosaria died, José stopped eating regularly, didn't care how he looked, made no attempt to keep the house clean, and stopped participating in the activities that he enjoyed while she was alive.

As you learned in Chapter 7, depression is not a weakness, a lack of courage, a poor constitution, or a natural part of getting old. It's an illness that can be caused by many things, and it's very treatable. José, for example, became depressed as a reaction to a significant event: He lost his role as a husband, a role he lived for 45 years. Responding to a loved one's death with sadness is normal. Personal losses should and do produce deep sadness, but the sadness should lessen over time. If it doesn't, more than likely the person is depressed.

You know from reading Chapter 7 what the signs and symptoms of depression are. You also know that many older people think there's a stigma attached to mental illness. Some say they have little use for psychiatrists. Some are particularly hesitant to admit that they have an emotional problem. They fear being thought of as crazy, "being put away," and/or thinking that they might have Alzheimer's disease. You should take both the severity of signs/symptoms and the length of time that the person has been exhibiting signs/symptoms into consideration when thinking about whether your loved one's emotional state needs treatment.

If you decide to approach the person, do it gently. Share what you've observed—for example, his or her wearing soiled clothes or the same clothes all the time, not enjoying a visit from the grandchildren, or not wanting to leave the house—using I-centered speech. Even if you do use this approach, your loved one may resist your attempts to help. In extreme cases you may need to ask family members or close friends to help you encourage the person to seek treatment. If this doesn't help, contact a geriatric mental health specialist.

There are numerous treatments for depression. Let's look at a few.

Treatment Options

Antidepressant medications probably are the most com-

Alert!

Signs/Symptoms of Depression

Seek medical attention if you notice the following signs and symptoms in the older adult in your life:

Sleep disturbances (too much or too little sleep)

Significant weight loss or weight gain

Restlessness, agitation, or irritability

Constant complaints of feeling exhausted

Feelings of worthlessness, self-reproach, and/or excessive guilt

Difficulty thinking or concentrating

Loss of interest in other things and other people, including oneself

Suicidal thoughts or attempts

monly prescribed intervention, although not necessarily the best, for older adults experiencing depression. Although these medications work well for some older people, many others can't use these medications because they're taking others that don't interact well with the antidepressant. There also are side effects associated with antidepressants that can be more detrimental than the depression itself:

- Postural hypotension (a sudden drop in blood pressure when changing position from seated to standing)
- Increased vulnerability to falls and fractures resulting from postural hypotension
- Heart arrhythmia
- Urinary retention
- Constipation
- Disorientation
- Skin rash
- Dry mouth

These side effects can present a dilemma—your loved one needs the medication, but he or she can't stand the side effects. You need to understand that not everyone who takes antidepressants experiences these side effects. Because they might occur, an older adult should be started on a lower dose than would a younger person, as much as 50% lower. Keep in mind that antidepressants sometimes take 2–3 weeks to take effect in the bloodstream, and they may be continued after the depression ends to prevent a relapse.

Most experts in geriatric care prefer to try treatments such as short-term, client-centered, directive talk therapy and behavioral therapies first rather than prescribe antidepressants. Unfortunately, when older adults are examined by health care professionals with no or little training and experience in geriatrics or the treatment of depression, many of them are given a prescription for antidepressants as a first line of attack rather than being referred for counseling, which actually may be more appropriate for them.

Secondary depression, the depression that occurs as a response to losses, like José's, responds well to short-term psychotherapy because this type of therapy allows the person to review and come to terms with the stresses and losses of late life. It also allows him or her to reestablish control over life and emotional stability. With this type of therapy, the depressed older adult can understand the source of his or her depression and related anxieties, fears, guilt, and apathy that have affected the person's ability to function effectively.

Electroshock (*electroconvulsive*) therapy is an effective treatment for people whose depression hasn't responded to therapy and/or antidepressants and who are at risk for harming themselves. Because of the effect on memory that electroshock therapy can have—reaching its peak about halfway through treatment and gradually subsiding over the next several months—however, many health care professionals are reluctant to prescribe this treatment. In addition, its long-term effectiveness remains unclear and requires further research.

What You Can Do

There is much you can do to support and enhance whatever professional treatment is recommended for the older adult in your life. An objective assessment of the person's ability to care for him- or herself is important. A person in the throes of depression may not be able to accurately judge his or her ability to do things. If the person clearly is unable to manage alone, you can provide the help that's needed or arrange for outside help. If the person is able to participate in self-care, you need to communicate your confidence in his or her abilities by being calm, patient, and firm with the person as you encourage him or her toward self-care.

People who are depressed often have little energy or interest in self-care. They think of themselves as incompetent and believe that you should "do for them." A helpful approach is to perform a task along with them and encourage them as you do the task, which may provide the initiative they can't generate on their own.

Your depressed older adult may refuse to get out of bed, eat, or dress and may say, "I just want to be left alone." Don't make the issue a power struggle, and don't argue with the person. Give him or her activity options. For example, if your mother wants to stay in bed all day, you could say, "Mom, it's important for you to get up. It'll help your circulation. Do you want to get up now or later?" Mom may say, "Neither," and you can reply, "Okay, but I really feel that you should take a little more time to think about your answer. I'll come back in a half hour." When all else fails, humor sometimes brings a different perspective: "What? You want to spend the whole day in bed? Maybe that'll help you to not get up on the wrong side of it!"

Encourage depressed older people to express their feelings, but don't give up too easily. Many people from the Great Depression and World War II generations find it difficult to express their true feelings—you may hear them say, "In my day, it just wasn't done." Make sure that you give them numerous opportunities to vent their feelings about their life experiences and to reminisce. If they're reluctant to share, point out that it takes a lot of energy to keep feelings and emotions inside and that sharing them with a trusted relative or friend reduces the stress they must be feeling. It's not always easy to listen to their negative feelings, but you need to do just that. Don't argue with them or cut them off. Reflecting on and talking about their life experiences validate their self-worth and confirm that they have a purpose in life.

Help the older adult in your life to schedule activities that are interspersed with rest periods. Set small goals, which gives the person direction and a reason to be involved in the activities. Introduce new goals as old ones are achieved. Replacing old goals with new ones adds variety to life, motivating the person and maybe giving him or her a new outlook on the present and future. Make sure that the activities are achievable and not competitive (or not overly competitive) so that the person can be successful at them.

Regular exercise is a vital part of treating depression. An added benefit of exercising is that depressive thoughts are difficult to maintain. Exercise distracts the person and makes him or her feel good, which ultimately enhances his or her response to other parts of the treatment. The person may not want to exercise, in fact, he or she may never have exercised, so your task is to encourage him or her to try it. The activity can be as simple as a housekeeping task, such as washing the kitchen floor, vacuuming, or raking leaves.

The individualized attention and interactions that you provide your loved one help to increase his or her feelings of self-worth. Reading aloud, writing letters, walking with the person, and conversing about current events can help generate interests outside the self.

Depression and Suicide

When older people attempt suicide, they usually succeed. The older adults who are most likely to attempt suicide are those who live alone, have a family history of suicide, have made prior suicide attempts themselves, and/or who are in the old-old age group (ages 85 and older). If your depressed loved one says things like, "I don't want to live any more," "What's the point of going on?" or "Now that my [spouse] is gone, there's nothing left to live for," don't ignore him or her. Insist that the person get help right away or get it for him or her.

Be alert for abrupt, unexpected changes in the person's mood, including changes that reflect feelings of peace with oneself. When a person finally decides to commit suicide, he or she may seem unusually calm and composed. Pay close attention to your loved one: This calmness and composure is a warning signal.

Observe the older person and his or her medication habits. If the person is taking antidepressants, is he or she continuing to take it as prescribed? Obsessive thoughts about suicide (suicidal ideation) usually stop when the person is taking an antidepressant correctly. It's also possible that your loved one is storing up medications such as sedatives or pain medication to use in committing suicide.

Actively listen to the older adult in your life. Encourage him or her to talk about any feelings, even negative ones. Knowing that someone cares may reduce the depression and anxiety and reduce thoughts about taking his or her life. To the extent that you feel comfortable doing so, try to help the person feel needed and cared for.

A person's spiritual and religious beliefs can help to relieve feelings of hopelessness. Support the person in his or her beliefs, even if you don't agree with or share them. A visit by a priest, minister, or rabbi may provide the person with an opportunity to share deep thoughts and beliefs and relieve unresolved grief and guilt.

Make sure that the person's environment is safe. Remove potentially dangerous objects such as large knives and guns.

Find the telephone number of the local crisis intervention line and give it to your loved one. If he or she seems reluctant to take the number, then use it when you feel that the person's depression is becoming overwhelming for him or her or if the person attempts suicide and you can't reach the primary health care provider or counselor/therapist.

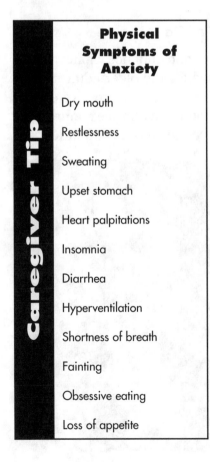

Caregiver Tip

Physical Symptoms of Anxiety

Dry mouth

Restlessness

Sweating

Upset stomach

Heart palpitations

Insomnia

Diarrhea

Hyperventilation

Shortness of breath

Fainting

Obsessive eating

Loss of appetite

ANXIETY

As you learned in Chapter 7, anxiety is a sense of uneasiness, apprehension, or tension that's caused by a vague, nonspecific danger or threat. You also learned that anxiety can create increased motor activity such as pacing, agitation, and irritability and that there are four categories of anxiety (mild, moderate, severe, and panic state). There are several treatment options for anxiety in older adults.

Treatment Options

As with depression, when anxiety becomes severe, medication and/or psychotherapy are the treatments of choice. One

type of antianxiety medication is benzodiazepines; the benzodiazepines Serax and Ativan are particularly effective for older
adults. Lower dosages must be prescribed for older adults than for
younger people because the physical changes of aging (see Chapters 6 and 9) cause the medication to stay in the body longer, and
this can lead to toxicity or overdose. Another type is nonbenzodi-
azepines, such as Equanil, Atarax, Vistaril, and BuSpar. Be vigilant
if your loved one takes these antianxiety medications because he
or she can become dependent on them when they're used long
term or prescribed in large doses.

In addition to or instead of medication, the older adult in
your life can relieve anxiety with slow, deep breathing, a warm
bath, a back rub, or a walk or some other exercise.

What You Can Do

There is much you can do to support and enhance whatever professional treatment is recommended for the older adult in your
life with anxiety. People who experience moderate to severe anxiety find it hard to concentrate on a problem and see connections
between details. You can help by directing his or her attention and

having the person work at a simple, concrete task or at least one piece of a large task at a time.

Some part of the person's lack of concentration may be related to living in an overstimulating environment. Decrease the noise level in the house—turn down the volume of radios and televisions. Lower the brightness of the lighting. Work out a daily routine with the person that takes into account the routine he or she used before the person became dependent on you. If you must make changes in bathing and eating routines, don't make them frequently, and give the person time to adjust to the new routine.

If your loved one lives alone and you live far away, he or she may experience anxiety stemming from fear of an emergency or a crisis, for example a sudden illness, a fall, or a robbery. You can calm his or her fears by arranging for a daily reassurance telephone call and/or a service such as LifeLine, which enables the person to summon help by pressing a button on a pendant. Your local Area Agency on Aging can give you further information on these services. You could arrange for a neighbor to check on your loved one regularly, for friendly visitors, or for him or her to eat a daily meal at a senior center.

Listening to and talking with loved ones about their anxieties also are very helpful activities. When you're trying to understand what's happening, focus on the feelings that they're expressing rather than on their symptoms. As you listen and respond to their feelings, use the same terminology that they use; don't give your own interpretation. Ask them if they've felt this way before and how they coped with it. When they're able to verbalize their feelings, it helps them recognize and label what they're experiencing. Using this method, you can help them make the connection between anxiety-provoking events and everyday situations.

For example, your father feels anxious when bedtime comes and has difficulty falling asleep. Talk to him; ask him what he's feeling at bedtime. Is he afraid he won't wake up? Is he afraid of being alone? Also, consider his health. Does he have a problem breathing when he lies down? Are his eyesight and hearing diminished in their capability of interpreting the environment and responding appropriately? A night-light might help him to orient to his environment if he wakes up; an additional pillow or open window could help him to breathe better; an open bedroom door might increase his feeling of safety and lessen any feelings of isolation, and an intercom placed next to the bed could soothe his fear of

Older Adults and Sleep

In later life, the quality of sleep declines, not the total sleep time. Researchers have found that sleep becomes more fragmented as people age. Many reports suggest that older people are less likely than younger people to stay awake throughout the day; older people also tend to take more naps than younger people do.

being alone. There are many more simple things that you can do; just keep in mind that it's important to be available to listen to the older adult in your life, gain a better understanding of the situation, and help the person find a solution.

INSOMNIA

What can you do when the older person in your life naps frequently during the day, isn't particularly active when awake, goes to bed early, wakes up frequently during the night, and has difficulty falling back to sleep? Your loved one may say to you, "I went to bed early, but I'm still so tired. I don't understand why." Some helpful interventions include the following. Assess the person's sleep pattern, noting how often he or she takes naps and when they are taken. Note the activities that the person engages in during the day. Suggest that the person change the cycle: take a walk in the afternoon, do some light chores—whatever activity or activities he or she would enjoy and would keep him or her awake during the day. Sometimes the older person who doesn't nap becomes overtired and finds it difficult to fall asleep at night because of overfatigue. Such an individual would benefit from a short nap in the afternoon.

Insomnia may be related to anxiety or depression. Some interventions that may help the person fall asleep are:

- Opening the window a little to increase air circulation in the room
- Listening to the radio or watching television
- Reading a good, relaxing book
- Sitting with the person before bedtime and sharing the day's happenings, focusing on pleasant events
- Drinking warm milk or a glass of wine (if permitted by his or her health care provider)
- Taking a warm bath and getting a back rub
- Turning on a night-light to help orientation (as well as enhancing safety should the older person awake at night).

Finally, physical difficulties may cause insomnia. For example, a person's impaired circulation probably makes him or her cold, especially at night. Wearing something on the head and feet can help the person stay warm in bed.

ANGER/AGGRESSION

Older people who are assertive maintain their self-image without hurting others. But when assertion turns into aggression and leads to unprovoked verbal or physical attacks on others, it not only hurts others but also turns others away from them. When people feel powerless, when their sense of authority or influence is challenged or diminished, they may respond with anger. In addition, when frail or displaced older people find themselves dependent on others for care, a sense of powerlessness and hopelessness can develop. You may find that they'll express their anger or frustration verbally or physically. Sometimes their anger is directed at you but it's really meant for someone else.

When a spouse or partner dies, the person who is "left behind" may feel let down and angry at the loved one who died. At the same time, the surviving spouse may feel guilty that he or she didn't do enough or care enough for the spouse or partner. On top of these feelings, the older person may feel even more anger and guilt because he or she is unable to care for him- or herself and depends on you and your family.

Some older adults also feel guilty because they think they've let you (the caregiver) down: "I'm the mother; I'm supposed to be caring for you and giving to you, not the other way around!" Because they may not know how to handle the confusion and anger these feelings bring up, they may vent their feelings on the one who's closest to them, the one who is most involved in their lives—you.

Aggression may be a defense mechanism. Older people may be belligerent, combative, and/or offensive in their actions. Remarks may be made that are challenging, demeaning, or critical. Sometimes, they may swear or make lewd statements or threats.

The following steps can help you handle angry or aggressive situations with the older adult in your life:

- Find out what is causing your loved one's outbursts.
- Encourage your loved one to talk about the aggressive behavior and reasons for it, and help him or her understand fully what the consequences of the behavior are.
- Help the person resolve the problem(s) that trigger the aggression.
- Provide a constructive outlet, such as exercise, for the energy that fuels his or her aggressive behavior. In particular, engage the person in an activity in which he or she can experience feelings of accomplishment.
- Give positive reinforcement to the person when he or she demonstrates the ability to change angry or aggressive behavior. Positive reinforcement instills confidence that life can improve if he or she takes responsibility to improve it.

PARANOIA/SUSPICION

Paranoia in older adults usually is associated with personal losses, vision and hearing deficits, social isolation, stress, and reactions to medications. For example, when older people have trouble hearing what's said, they may misinterpret it, which can result in the paranoid thought that others are talking about them. This paranoid thought can translate into a sincere belief that something bad will happen to them. Such a belief can affect their food intake (when they believe that their food is poisoned) or hygiene practices (refusal to bathe because they believe that someone's watching them).

Having experienced many losses in life and stresses in their later years, some older people may suddenly become suspicious of the motives of those caring for them. They may fear that the caregiver or others are "out to get them," that whatever is said to or done for them is not to be trusted, that all the caregiver wants is their money or belongings. It's sad that in some cases, older people have good reason to believe these things.

The way that you can help your loved one is to assess whether his or her paranoia is based in fact. This assessment is especially important when you are a long-distance caregiver. Ask yourself, is there a real threat to him or her? Is he or she living in a high-crime area? Once you've assessed the situation, you can intervene as appropriate. Interventions may include suggesting to the older person the idea of relocating or installing strong deadbolts on doors, installing a burglar alarm system, and reinforcing instructions about not opening the door to strangers. Many times, just your acknowledgment of what he or she is feeling, that it's not "all in your head," may diminish his or her paranoia.

If you determine that the person's paranoia isn't based in reality, then your loved one needs to be taken for professional consultation with his or her primary care physician or a geropsychiatrist, an expert in the emotional problems of older people.

HOARDING

Many older people grew up during the Great Depression and World War II, times of severely limited resources. Their experience is one of "making do" with what one has and making things last. Although they may now be able to afford to replace items or buy new things, their habits and worries may be so ingrained that it's difficult for them to throw away anything. Because you don't share their experience directly, you may feel that they're hoarding these items. You may be concerned about the older person's safety because the house is overcrowded with clutter and he or she risks falling, or you may be concerned about the risk of fire. Keep in mind, however, that what you call "hoarding" may be defined by the older adult in your life as "being thrifty" and "saving for a rainy day."

Many older people feel sentimental attachments to their possessions, and it may be hard for them to "let go." Help them to review the items and share with them the meaning that each piece has/had. Doing this may enable them to let go, to keep those things that are truly important as memories of days past and relinquish the rest, maybe donating these possessions to charity. This shared experience allows you to maintain your link with the past and strengthens your link with them, and it can provide you with cherished moments that you can share with the next generation. And, donating to charity helps older people to part with things, knowing that they can be useful to others who are less fortunate than they are. As always, your goal is to allow them to maintain their respect and personhood as you decrease your stress level and concerns for their safety and well-being.

IV

Getting
Help

15

Navigating Community Services

Many readers probably won't pick up a book like this until the older adult in their life has developed some serious health problems and become a source of concern for them. This chapter is here because your loved one may recover sufficiently to be independent again, at least to live in the same house or apartment as before with just a little extra help, and many of the resources described in this chapter are useful even after he or she recovers.

The U.S. health and social services systems have grown rather haphazardly. A diagram of the connections among all of the services a person might use during a lifetime or even one's "golden years" would look like one of those Rube Goldberg machines people used to joke about. These machines were incredibly complex contraptions that seemed to be designed to accomplish a simple task in the most complicated way possible. Every time a new health or social need was identified, a new service was created. Each new service was connected in some way to existing services but not necessarily in the most logical or efficient fashion. The result was and is an incredibly complex system, a maze of services and eligibility requirements that even health care professionals find confusing. Most of the time this system works for people despite its complexity, but when it fails, the result is bewilderment and frustration.

To maneuver skillfully through this maze, you need to know what services are available in your community and how to become a more active consumer of them. Because you picked up

*Because website addresses change frequently, some of the addresses provided here may no longer be valid. If you get a 404 message, try one of the Internet search engines to search for the organization by name.

this book, you've already begun to take charge of the care of your loved one. The information presented here is meant to help you take an even more active role.

One of the confusing aspects of community services is that the same service can have one or more names, different eligibility requirements, and various degrees of responsiveness to people's needs in different communities. "Dial a ride," for example, could be a commercial service developed by a local taxicab and limousine company or it could be a service that's supported by city or county taxes. "Meals at home" could be elegant but expensive or it could be plain but free. "Special transport services" could be for children, older people, or both. They could be prompt and courteous or rude and undependable. You simply can't tell from the name alone.

Getting the best-quality help requires effort. If our system were better integrated and more consumer oriented, it wouldn't require so much effort. Caregivers and their loved ones must become active, informed consumers. Persistence pays. Don't give up; you *can* make the system work for you.

BEING AN ACTIVE, INFORMED CONSUMER

Modifying the doctor–patient relationship is one way to explain how you can become a more active consumer. People in the medical profession inspire a certain amount of respect, even awe, that leaves most of us at a loss for words, especially challenging or disagreeing words. Part of becoming an active, informed consumer-caregiver is understanding what's going on—ask questions when you don't understand something, and encourage the older adult in your life to do the same. Despite the godlike image that's been built up about doctors, they don't know everything, and they do make mistakes. Medical knowledge has expanded so rapidly that no one, not even the most qualified physician, can be totally knowledgeable about every problem and every treatment, including surgery, medications, diet, exercise, and stress reduction.

When we're sick, these aren't comforting thoughts. We want someone to make us better as soon as possible. We want to place ourselves in the hands of someone whom we trust and respect. The idea that a doctor might not know something or could make a mistake is unsettling, but it's reality. It also may be unsettling to think that we have to make an effort to get to the bottom of things, but remember that the rewards, including peace of mind and higher self-esteem, outweigh the negative aspects.

Choosing a Doctor

Most people have several doctors—an eye doctor, a podiatrist, a heart specialist, and so forth—but it's still important to have a starting place when seeking health care, an entry point into the system, somewhere to go for checkups and preventive screening, a place to go to get ordinary problems taken care of and help for more complicated problems. This starting place is called primary care, which usually is provided by a primary care physician, a nurse practitioner, a family practice group, an internist, or a doctor at an ambulatory care center. How do you choose a primary care provider? Here are some suggestions:

- Ask acquaintances, friends, and relatives who are in the health care field whom they would recommend. They often know by experience or by word of mouth who are the best primary care providers. Other friends and relatives may be helpful, but their advice may be influenced more by the care provider's personality and reputation than by his or her actual expertise.
- Check with the local medical society. You can find the telephone number in the telephone book (look under "Physicians: Information Bureaus" or a similar listing). The medical society provides names and qualifications such as board certification but not a real evaluation of the individual's expertise.
- Check the Internet. For example, select a search engine, click on your state and locality, request doctor or physician listings, and find a site or sites that'll direct you to detailed information about the health care providers in your area.
- Consider the type of practice that you're most comfortable with. Do you want an old-fashioned family physician, a less-traditional wellness-oriented center, an impersonal but efficient clinic setting, or a more experienced but probably more expensive internist or geriatrician (a doctor who specializes in the care of older people)?

- Consider the cost of care. Can your loved one afford to pay for care? What kind of health insurance does he or she have? What limits does the insurance company place on types of care?

Once you and your loved one have selected a primary care provider, it's important to find out whether you've made a good choice. Consider the following criteria after visiting the practitioner several times. Is he or she:

- Easy to talk with so that you're comfortable discussing your concerns?
- A real listener, not someone who jumps to conclusions or tends to categorize patients by age, gender, personality type, or the like?
- Willing to refer you to another care provider—in other words, is he or she willing to admit having limits?
- Open minded and flexible, not rigid in his or her diagnostic or treatment approach?
- Knowledgeable, up to date, and willing to discuss alternatives with you?

Changing or Adding a Doctor

Some older people stay with the same physician they've had for years even though that physician isn't the best one for them. They're comfortable with the doctor, the office, and the routine. Simple inertia comes into play here—it's easier to keep doing the same thing than it is to make a change. There are good reasons to escape from this comfortable routine: when you or the older adult in your life isn't satisfied with the care provided, when you or the person no longer have full faith and trust in the physician, or when your loved one isn't getting better despite treatment.

At times, treatment is ineffective and can be improved but isn't because doctors are rushed, impatient, or don't want to "fine tune" the regimen. Some doctors, because they're only human, become discouraged. They may give up on the person psychologically; at this point they're no longer helpful to him or her. They may begin to question how much pain or how many symptoms your loved one really has if they can't figure out what's wrong. Even worse, they may decide that the person is simply old and that, whatever the problem is, it's just a sign of old age so there's nothing to be done. It may be difficult for you to act at such a demoralizing time, but you and your family member must not give up. Instead, find another doctor.

Adding a doctor sometimes is as simple as getting a second opinion. For example, your loved one has a problem that's difficult to diagnose. Some problems are very easy to diagnose—the symptoms present a clear pattern, and lab tests confirm the doctor's suspicions. Other problems aren't so easy to diagnose. When this happens, your loved one may need to consult a specialist, someone who specializes in particular types of problems.

You and the older adult in your life may find yourselves in the difficult position of being told that nothing more can be done for the person's condition. This is especially hard when you think that the treatment that's already been given should've been more effective. Don't accept the physician's opinion on face value—ask questions:

1. Why do you think nothing else can be done? This question is often avoided because we don't really want to hear an honest answer.
2. Is there anything that can still be done? Without consulting you and your loved one, the doctor may have concluded that he or she is too old, frail, or unmotivated to continue with more experimental, expensive, painful, or uncomfortable treatment.
3. Is there anywhere locally or across the country where research is being done on this problem? The doctor may not know, so contact the organization associated with the disease (for example, the American Cancer Society, the American Lung Association, the Alzheimer's Association, the National Parkinson Foundation) to find out who's doing research in your area. You can contact the National Institutes of Health (NIH) in Bethesda, Maryland, and request a list of active research programs on this particular problem (NIH also has a website, http://www.nih.gov). You may still find out that either there's nothing that can be done or the remaining alternatives really are too painful or exhausting for your loved one. At least you have the satisfaction of knowing that you've tried everything possible.

Getting the Most Out of an Office Visit

Think of a visit to your doctor or nurse practitioner as a consultation: Your loved one is concerned about his or her health and has come to the expert for advice and assistance. Because everyone responds to health concerns and problems in his or her own way, the health care practitioner needs to take enough time to assess the person's response and relate it to any other health problems he or she may have. Unfortunately, this doesn't always happen in the brief, often-hurried encounter that is called an office visit. A health care provider's quick, general examination, failure to ask enough questions or to listen to the answers, and a rush to judgment may lead to inappropriate treatment or treatment that conflicts with other treatments the person already is receiving.

You and the older adult in your life don't have to settle for inadequate care. Simply asking good questions often leads to better, more holistic care. The following are suggested, general questions either you or your family member can and should ask during an office visit:

- What do you think the problem is? What's wrong?
- Why do you think it's that particular problem?
- What are the symptoms so I can watch for them myself?
- What's the plan from this point on?

If the plan is to begin treatment or to continue seeking a diagnosis, ask these questions:

- What'll these tests tell you about the problem?
- What are the risks of these tests?
- What are the risks of this treatment (tests/drug)?
- What treatment do you recommend?
- How will this treatment take care of the problem?
- Is there anything I should know about preparing for treatment?
- How much will this cost?
- How will I know if it's working?
- How long should I continue with this treatment/drug before coming back? (Ask especially if it doesn't seem to be working.)
- Is it time to consult a specialist? If not now, when?

If your loved one is just going in for a checkup, you or the person can ask the following questions (these questions are especially important when the person is taking medication regularly or is being followed for a particular chronic problem):

- What is the overall plan for keeping (loved one/family member) as healthy as possible?
- How often and for what reason should (loved one/family member) return for preventive care (for example, occult blood test, blood pressure check, mammogram, prostate examination, cholesterol level)?
- What else in terms of diet, exercise, activity, stress reduction, lifestyle changes, and so forth should (loved one/family member) be doing to stay as healthy as possible?

Now that you have a good idea of what we mean by being an active consumer and advocate for yourself and your loved one, let's look at the most important services that are available to an older person.

FINDING HEALTH CARE SERVICES

Health Maintenance Organizations (HMOs)

HMOs were designed to save money based on the belief that prevention and early treatment and diagnosis would reduce the need for later, more expensive treatment. As HMOs have grown and prospered, their emphasis has shifted to saving money across the entire spectrum of health care services, from prevention to long-term care and, for some, making a tidy profit for their shareholders. When people join an HMO, they are asked to choose a primary care physician from the HMO's list. All of their care is arranged through this primary care provider. Even if the older adult in your life knows that a visit to a specialist is necessary, in most cases he or she must be referred by the primary care provider if the person wants the insurance plan to reimburse him or her for the consultation with the specialist. Sometimes approval from the HMO's home office is required as well.

Many older people are attracted to HMOs because they offer free or low-cost prescriptions and eyeglasses, a great benefit to people with chronic conditions that require continuing medication therapy. This attractiveness has limits, however. For example, in order to save money, some HMOs reduce the amount they pay their doctors or don't reimburse at all if the doctors order too many expensive lab tests or treatments for their enrolled patients. Approval of expensive surgical procedures and post-surgical therapies may be difficult, sometimes impossible, to obtain. People also may find themselves hurriedly discharged from the hospital or rehabilitation unit before they're ready to go home. Finally, some HMOs use high-pressure marketing tactics to enroll new members. These tactics may include gifts, free offers, and misleading information about the benefits of an HMO.

Despite these problems, some HMOs provide excellent care. Again, it is up to the consumer—you and/or the older adult in your life—to shop around and find the best plan. Your local newspaper or library may have the state regulatory agency's evaluations of the HMOs in your locale. You also can write or call the National Committee for Quality Assurance (NCQA) to find out the HMO's accreditation status (see the list of associations at the back of this book).

Preferred Provider Organizations (PPOs)

A different type of health plan also designed to save money is the PPO. PPOs provide a little more choice in physicians than HMOs do, but they may pay less of the final bill. For example, if your family member goes to a physician who's part of the PPO network, about 80% of the bill would be paid by the insurance plan, but only 60% would be paid if the physician weren't part of the network. Your state's department of insurance or insurance commissioner, local library, and the National Insurance Consumer Helpline may be able to help you choose a good plan (see the list of associations at the back of this book).

Public Health Department

The public health department is responsible for protecting the health of the community. Among its many tasks are testing water quality, inspecting restaurants, and educating the public about the transmission of AIDS. Most health departments offer services to individuals, although the type and amount vary widely from place to place. They usually offer free screenings for glaucoma, oral cancer, diabetes, and so forth, and free or low-cost flu and pneumonia immunizations.

Emergency Services

Like many of the other services described in this chapter, emergency services differ by locale. Living close to a major trauma center usually isn't necessary, but the response time of the local emergency team and distance to the nearest full-service hospital could make a difference in case of a heart attack, stroke, or other major medical crisis. Emergency telephone numbers should be posted next to the telephone in the kitchen and bedroom. You also should identify a person whom your loved one can call in case you're not available and write his or her telephone number in the same place as the emergency telephone numbers.

Telephone reassurance services, either automated or personal, can be used to check once or twice a day on the older person who lives alone. There's a predetermined procedure for notifying family, friends, or emergency services if the person fails to respond to the call. Check with local hospitals and referral services (see p. 263) if you can't find one nearby.

Your loved one can wear a Medic Alert identification bracelet or pendant, which contains information about his or her known allergies or chronic conditions. In case of an emergency, these bracelets or pendants provide vital information to the rescue team. Another alert system is a vial containing medical information similar to that on the Medic Alert bracelet that's placed in the person's refrigerator. Emergency personnel check the vial when they're called to the person's home.

Alarm systems are more expensive but provide added security for older people who live alone. In some assisted living facilities, bathrooms have an alarm button that, when pressed, summons immediate help from facility personnel. A different system uses a small alarm that the person can wear. Pressing the alarm activates a call for help. This is especially useful when a person has fallen and can't get up without help.

FINDING OTHER COMMUNITY SERVICES

Area Agency on Aging (AAA)

AAAs usually provide or support a wide array of community services from transportation to chore services. The staff of most AAAs know virtually all of the services that are available to older adults, and if they don't have the information, they can tell you where to find it. The telephone number of the local AAA is in the telephone book.

American Association of Retired Persons (AARP)

Anyone age 50 and over can become a member of AARP, even if they're not retired. AARP doesn't provide or support the kinds of hands-on help that AAAs do, but they do provide an array of useful services to older adults. Members receive a monthly news bulletin concerning important issues to older adults, including health care issues, and a magazine called *Modern Maturity*. AARP produces a number of helpful booklets and pamphlets on health insurance, home health care, long-term care, and the like. The organization also provides a pharmacy service that may reduce the cost of the older person's medications. AARP also offers group health, automobile, and home insurance policies. The health insurance program includes long-term care and home health coverage. The listings for AARP can be found in the list of associations at the back of the book.

Public Library

Your local public library contains a wealth of useful information for you and the older adult in your life, including government publications and reference books. The reference librarian can help you find the names and addresses of health-related organizations that may not be included in the list of associations at the back of this book. You may also find copies of the guidelines for care that are published by the federal Agency for Healthcare Research and Quality (formerly the Agency for Health Care Policy Research) and the American Medical Association's drug evaluations.

If you're seeking highly technical information (especially information about medications and the treatment of uncommon or unusual diseases), you may need to go to the nearest regional medical library or university library. The average person will find these libraries more complicated to use, but the librarians can help you get started. Unlike the public library, however, they may charge you for some services.

Referral Networks and Hotlines

During your information search, you'll probably find a telephone hotline or referral source that specializes in information for older adults and their families. Your local Area Agency on Aging may operate such a network or telephone hotline. Think of these hotlines as access to enormous lists of people and organizations to which you can turn for information about your particular problem.

If you have a computer, you can search for information on the Internet using one of the search engines and use the National Library of Medicine's information website Medline (access Medline for free from http://www.ncbi.nlm.nih.gov/PubMed) to find articles that are written for health care professionals.

Be careful using any information you find on the Internet, particularly from sources that aren't familiar to you, because not all of the information is accurate, and the source of the information may not be identified—usually a good sign that the material isn't very reliable.

Special Health-Related Community Organizations

All kinds of organizations have been created to help people with a particular problem. These include Alcoholics Anonymous, the Multiple Sclerosis Foundation, the American Diabetes Association, and the National Kidney Foundation. They can be even more specialized, such as the National Organization for Rare Disorders.

These organizations provide information, referral, and support and educational groups. Some publish high-quality, readable materials on health-related issues. Most keep current with research treatment options and policy issues but don't provide hands-on care, supplies, or equipment.

We've compiled a list for you (see the back of this book), but it's not comprehensive. Remember, you're an active, informed consumer—don't give up your search just because the organization you seek isn't on our list.

Support Groups

From groups that help people stop smoking to groups that help people deal with a diagnosis of terminal cancer, support groups can benefit both you and your loved one. Some support groups form to share information among their members, some to help people get through a crisis, and others provide continuing support. Longtime group members can offer practical tips, local information, and the wisdom that comes from experience.

If you or the older adult in your life decide to join a support group, choose one carefully. Some are organized primarily for the purpose of marketing hospital or physician services; some are led by incompetent, even destructive, individuals. The majority do just what's advertised—provide the support you and your loved ones need to get through a life transition. If making it to a meeting is difficult, you may be able to find an appropriate group on the Internet. The same caveats apply to these groups as to community groups.

FINDING FINANCIAL HELP

From income assistance to senior citizen's discounts, alert older people and their families can take advantage of quite a few sources of financial advice and assistance that are designed especially for older people. Advice from individuals or organizations who stand to gain financially from the relationship needs to be evaluated very carefully: stockbrokers, insurance salespeople,

HMO representatives, mortuary representatives, and a host of others may be honest, caring people or they may be thieving liars. A piece of advice often given but also often ignored may be helpful here: If it sounds too good to be true, it probably is.

Social Security

Explaining the Social Security system is a book unto itself. Instead, we'd like to clear up some common misunderstandings about Social Security: the source of the money that's used to pay for it, its original purpose, and the eligibility criteria for it.

Social Security benefits are the best-known and most widely available source of financial support for older people. Unlike some other sources of financial help, Social Security benefits are earned in much the same way that any insurance benefit is earned—they're not based on need but on age and earnings. The amount an older person receives is calculated from the length of time that the person worked and the amount that he or she earned. If the wage earner dies, his or her spouse is entitled to the earned benefits.

The Social Security taxes that are paid by people in the work force and by their employers are used to pay current benefits. Many people are concerned that the number of contributors to the Social Security fund may be too small in the future to support the large numbers of potential beneficiaries. As of this writing, the Social Security system is fully funded and a reliable, though modest, source of income for many older people.

Disability benefits also are available through the Social Security system but on a different basis. To be eligible for disability benefits, a person must have 1) enough earned work credits; 2) a disability, including very low vision, that prevents him or her from doing any kind of work; and 3) a disability that's expected to last 1 year or more or lead to death. The eligibility criteria are quite strict, but if you believe that your loved one is eligible, it's worth the effort to apply for the benefits. If benefits are denied, you or the older adult in your life has the right to appeal the decision.

Medicare

Medicare is a two-part (Part A and Part B) health insurance bene-fit for older people. Each part covers different things. People who are eligible for Social Security benefits are automatically eligible at age 65 for Medicare Part A (Part B isn't automatic). It's also pos-sible to pay for Part A if the person is 65 but not automatically el-igible. This may be a good idea if the person doesn't qualify for another type of health insurance. Part A pays for a portion of an older adult's hospital care, rehabilitation, and home health care after hospitalization, and hospice care for people with a terminal illness. Most people are surprised by the limitations of the cover-age. It's probably more accurate to say that Medicare *helps pay* for these basic health care needs than to say it *covers* these services. Getting supplemental health insurance that helps cover what Medicare doesn't is a good idea for most older Americans.

Medicare Part B is voluntary and available to anyone over age 65 who wants to enroll and pay the premium. Part B helps cover some services that aren't covered by Part A, including physicians' services.

Watch for Medicare enrollment periods and make sure your loved one is enrolled for both Part A and Part B. The older person in your life needs to apply for Medicare (if he or she isn't receiving Social Security or Railroad Retirement Board benefits) 3 months before his or her 65th birthday (that's the beginning of the 7-month initial enrollment period) or if the person needs regular dialysis or a kidney transplant. By applying early, the person avoids a delay in the start of Part B coverage. Your loved one can apply by contacting any Social Security Administration office or, if the person or his or her spouse worked for the railroad, the Rail-road Retirement Board. If the person doesn't enroll during this 7-month period, he or she will have to wait to enroll until the next general enrollment period. General enrollment periods are held from January 1 to March 31 of each year, and Part B coverage starts the following July. If he or she waits 12 months or longer to sign up, the premiums generally will be higher.

Careful record keeping is important when filing for these benefits. Although the time limit for filing claims is fairly generous, time can go by quickly when an older person is ill, so it's best to deal with the claim immediately. Make sure that your loved one is billed only for the services that he or she received. A considerable amount of billing for services not received has occurred in the past. Alert citizens can reduce the amount of fraud related to these programs by reporting it immediately to the Inspector General's Office hotline (800-368-5779). Eliminating fraud helps keep Medicare costs down. You can get more information about Medicare from the Health Care Financing Administration (HCFA) website (http://www.hcfa.gov/medicare/mcarcnsm. htm), but keep in mind that regulations change frequently.

Supplemental Security Income (SSI)

SSI often is confused with Social Security because of the similar name and because it's administered by the Social Security Administration. As the name indicates, SSI provides additional or supplemental monthly income payments to low-income people who are old, blind, or disabled. It's not funded by the payroll taxes that are paid into the Social Security fund.

A very careful assessment of the older person's income and assets determines his or her eligibility for SSI benefits. Very few assets are exempt: the home the person owns, a modest car, a burial plot, and some insurance policies. Money in savings accounts is not exempt. The precise amounts and sources allowed change frequently. To find out what they are and how to apply for SSI, call the local Social Security office or speak to the person's social worker or case manager.

One of the frustrating aspects of these eligibility requirements is their strictness: If your loved one's income or assets are just a few dollars over the limit, he or she will be denied benefits. Inquire about transferring assets to another account. The rules about transferring assets also change frequently, but, if done correctly and legally, they may be some help in eventually meeting the eligibility requirements.

Your loved one can't receive SSI benefits unless he or she applies for them. It's estimated that more than 2 million older people who are eligible for SSI benefits have never received any because they've never requested them. The same is true for food stamps and subsidized housing. The eligibility requirements are similar to those governing SSI.

Medicaid

Medicaid provides assistance in paying health care costs for low-income people, usually those who are eligible for SSI. Because Medicaid is a joint program between federal and state governments, a person's eligibility criteria and benefits will vary from one state to another. For example, Arizona has its own state program and doesn't offer Medicaid at all.

In general, Medicaid will pay for the following services if they're determined to be necessary and the older person can't afford them:

> Hospital stay
> Nursing facility care
> Home health care
> Clinic and doctor visits
> Dental care
> Prescription medications
> Eyeglasses

FINDING TRANSPORTATION

Limited vision, shaky hands, slow reflexes, or a crisis of confidence after a minor accident or close call can cause an older person to give up driving or be asked to give it up. Once-trivial tasks such as picking up a prescription or shopping for groceries become major undertakings without access to a car. Independent living is threatened. Because you want to encourage independent living, it's worth the effort to find alternatives to the person driving or your driving the person everywhere. The following suggestions may help you and your loved one put together a workable transportation system:

- Talk with other older people in the neighborhood, especially those who don't drive. Find out how they get around.
- Call the Area Agency on Aging. They may have some suggestions or be able to refer you to another agency that can help.
- Find out if the community has a senior center. Many senior centers offer bus or van transportation.
- Check the local city or county bus schedule. They may offer senior citizen's discounts on off-peak hours.
- Call a local taxi company. They may offer senior citizen's discounts.
- Find out if your community has jitney or car services that carry people to local malls, supermarkets, and doctor's offices.
- Call the local hospitals, health centers, and doctors' offices; some offer transportation. Beware of choosing a health care provider on this basis alone, however.
- Investigate home delivery services. Meals, medications, and other items can be delivered to the person's door.
- Banking and shopping, even for groceries, can be done by telephone, mail, or computer.
- Arrange emergency backup transportation with a friend or neighbor. Although it's difficult to depend on them for routine transportation, they're usually willing to help out in a pinch.

FINDING SOCIAL AND RECREATIONAL RESOURCES

Living a full life requires human contact and purposeful activity as well as maintenance of mental, physical, and financial health. There are so many activities in which an older adult can participate that the best that we can do is list those that are designed specifically for older people. The choice of group to get involved in or even to get involved at all should be left to the older person.

Golden Age clubs and senior centers can provide all of the activity a person could ask for, including crafts, trips, entertainment, and parties. Frequently, a nutritious lunch is served, which is especially important for the older person who no longer wants to cook or who doesn't eat well at home alone. Many churches and temples offer congregate meals at which older adults can share food and companionship several times a week.

Using the talents and skills they've acquired over the years, people belonging to groups like the Retired and Senior Volunteers

Program (RSVP) and Service Corps of Retired Executives (SCORE) provide assistance to younger people who want to start their own businesses. Likewise, Foster Grandparents offer love to children whose grandparents don't live nearby or don't have grandparents at all. (For more information on these programs and Senior Corps, contact the Corporation for National Service at http://www.cns.gov.) Many political, religious, and civic groups depend on older adults for staffing. Volunteers in schools, nursing facilities, and hospitals often are retired people who want to give something back to the community.

16   Finding Home Health Care Services

The importance of home health care often is underrated. Maybe it's because it occurs behind the closed doors of people's homes, or maybe it's because few people realize how much care can be provided at home. Home health care may become the core of the U.S. health care system because so many services that have been provided in hospitals and nursing facilities can be provided at home, and many people do as well or even better when cared for at home.

Although people of all ages can receive home health care, a large portion of people getting home health care are older people. We've often heard caregivers say things like,

> My father called us from the hospital. He said, "I'll be going home tomorrow." I asked, "So soon?" He said, "Yes, and they want to know if there'll be someone who can stay with me."

As people leave the hospital quicker and sicker than ever before, families often are called on to provide help at home. Another story that we've heard frequently is one that we first heard on the radio:

A man took his wife to an outpatient surgical center for an abdominal procedure. He saw her briefly after she came out of the operating room and then settled back to wait for what he thought would be hours before she was ready to go home. A few minutes later, a nurse approached him and said, "Your wife is ready to go home." The man was shocked. "Already?!" he asked. The nurse looked at him without expression and said, "Yes, we need the bed." The stunned husband asked, "Is she really ready to go home?" The nurse replied, "She'll be just fine. Bring your car around."

His wife was still groggy as the man and the nurse bundled her into the back seat of the car for what he feared would be an uncomfortably bumpy

271

ride home. Before they left the surgicenter, his wife began to vomit. The man ran inside the building and told the nurse that his wife was retching. The nurse gave him a bucket to catch the vomit and sent him on his way.

The man then described how he had to arrange for nurses to stay with his wife for several days because he had to work and couldn't stay home to care for her.

Nowadays, people leave hospitals, nursing facilities, and clinics with staples, drains, catheters, IV's, and other equipment still in them/attached to them—equipment that used to be considered reason enough to keep them in a care facility. The shift from hospital to home has been neither slow nor subtle. Instead, it's been a swift and powerful response by care facilities to their need to save money by reducing the number of days a person spends in a hospital or nursing facility. This across-the-board policy change has moved a lot of care into people's homes and placed more responsibility on the person and his or her family, many of whom aren't prepared to handle scenarios similar to the one in the preceding paragraphs.

HOME HEALTH CARE PROS AND CONS

The shift from hospital and nursing facility to home care has advantages and disadvantages. Under the right circumstances, home health caregiving can be far more satisfying for both the care receiver and caregiver. These circumstances vary for every older adult and his or her family.

Pros

People Prefer Home over Hospital

Most people would rather be cared for at home than in a traditional care facility, unless they're truly unable to manage at home, are afraid to be alone, or have very poor living conditions. It's surprising how often families and health care professionals ignore this preference when they're trying to help an older person choose between home and inpatient care.

More Control

Older people have much more control over their lives at home than in an institution. From being able to lock the bedroom door to having a midnight snack, care at home allows older people their privacy, independence, and choice, all very precious commodities.

More Personal and Individualized Care

It's hard to imagine any place that's more personal than one's own home. Personal possessions and individual style are much more easily accommodated at home than they are in a care facility. More important, whether care is given by informal (family, friend, or other) or formal (paid) caregivers, it's given to one person at a time, not to a group of people. The focus on one individual is likely to result in a more comprehensive assessment and tailoring of the treatment to the person's needs. It's also likely to be more holistic because the individual is seen in his or her own surroundings, which makes it far more likely that the person will be treated like an individual than like a case. Formal caregivers also are more likely to recognize the contributions and needs of the family members who are providing assistance.

At home, the older person is far more likely to be involved in housekeeping and other ordinary activities of daily living, all of which help a person maintain a feeling of belonging and usefulness. And, with some exceptions, home is a far more healthful environment than institutions are. Being at home encourages people to function and be involved at the highest level that's possible for them rather than just being a passive recipient of caregiving.

It's Easier to Maintain Attachments

Family, friends, and neighbors are more likely to be close by when the older person is cared for at home. The person also has more opportunities to continue to feel like he or she is a part of family life. Visits don't have to be planned ahead of time, and they can be as long or as short as both parties want them to be. This arrangement is less tiring for both the older person and his or her family.

It's Less Expensive

Unless your family member needs round-the-clock nursing care and expensive equipment, home health care usually is less costly than the care provided in an institution. This is because a lot of health care is given at home by informal providers, primarily the older person's family members and friends.

Lower Infection Rate

People are less likely to develop infections at home than in the hospital (*nosocomial infection*). The recent increase in the number of antibiotic-resistant infectious organisms makes it even more important for an older person to recuperate at home rather than in a hospital or nursing facility.

Cons

Despite the many advantages of health care at home, the disadvantages will outweigh the advantages for some people.

Increased Family Responsibility

There's no question that older adults, their families, and other loved ones find themselves with more responsibility for caregiving if the infirm older person is cared for at home. Although much of this work can be delegated to others if the older adult is eligible for government- or insurance-covered home health care services or can afford to pay for formal caregiving, the ultimate responsibility usually remains with the family. Some families handle this very well, and even prefer it. Other families find it stressful.

Household Disruption

The older person's mental and physical conditions, in combination with the dynamics of the household in which care is given, determine the degree to which home care is easy or difficult to incorporate into the household routine. Another factor, of course, is whether the older person will stay in his or her own home or will move in with other family members. The latter situation may create more discord unless it is planned well and both parties are flexible. The daily routines of family members and the amount of space available in the house also can make a big difference.

Weekend and Night Coverage

The older person who needs round-the-clock assistance is much harder to care for at home than the individual who needs help only during the day. Obviously, the daily expense of paying three 8-hour shifts is much greater than one 8-hour shift or one 4-hour shift, which usually is sufficient for older people who need help with their morning personal care routines. It's easy to understand why hospital and nursing facility care is so expensive when the cost of weekend and holiday care is added to round-the-clock care. Many families solve this problem by providing night and weekend care themselves or by hiring live-in help.

Coordinating Care

Coordinating complex total health care at home can be quite daunting. Imagine hiring and scheduling an aide to give a bath, a nurse to check heart and lungs and give pressure sore (*decubitus*) care, and a physical therapist to teach the person how to walk again (*gait training*), add obtaining all of the equipment, supplies, and medications that will be needed daily, and then add doing the laundry, cooking meals, paying the bills, and housekeeping to this list. Obviously, there's a lot to coordinate.

Supervising Care

Someone has to make sure that all of the caregivers show up as scheduled and provide the care contracted for. A frail, ill older person may not be able to do these things effectively, so the family or the person's care manager often assumes this responsibility. We'll talk a little more about care managers (perhaps more familiar to you as "case managers") later in the chapter.

Quality Control

The care that's provided by this long list of health care providers, all having different skills, is harder to supervise when it's provided in a person's home than it is on a nursing care unit of an institution where it can be readily observed. Home health care agencies supervise their staff, but it's a more random and less-continuous kind of supervision than it is in an institution.

Slower Emergency Response Time

Informal and formal caregivers have to be prepared to deal with an emergency in the home. Unlike in a hospital or nursing facility, in the home, emergency response teams aren't immediately available. You may be the only person available to call 911 or take the older adult in your life to a hospital emergency room.

WHAT KIND OF CARE CAN BE GIVEN AT HOME?

The kind of care that can be provided at home is expanding rapidly as more and more ways to provide complex care at home emerge.

Post-Hospitalization Care

It wasn't too long ago that the main reason for home care was follow-up care after a person was discharged from a hospital. The individual might need blood pressure or blood sugar monitoring, complex dressing changes, help in learning how to manage a colostomy (an artificial opening through which bowel elimination occurs), or other continuing care. Sometimes, an aide to help the person bathe or shower is needed as are therapies of various kinds, depending on the original reason for hospitalization.

Post-Nursing Facility Care

Nursing facilities are offering more rehabilitative and post-hospital recovery care (subacute care) with the expectation that the person will go home. Continuing care at home often is needed after discharge from a nursing facility, just as it is for people who are discharged from a hospital.

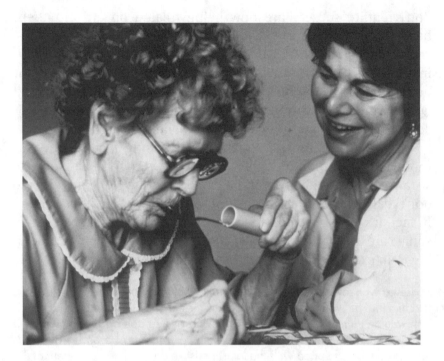

Rehabilitation

Many people who are discharged from a hospital or nursing facility still need a great deal of rehabilitation to return to their previous level of independence. Much of this rehabilitation can be provided either in the person's home or at an outpatient clinic that the person visits several times a week. This type of care is particularly valuable for frail older people who can't maintain the rapid pace and high demands of inpatient rehabilitation but can progress if they're allowed to do so at a slower pace.

HOME HEALTH CARE AS AN
ALTERNATIVE TO HOSPITAL OR NURSING FACILITY

Older adults with problems that once meant automatic admission to a hospital are now being cared for at home. For example, people who have had small strokes or acute abdominal problems that don't require surgery are now being treated on an outpatient basis. Immediate care is given in the emergency room (trauma center) or a surgicenter, and then individuals are sent home with instructions on how to care for themselves and when to call for help or return to the hospital. Some people think that this trend will continue to the point that only major surgery, trauma care for accident victims, and intensive care will be done in hospitals.

The same thing is happening in nursing facility care, although not as rapidly. People who don't need round-the-clock assistance and monitoring can be cared for at home. Many people don't realize how much can be done at home for an older person. In fact, it's possible to arrange for in-home round-the-clock personal care assistance and daily check-ups by a nurse. The following is an example of what can be done at home:

Roosevelt was severely injured in a car accident when he was 18. His doctors told him that he would be in a wheelchair for the rest of his life but that his injury wouldn't limit his ability to earn a living or manage on his own. After 3 years of intensive rehabilitation, Roosevelt was ready to be on his own. His apartment was equipped with the latest assistive devices, and a student at the local community college was hired to help him get out of bed and shower and dress in the morning and help him with the reverse process in the evening. Roosevelt had a good job and felt confident about his future.

Roosevelt's family lived nearby and visited often. During one visit, his mother told him that his diabetic grandfather had to have his leg amputated below the knee. "I guess he'll have to go to a nursing home now," his mother said. "Why?" asked Roosevelt. "He won't be able to take care of himself any more," his mother replied. "Why not? He'll still have one leg that works, won't he?" asked Roosevelt. "Neither of my legs work, and I'm doing just fine. Why can't he?"

Roosevelt's grandfather succeeded in learning how to walk using his artificial leg and returned to his own home. However, he continued to have trouble controlling his diabetes and needed supervision for this and several other chronic health problems. His family arranged for him to receive maintenance care, a type of home health care.

Maintenance Care

Many older people need just a little help with personal care or guidance in managing their health care needs—reminders to take their medication or someone to monitor their condition and make adjustments in their regimen. This can be managed very easily at home. Others are in stable condition but need much more intensive therapy. For example, people with chronic kidney disease often can be maintained on home dialysis; people with cancer may need intravenous nutrition or chemotherapy. These treatments can be given at home. In fact, there are home health care agencies that specialize in providing these intensive therapies.

Respite Care

Home care agencies can provide temporary substitutes for family members who need a rest, or respite, from their caregiving responsibilities. From volunteer companions who stay just a few hours so that the primary caregiver can go shopping to round-the-clock help so that the family can go on vacation, respite care provides a welcome break.

Hospice Care

People with terminal illnesses can be cared for at home rather than in an institution through hospice care. Hospice care allows them to die peacefully at home rather than in an emergency room or operating room. Both the person with the illness and his or her family members have an opportunity to prepare emotionally and spiritually for death with the guidance of hospice chaplains and counselors. Necessary care isn't withheld but is focused on keeping the person as comfortable as possible rather than on trying the most extreme kinds of treatment to keep the person alive. This is called palliative care.

AVAILABLE SERVICES IN HOME HEALTH CARE

Most people who choose to be cared for at home really need a package of services, not a single service. These services may include the following:

1. *Personal Care.* Personal care is help with bathing, grooming, getting dressed, using the toilet, and eating, which usually is provided by nursing assistants or home health aides.
2. *Diagnostic Work.* A nurse can draw blood and collect urine, stool, and wound drainage specimens during a home visit. Portable

X-ray machines can be brought to the home as can heart monitors that are connected to the doctor's office by telephone. Laptop computers can be used to discuss problems with a nurse or doctor who's miles away. Doctors even make home visits in some communities.

3. *Treatment.* Treatment services usually are provided by health care professionals, many of whom specialize. Intravenous therapy, home dialysis, ostomy care, heart monitoring, skin and wound care, physical therapy, speech therapy, psychotherapy and counseling, health instruction, nutritional guidance, spiritual guidance, and more can be brought to the person's home.

4. *Equipment and Supplies.* Medications, oxygen, intravenous equipment, heart monitors, breathing equipment, canes, walkers, wheelchairs, hospital beds, lifts, commodes, and other supplies can be rented or purchased for the home.

5. *Home Maintenance.* Homemakers can be brought into a person's home to help with laundry and housecleaning. Some homemakers shop and prepare meals for older, homebound people. Home repair services and transportation services also may be purchased.

If the older adult in your life is in a hospital or nursing facility, a social worker or care manager will help you decide which services he or she will need at home and make arrangements for them. If your loved one is at home, however, his or her doctor probably will direct you to a community agency that can arrange for home health services. However, because they can afford private assistance, their particular problem isn't covered by the available services (for example, Alzheimer's disease), or there's no service available in their community, some people with home care needs "fall between the cracks"—they're not eligible for this kind of assistance. When this happens, family members can make the arrangements themselves or they can hire a private care manager to help them.

CARE MANAGEMENT

Many older people complain that they are exhausted by the "parade" of formal caregivers coming to their home. The home health nurse, home health aide, physical therapist, occupational therapist, equipment supplier, and care manager may appear at various times during a single day. Unless all of this is well coordinated, it can seem like a three-ring circus in desperate need of a ringmaster. The "ringmaster" who coordinates all of the various caregivers and suppliers may be a family member, a home health nurse, a social worker, or a care manager.

You may ask why the person's doctor isn't the coordinator. Although doctors usually sign the orders for home health care services, in general, they aren't involved in arranging and coordinating them. In fact, often they aren't very well informed about the details of home health care services and the eligibility requirements, which is a specialty in itself. Instead, they depend on whomever takes responsibility for the coordination of these services to report any problems to them.

The care manager is a new kind of health care professional. As is typical in health care, you can't just ask for a care manager because there are so many different kinds. We'll begin with a description of an ideal care manager and then list some of the things you and the older adult in your life need to know about his or her care manager.

The ideal care manager is a health care professional who has an in-depth understanding of the person's health problems, the kind of care that's needed, and the entire spectrum of services that are available. The care manager also should be able to help your loved one meet eligibility requirements for these services, put together the most economical package of services without short-changing the person's health needs, pull these services together so that they don't conflict or leave gaps, supervise the care to make sure it's of the highest quality, and act as an advocate for your loved one if a problem arises.

Not surprising, many care managers fall far short of this ideal. The following are some questions grouped in categories that you can ask to gain a better understanding of what you can and can't expect from a care manager.

Preparation

Care managers may be social workers, nurses, or generic care managers. Social workers understand the economic implications of the person's health care needs particularly well, but a nurse is likely to better understand the course of the illness. Generic care managers probably are most familiar with the different services available and how to obtain them.

Employer

Does the care manager work for you or for someone else? You'll want to know whose interests are primary to the care manager: the older person's interests or those of the insurance company, health care organization, or HMO that hired the care manager.

Goal of Care Management

Although every health care provider tries to help a person get better or at least to be as comfortable as possible, there are other goals that may not be as obvious but are important. Is the care manager trying to find the highest-quality services available at any cost, or is the care manager trying to put together the most economical package, with its quality secondary? Will the care manager cut corners to keep the cost down, or will he or she ignore cost implications? Will the care manager consider every agency in the community or only the ones that are associated with his or her employer or the ones that are most familiar to the care manager?

Scope of Care Management

Will the care manager continue to work with you and your loved one, or is this a temporary relationship? Although there's a lot of talk about "the seamless continuum of care," in fact, there are many beginnings and endings to relationships with various caregivers when a person moves from one care setting to another.

You'll also want to know whether the care manager can help your loved one with the whole range of needs that he or she has or can help with only one aspect. For example, some are experts in long-term care but they aren't prepared to help in an emergency or if a complex problem arises that requires the attention of medical specialists.

Sources of Home Health Care Assistance

It's helpful for you and your loved one to know a little about the types of organizations that provide home health care services. This section doesn't list every source, but you'll get an idea of the various sources that are available in the community. Keep in mind, however, that the older adult in your life may not be eligible for them or may not be able to afford all of them.

There are many nonprofit agencies that provide home health care. Many depend on contributions as well as fees and support from local governments to operate and are likely to focus on meeting the needs of underserved people in the community. Visiting Nurse Associations (VNAs) are the main nonprofit agency. VNAs are nonprofit organizations that are supported by the fees they charge and by contributions from sources such as the United Way. Usually they're accredited in the same way as are most hospitals and are committed to serving the needs of people in the community.

The wide array of government-operated services have strict eligibility requirements based on where a person lives, his or her income level, and the person's particular health problem. These agencies often provide a package of services to those who are eligible, however.

Almost half of the home health care agencies in the United States are run on a for-profit basis. This operating style produces a tendency to focus on the most lucrative part of the market: the care that's reimbursed by private insurers, HMOs, and Medicare. Some for-profits are local, whereas others are part of regional or national chains.

Hospitals and nursing facilities have become interested in providing home health care, as have HMOs, although they frequently contract with other agencies rather than provide the care themselves. The opportunities to improve the continuity of care between institution and home are a potential advantage of this kind of arrangement.

Judging the Quality of Home Health Care

Good quality is particularly elusive in home health care. It's hard to define and even harder to judge, especially by the consumer. Is it worth the effort? Consider the following example of a woman who got poor-quality home health care because of inadequate care management:

Elvira lived alone in a small apartment that was part of a huge public housing complex for older people. The low rent and her frugal ways made it possible for her to get by with a very small Social Security check. Her husband had been killed in a construction accident years ago, and Elvira was used to taking care of herself.

Elvira developed a few chronic health problems, but she took good care of herself and the problems were under control. Then, she fell and broke her hip. It required extensive surgery.

Elvira was discharged from the hospital to a nursing facility for 6 weeks of rehabilitation. Her progress was slow but steady. The social worker at the nursing facility told her that, although she had to be discharged because her HMO would no longer cover the expense of her stay at the nursing facility, she could continue to receive therapy at home. Elvira looked forward to going home and was so excited about it that she forgot to ask questions about how she would manage at home.

Elvira went home in a taxi. She was proud of the way that she could get around with her walker and that she needed only a little help from the taxi driver. She was tired when she got to her apartment and fell asleep almost immediately. Elvira woke up at 6 P.M. She didn't have much food in her apartment, just some frozen bread and instant coffee. After fixing a couple slices of toast and a cup of coffee, she went to bed and slept until morning.

Elvira awoke stiff and achy. She made more coffee and toast and went back to bed. She expected a therapist to call on her, but no one came all weekend. Elvira tried to call the social worker at the nursing facility, but no one was available during the weekend. Her pain was worse, and her medication had run out, so she slept most of the day.

By Monday, Elvira was frantic. Her pain was almost unbearable. She was stiff and sore and feeling lightheaded from having eaten so little. She didn't know who was supposed to help her so she called the nursing facility again and left a message for her social worker. Later that afternoon, the social worker returned Elvira's call. Elvira burst into tears as she tried to describe what had happened. The social worker investigated the problem and found that a new secretary had typed in the wrong discharge date on the requests for home health care services.

Elvira's problem was solved the following day. All of the equipment and therapists arrived. The home health care nurse told her that it was a miracle she hadn't fallen again from lightheadedness. She also said that it'd take some time for her to regain the strength and flexibility that she'd lost since being discharged and to heal the skin areas that had begun to break down from lying on them so long. Luckily, no permanent damage had been done.

The following are guidelines (adapted from professionals' guidelines, including care managers') you can use to judge the quality of a home health care agency (see also the handy checklist at the end of the chapter):

1. A license from the state is required, but it's only an indication that the agency has met the basic (minimum) standards.
2. Certification from Medicare and Medicaid indicates that their basic standards have been met.
3. Accreditation from the Joint Commission on Accreditation of Health Care Organizations (JCAHO) and the Community Health Accreditation Program (CHAP), which accredit home health care agencies—an agency's willingness to undergo the rigorous scrutiny of these accreditors is a sign of good quality.
4. Recommendations from objective doctors, social workers, nurses, therapists, care managers and other health care professionals—be skeptical of the recommendations of people with a financial stake in an agency or who have friends and colleagues who work for the agency.
5. Recommendations from wise and knowledgeable friends based on their own observations and experience with an agency.
6. Availability of services 7 days a week, including evenings, nights, weekends, and holidays—illness does not take a day off!
7. Family-centered care—interest in the entire family, not just in the older person
8. The agency's responsiveness to inquiries, concerns, and needs
9. That continuity of care is provided—it's important for you to see the same nurse, aide, or therapist each time one is sent to your home. They shouldn't be rotated.
10. A philosophy of service to the older adult, his or her family, and the community; and pride in the high quality of these services, not just an emphasis on the agency's ability to turn a profit or to pinch pennies.

Checklist for Good-Quality Home Health Care

Ask the individual who is arranging the home health care services for an evaluation of the agency or agencies that have been chosen, and discuss this with your loved one's doctor, social worker, nurses, therapists, and care manager. After service begins, observe the caregivers and discuss with the older person what level of quality is being provided. It's important to be an active advocate, not a passive bystander or one who just pays the bills without asking questions.

Licensing and Accreditation

❏   Is the agency licensed in your state?

❏   Is the agency certified by Medicare and Medicaid?

❏   Is the agency accredited by JCAHO or CHAP?

❏   Is this agency recommended by objective, knowledgeable sources?

Responsiveness to Needs

❏   What type of care is available?

❏   Are services available 7 days a week, including evenings, nights, and weekends?

❏   Do staff concern themselves with the whole family, not just the older adult?

❏   Will you see the same nurse, aide, or therapist, or are they rotated?

❏   How are the concerns and complaints of the person and his or her family handled?

❏   How often do agency staff communicate with the older person's primary care provider?

❏   Do staff respond to all of the health care needs of the person or only to those for which they were originally sent to the home?

Once Service Has Begun

❏   Do staff arrive on time?

❏   Are staff responsive to the person's needs?

❏   Do staff discuss the person's concerns or problems willingly and knowledgeably?

❏   Are staff courteous to and respectful of the older person and his or her family members?

17

Making the Nursing Facility Decision

Ten of the most dangerous words in the English language are, "Promise me you'll never put me in a nursing home." Ten even more dangerous words are the response, "I would never do that to you, no matter what." Consider Tomoko's dilemma:

The idea of being placed in an American nursing facility terrified Tomoko's mother. Tomoko thought, "She'll never be comfortable there. Strangers will do intimate things to her. The heavy American food will make her ill. No one will understand her." Tomoko assured her mother that she would never put her in a nursing facility.

Last year, Tomoko's father died after a long battle with pancreatic cancer. Her mother took care of him the entire time, and he died peacefully at home. Since that time, Tomoko's mother had a third stroke. The first two left little residual damage, but the third stroke was a major one that left her unable to speak or care for herself. Her mother was about to be discharged from the hospital, and Tomoko wanted to bring her home.

Tomoko and her husband have three young children. The oldest child is very ill with leukemia. They live in a tiny house that they can barely afford because of the medical bills. Her husband works 15 hours a day so that Tomoko can stay home with their youngsters during the week. On weekends, when her husband is home, Tomoko works two 12-hour shifts as a registered nurse. The financial problems have placed a great strain on their marriage and Tomoko fears they may separate, leaving her with full responsibility for the children. Her husband believes that her mother belongs in a nursing facility and will not listen to Tomoko's pleas that "it would kill her to be in a nursing home."

Tomoko is distraught. Her loyalties to mother and husband seem to be in direct conflict. Should she break her promise and place her mother in a nursing facility? Or should she upset her husband by bringing her to live in their small house? Even if she doesn't consider her own needs (and she should), Tomoko can't come up with a solution to her dilemma that meets the needs of her husband and her mother, both of whom she loves very much.

Tomoko's dilemma is a common one. She wants the best for all of the members of her family, but she feels caught between her parent and her spouse and bound by her earlier promises. Sometimes these dilemmas can be worked out by sitting down with everyone involved and discussing the problem. At other times, a caring and concerned outside party brings a new perspective:

Fortunately, Tomoko had a good and wise friend who had recently experienced a similar dilemma. Her friend had done a lot of homework, reading books from the library, publications from AARP (the American Association for Retired Persons), speaking with her own mother's care manager, and visiting nearby nursing facilities. Tomoko's friend found a very small, well-run facility that catered to older Japanese Americans who needed personal care and 24-hour supervision. The meals they served were a combination of Japanese and American dishes that seemed to please the residents and conform to their dietary restrictions. Their mothers could share a room, and the two friends could share the job of visiting and ensuring that their mothers were well cared for. The facility had none of the stereotypical characteristics of a nursing facility that had frightened Tomoko's mother. With her friend's support, Tomoko felt that she could place her mother there without violating her mother's trust.

Making the Decision

Making the decision to place a loved one in a nursing facility is a very personal experience. What works for one family may not work at all for another family. Even within a family, what's best for one family member may not be best for another. This chapter looks at this often-emotional time in some detail, beginning with making the decision for or against nursing facility placement, carefully selecting a nursing facility, preparing the older person for the transition, active visiting after placement, and, finally, considering the reasons why a family member may be taken out of a nursing facility.

The use of nursing facilities to care for older and disabled people as well as for rehabilitation and short stays after hospitalization has increased dramatically in the United States. There were five times as many people living in nursing facilities in 1990 as there were in 1950: 15 million in 1990 versus 300,000 in 1950. There are more nursing facility beds in the U.S. than there are hospital beds, and 20% of all health care costs for people over age 65 can be attributed to nursing facility care—not an inconsequential piece of the health care pie.

Why People Fear Nursing Facilities

Of all of the health care decisions we make for ourselves and our loved ones, deciding whether to place a loved one in a nursing facility often is one of the hardest to make. This decision is fraught with emotional trauma for both the family and the older person for many reasons.

Specter of the 19th-Century Poorhouse—The specter of the 19th-century poorhouse, where destitute older people ended their days continues to haunt us. These poorhouses were dumping grounds for unwanted elderly people—warehouses in which to store them until they died. They were dismal, depressing places that most people avoided if they could.

Unscrupulous Operators—Several events led to an increase in the number of nursing facilities and a much greater entrepreneurial interest in them as possible sources of profit for their owners:

- The advent of Social Security reduced the number of destitute older people.
- Federal support of hospital construction was expanded to include nursing facility construction.
- The creation of Medicaid, which pays for almost half of all nursing facility costs.
- The emptying of state mental hospitals, which once housed many cognitively impaired older people (people with dementia).

The outcome of these and other events was a great increase in demand for nursing facility beds and a better, although still inadequate, way to pay for them. Unfortunately, the profit motive overwhelmed the caregiving motive for some nursing facility operators. Attempts to save money led to practices such as cramming three meals into an 8-hour shift so that the facilities wouldn't have to pay additional workers, neglecting and abusing residents, and embezzling their assets. Although media attention and government regulation have eliminated the worst of these practices, the negative image of nursing facilities persists and, in fact, taints the entire industry. It also frightens people considering nursing facility placement for themselves or their loved ones.

Promises Made Long Ago—Like Tomoko in the vignette, many people have promised older family members who are afraid of nursing facilities that they would never have to live in one. Although these promises were made in good faith, circumstances change, and it sometimes becomes difficult or impossible to keep these promises. This leads to feelings of guilt on the part of the caregiver and of abandonment on the part of the older person.

Abandonment—The history of nursing facilities as dumping grounds for unwanted older people and the effects of promises made long ago together can make the older person feel abandoned by his or her family if the person is placed in a nursing facility. For the same reasons, many families avoid placing an older relative in a nursing facility because they think it's tantamount to abandonment. The sense of abandonment is only reinforced by families and loved ones who fail to visit the person.

A Place to Die—Again, the image of the nursing facility as a place to go to die haunts people who anticipate placement. Most people don't know that the number of so-called live discharges home, that is, people who return home after a short stay, has increased steadily since the early 1990s.

Reminder of One's Own Mortality—Placing an older family member in a nursing facility reminds younger family members of their eventual fate: old age and possible nursing facility placement. This confrontation with the possible future can be very unsettling, especially in America's youth-oriented society.

Loss of Cherished Freedom and Independence—Older people with chronic illnesses and disabilities can find themselves giving up many of the privileges and freedoms of adulthood after being placed in a nursing facility. So long as they remain at home they get to keep the freedom and independence that most of us don't appreciate until they are taken away—for example, the freedom to eat a meal at whatever time we like, the freedom to bathe at night instead of in the morning, the freedom to stay in bed until noon on Saturday just because we feel like it, the freedom to watch television at 3 A.M. In all but the most homelike facilities, these freedoms are lost.

Understanding why we have so many negative feelings about nursing facility placement helps us sort out which concerns

Is a Nursing Facility the Right Choice?

Yes, if the older person needs:

Special therapies or equipment that can't be provided at home

24-hour monitoring because of an unstable medical condition

Round-the-clock assistance that can't be provided at home

Care that would be more expensive to provide at home

Companionship that can't be provided at home

Safety precautions that can't be provided at home

No, if the older person:

Is very private, a "homebody"

Doesn't need help during the night

Values his or her freedom and independence highly

Is in stable physical condition

Needs only intermittent help

Is a low safety risk

are justified and which aren't. It also lets us more objectively consider the advantages and disadvantages of nursing facilities before making a decision.

Advantages

Nursing facilities have some advantages over being cared for at home. Many of these advantages are related to their ability to bring together staff with a number of different health care skills in one place.

24-Hour Monitoring—Probably the greatest advantage of nursing facility care is the round-the-clock availability of trained staff. Unlike family caregivers, staff work 8-hour shifts and are awake at night, checking periodically on the condition of all of the residents. They're also trained and prepared to summon help when it's needed, particularly important for the person whose condition is unstable.

24-Hour Assistance—Again, the availability of staff who can provide help at any hour is an advantage over being cared for at home by loved ones. Older people who need help to get to the bathroom at night, and who need frequent wound care, intravenous antibiotics, tube feedings, or any other treatment may be better cared for in a nursing facility.

Reduced Family Caregiver Responsibility—The availability of trained staff relieves family of much of their caregiving responsibilities. To some people's surprise, however, it doesn't completely relieve them of all of their responsibilities (see "Active Visiting" below).

Greater Safety—Older people who have problems with dizziness, fainting, falls, or wandering need a secure environment, whether with family members, in an assisted living setting, or in a nursing facility, depending on the severity of their problem(s). Even more important is that staff is able to respond quickly to medical emergencies.

Companionship—Like adult day services and assisted living settings, nursing facilities offer opportunities for companionship. Some people find this more important than being able to remain at home. Not all families or residents feel this way, however.

Less Expensive—Virtually any care that's provided in a nursing facility can be given at home as well. However, if the care is complex and requires a large number of different specialists (for example, occupational, physical, or speech therapists, psychiatrists, kinesiologists, and so forth), it may be less expensive to provide the same care in a nursing facility. Accurate estimates of the costs involved require careful calculation because there are many hidden charges in nursing facility care (such as laundry, medications, laboratory tests, and physician visits) and many unforeseen costs for at-home caregivers (for example, not being able to go to work).

Disadvantages

Many of the disadvantages of nursing facility care are related to the impersonal nature of the care that's provided in most institutions. Impersonal care is pervasive despite the attempts of some facilities to make the environment more homelike.

It's Impersonal—The care given in a nursing facility is care that is given by strangers. Some people prefer detached care, whereas it's abhorrent to others. In general, the larger the nursing facility, the more impersonal the care provided, but a warm, caring staff can counteract the impersonal quality of even the largest facility. Facilities that are located in small towns seem to go against this tide because often the staff aren't strangers at all, but the sons and daughters of friends and neighbors.

Limits on Freedom and Independence—Nursing facilities have rules—lots of them. Most rules are necessary either to protect the residents or to protect the facility. The result, however, is a considerable amount of restrictions on personal freedom. Residents of most facilities aren't allowed to walk out the door and stroll down the street, for example, or to keep a bottle of scotch in their bedside table or bureau.

Loss of Privacy—Few nursing facility rooms are private. The majority of residents share a room with a person they had never met before they came to the facility. Although compatibility is a desirable goal, it's not often achieved. In addition, some residents experience the shock of seeing a roommate die or watching him or her being taken away to the hospital or another facility, certainly not a common occurrence at home. A thin curtain that doesn't meet at either end is the extent of the privacy afforded in a room, apart from the privacy of the bathroom. Shower rooms are not private spaces, and the failure to knock before opening a door is common.

Many residents don't have a telephone in their own room. Instead, they're forced to borrow the telephone at the nurses' desk or to use a public telephone in the hallway. Residents who can't ambulate independently have to ask someone to help them to get to the telephone and then wait until someone's free to do so.

Different Lifestyle—A nursing facility is a different world than home is: cultural differences between staff and residents; regimented mealtimes, bath times, and bedtimes; structured activities; limited access to the world outside; and lots of people in wheelchairs and with mental impairments.

It's Not Home—All of these disadvantages can be summed up by this one: despite the traditional name, nursing homes, they aren't home. Some facilities are more homelike and personal than others because they're very small. Others have made some valiant attempts to create a homelike atmosphere: small living areas for visitors to gather, kitchens that residents can use, television and music rooms, quiet nooks for a little privacy outside of the bedroom and bathroom. For some people this is enough; for others it doesn't suffice.

It's Expensive—If the older adult in your life doesn't qualify for Medicare or Medicaid, the cost of nursing facility care can easily be $40,000–$60,000 a year or more. A great deal of home care can be purchased for this amount, especially if family caregivers pitch in.

SELECTING THE RIGHT NURSING FACILITY

Nursing facilities provide 24-hour care for young, middle-age, and older people with chronic illnesses and disabilities that require more care than they're able to get at home. In general, residents of nursing facilities aren't as ill or don't have the kind of unstable health conditions as hospital patients. Nursing facilities provide nursing care, dietary services, social services, physical therapy, occupational therapy, speech therapy, recreational therapy, and chaplain services. Unlike hospitals, they don't provide pediatric or maternity services, surgical treatment, emergency care, or intensive care of any type. In fact, nursing facilities transfer their residents to a hospital if they require any of these acute care services.

Although some nursing facilities are operated on a not-for-profit basis (often by religious groups), the majority are operated for profit. About 75% of the nursing facility beds in the United States are in for-profit facilities.

Nursing facilities differ in size, levels of care provided, age and condition of their buildings, philosophy, style of management, attitude of staff and administration, resident population, and quality of care. Although all of these factors are important in selecting the right nursing facility for the older adult in your life, the quality of the care given is the most important and probably the most difficult factor for a family member or loved one to evaluate.

Because there's a wide range in the quality of nursing facility care, a thorough investigation of every facility you're considering is necessary. Most of these facilities are run on a for-profit basis, so you should keep in mind the term *caveat emptor* (let the buyer beware). Passively accepting the advice of a physician or social

> ## The 10 Most Important Indicators of Nursing Facility Quality
>
> Rating by the official state agency
>
> Attitude of the staff toward residents
>
> Condition of residents' rooms
>
> Quality of the care given
>
> Adequacy of staffing
>
> Quality of the food served
>
> Location
>
> Cost
>
> Condition of daytime (public) areas
>
> Your overall impression of the institution (your gut feeling)

worker may work out well, but without investigating for yourself, you won't be able to judge the quality of the advice given. There are times when these suggestions are based on a financial interest in the facility, a close connection with someone in the facility, convenience, or plain old laziness.

The quality indicators that follow may not be relevant to your particular situation, but all are relevant to some situations. Those that we believe from our experience to be the most important are listed in the display above.

Organizational Characteristics

Licensure—Licensure by the state is a bare-bones, minimum requirement for nursing facilities. Possession of a license for the facility and its administrator, medical director, and director of nursing simply means that they've met the basic requirements of the state. An unlicensed facility might be adequate, but why take the chance?

Rating—The rating by a state's official inspection agency is a better indicator of a good-quality nursing facility. It's possible for a facility to fake the level of quality to some degree by meeting the letter of the law but not the spirit to achieve a superior rating. However, that they even made the attempt to win such a rating usually is a good sign. Obviously, a poor rating is a clear warning signal, no matter how the nursing facility's representative rationalizes it. Ask the nursing facility operator to show you a copy of the latest report or call the state agency for this information.

Inspection Reports—Reports that list deficiencies found by state inspectors are public record. Ask to see these reports. Few facilities are perfect, so one or two minor deficiencies (in resident charting or building maintenance, for example) shouldn't scare you, but major deficiencies (in staffing, quality of resident care, or a serious safety deficiency, for example) are cause for concern.

Posted Residents' Bill of Rights—A copy of the nursing facility's residents' bill of rights should be posted in a conspicuous place on every unit. In addition, the telephone number of the local ombudsman's office also should be posted conspicuously. (Ombudsmen are trained volunteers who investigate resident and family complaints about long-term care facilities.)

Location

Close to Home—A long car or bus ride may not seem to be an important factor at first, but it can become one after weeks or months (or longer) of traveling to the facility to visit your loved one.

Close to Emergency Services—A country or rural setting has many psychological and physical benefits for residents, but proximity to hospital emergency services may be more important to older people whose health condition is unstable.

Neighborhood—The neighborhood in which the nursing facility is located may encourage or it may discourage visitors. If the neighborhood is near a busy highway or in a high-crime area, free movement in and out of the facility might be restricted.

Physical Plant and Grounds

Repair and Maintenance—Well-maintained buildings are often a sign of the facility's financial health as well as of the operator's commitment to high standards, however, it's not a guarantee of either. A beautiful exterior may disguise a disgruntled staff or represent the owner's profligate spending, so don't judge the facility on this alone. Maybe you've only seen a picture of the facility. Investigate further. Go to the facility. Look for water leaks, cracked walls or ceilings, broken fixtures, and level of cleanliness.

Safe, Attractive Grounds—Opportunities for residents to go outdoors often are limited in nursing facilities, especially in multi-story buildings. This limitation can reinforce the feeling of prison-like confinement, especially for restless residents. The availability of outdoor areas for visiting, pacing, exercising, bird watching, contemplating, and any number of other activities can make the difference between a facility that's barely tolerated and one that's pleasant. Wheelchair accessibility is an important feature for many potential residents and their families. Loved ones with Alzheimer's disease need safe outdoor areas in which they can feel free to move around and yet can't wander off the grounds.

Comfortable Temperature—Adequate heating and air conditioning are especially important for frail older adults because their internal temperature-regulation mechanisms are less efficient than those of younger people.

Proper Lighting—Bright lighting without glare is important to older people with diminished vision. Warm, sunny rooms and cool, dim rooms are both welcome at different times and for different purposes. Both types should be made available to residents.

Interior Spaces

Residents' Rooms—Check residents' rooms for good-quality mattresses, clean linens, personal possessions, proper location of call light/buttons, adequate storage, privacy curtains, comfortable chairs for residents and visitors, pleasant window views, adequate, proper lighting for reading, accessible sink and toilet, and a telephone. These are all desirable, if not essential, to residents' comfort and care.

Hallways—Hallways should be free of clutter. Often, dirty sheets or clothing left too long in hallways are the source of unpleasant odors and clutter. Sturdy handrails mounted along the walls of the hall provide a sense of security and help to prevent falls.

Bathrooms—Bathrooms must be outfitted for privacy and safety. Toilet seats should be raised for residents who use wheelchairs to make transfers easy. Safety rails should be mounted close to both the toilet and shower, and a call light/button should be located within residents' reach.

Dining Room and Activity Areas—Wheelchair access is important in the dining room and activity areas within the facility. Try to arrange your visit around a mealtime so that you can observe how and what meals are served and/or around an activity hour so that you can determine suitability for your loved one. Ask yourself, Would my loved one be comfortable here? Would he or she enjoy the types of activities offered?

Kitchen—Health department regulations may prevent you from entering the kitchen, but you should be able to see it from the doorway. Cleanliness and freshness of the foods being prepared and served are your main concerns. Also, ask to see the health department reports on the kitchen at the facility.

General Atmosphere

Attitude of Staff and Administration—You're very unlikely to see a staff member abuse or neglect a resident in your presence even if a facility has a problem in this area, so you need to watch for other signs of staff attitudes toward residents and one another. Be wary of a facility in which staff or administrators talk to or about residents as if they were young children. Watch for any evidence of anger or intimidation, however mild, when staff talk with residents. Staff should be caring and courteous to residents. If possible, speak to residents and visitors out of earshot of facility employees; they'll tell you how caring staff really is. The amount of caring about residents is hard to measure, but you can at least get a sense of whether it's occurring.

Respect for Residents' Rights—Ask about the policies regarding residents' going home for a weekend or holiday, smoking, and drinking alcohol; the facility's problems with theft of personal possessions; placement of married couples in the same room; self-medication; and residents' telephone use. Observe the attitude of the person you're talking with—the general attitude conveyed in his or her answers may be even more important than the actual policy.

Choice of Roommates and Room Changes—Some facilities move residents around so much that they never feel settled. This will upset an individual with strong nesting instincts. Also, roommates can make or break a nursing facility stay. They can provide comfort and companionship, or they can be so disturbing that your loved one can't eat or sleep. Observe the roommate pairings that are already in place, and ask residents and their visitors as well as employees about roommate selection.

Staffing

Adequacy of Nursing Staff—A superior nursing facility will exceed the minimum staffing requirements set by regulatory agencies. State minimums are just that: the very least number of staff that are necessary to keep residents safe.

Preparation of Nursing Staff—A nursing facility that employs a Director of Nursing who holds a master's degree (indicating special preparation beyond the minimum requirements) is a good sign. Also ask about the training program or requirements for nursing assistants because they do the bulk of the hands-on care in nursing facilities. Many nursing facilities provide extra training and opportunities for promotion for their best nursing assistants.

Staff Morale—Staff turnover is a problem in many nursing facilities. Ask about the turnover rate at the facility and compare it with others you've visited. If the facility is willing to let you wander about freely (many won't), try a favorite inspector's test: Go into an empty resident's room and press the call button. Clock the response time. Slow staff response to calls for assistance leave residents feeling insecure and frequently contribute to unnecessary incontinence, a source of great discomfort for residents.

Residents' Grooming—Residents' grooming is an easily-observed indicator of both staff morale and the adequacy of staffing, which go hand in hand in many facilities. Observe and ask yourself: Do most residents have clean, neatly combed hair? Are they wearing clean, matching clothing? Are the women wearing at least a little makeup? Are the men clean shaven? Look at the residents' hands.

Dirty fingernails are a sign of inadequate personal care. If possible, observe how often residents who need help are helped to go to the bathroom. A facility's overdependence on adult diapers is a sign that it's understaffed or it doesn't value rehabilitation.

Availability of Important Services

Medical Services—Can your loved one keep his or her own physician after being admitted to the nursing facility? Is the physician willing to visit the nursing facility? Many families are surprised when the answer to one or both of these questions is "no, not here." A physician should be on call to the facility at all times in case of an emergency.

Dental Services—Many nursing facility residents have few teeth. Even more have teeth that are so decayed that they hurt. As a consequence, they avoid eating any food that needs to be chewed. Arrangements with an outside dental service or dentist is essential if the facility doesn't have its own.

Pharmacy Services—Ask the facility's representative about the way in which medications are reviewed, ordered, obtained, and charged to the resident. At one time, nursing facilities abused tranquilizers and sedatives, using them to control resident behavior. Although this practice is much less common, there are still instances when residents receive more medication than they should.

Activities Program—During a brief stay in a nursing facility, a person may feel purposeless or bored. During an extended stay, however, a person can become passive, lethargic, even depressed. Try to get a detailed account of the facility's activities program. Most facilities have plenty of activities for healthier residents, but have few for people who are bedbound or have cognitive impairments. Suitability is a particular concern, especially if your loved one is a man and dislikes the typical arts-and-crafts programs and Bingo games offered by most nursing facilities.

Rehabilitative Therapies—The older adult in your life may need physical therapy, occupational therapy, speech therapy, recreational therapy, psychological counseling, or all of these therapies. The quality of these services runs from poor or nonexistent in some facilities to extensive and highly professional in others. Quality may be the factor that determines whether your loved one improves enough to be moved to assisted living or to return home.

Social Work—In the past, people thought of social workers as helping only the neediest families. Today, however, the complexity of services and eligibility requirements makes their services essential to almost everyone. A knowledgeable social worker can help you and your loved one cut through the confusion of eligibility rules to get the most appropriate services at the lowest cost.

Food Service

Quality and Nutritional Value— We are learning the truth of "you are what you eat." A well-balanced, nutritionally sound meal plan is essential to your family member's continued health.

Acceptability—Good food nourishes the spirit as well as the body. Cultural and religious needs are more difficult to meet than nutritional ones. Some facilities cater to the preferences of specific ethnic or religious groups. These needs may be more important to your loved one than you realize. It's important to ask him or her about these needs before you select a facility.

Special Needs—Low-sodium, low-cholesterol, or diabetic diets usually are easily accommodated in nursing facilities. However, specialized diets such as wheat-, egg-, or dairy-free diets may be more difficult for some facilities. Eliminating these items is only part of the solution; the facility must also provide acceptable substitutes to round out the diet.

Finances

Basic Costs—Good-quality nursing facility care is expensive. Inquire about financial assistance to pay bills from Medicare, which usually covers only short-term rehabilitative or subacute care; Medicaid, which covers long-term care for people with very limited assets and income; and your loved one's long-term care insurance carrier.

Additional Charges—The list of additional charges often shocks families who take care of their loved one's finances while he or she is living in the facility. Before you consider placement, ask to see a comprehensive listing of all possible additional charges, and talk with the nursing facility's representative about the ones your loved one is likely to require. Ask how you can keep these charges to a minimum. For example, you might be able to save some money by doing his or her personal laundry rather than paying the facility to do it.

Lost Items Policy—Eyeglasses, dentures, hearing aids, television sets, radios, sweaters, and valued personal possessions disappear frequently in some nursing facilities. Even flower bouquets disappear in some places! Many of these items end up in the laundry or kitchen on a food tray, but some are stolen by staff members. Inquire about replacement costs and who pays for items, not just for the first pair but also for the second and third pair of eyeglasses, dentures, and so forth.

Preparing for and Adjusting
to the Transition to the Nursing Facility

Often, preparing for the person's move into a nursing facility is the least-well-done step in making the nursing facility decision. People underestimate the impact of such a move on the older adult and his or her family. In addition, caregivers have difficulty dealing with the issues that are involved in the move. Here are some examples:

Lucille took her mother out to lunch and then dropped her off at a nursing facility without a word of warning. She thought that the nursing facility staff would explain the move to her mother better than she could.

Roberto followed the nursing facility's (poor) advice not to visit his father for the first 6 weeks of his stay. When he finally visited his father, Roberto found he had lost 20 pounds and was so despondent over his son's apparent abandonment that he could barely speak.

Maryann spent several weeks hunting for a good nursing facility for her husband. When she finally found the right one, she asked him to visit it with her. She was surprised at how upset he was: "Why did you do this behind my back?" he asked her over and over.

None of these family members meant to hurt or upset their loved one, but all of them failed to deal with the placement issue in a direct, caring, and timely way. Some people think that they are protecting their loved one from unnecessary pain by not discussing the move to a nursing facility. They mean well, but they are mistaken. As the examples illustrate, they risk greater pain later by avoiding it initially.

Involve Your Loved One in the Decision

Some older people are more willing than their spouse or adult children to face squarely the necessity of going into a nursing facility. Ideally, the older person is involved in the discussion from the very beginning. Involvement should be active, not token—the person should be actively involved in every aspect of the decision and should help to make arrangements for the move. He or she should be allowed to consider alternatives and to visit several nursing facilities before a selection is made, if possible. In other words, don't take over unless it's absolutely necessary. For example, if the older person is too sick to visit the nursing facilities, you can visit them, make notes, and collect brochures, or you can take photos and describe the results to your loved one. The only reason not to involve the person is if he or she is unable to participate.

Once the decision is made, one of the most difficult caregiving tasks can be sorting through and perhaps disposing of the person's possessions accumulated over many years. If no other aspect of caregiving has yet brought tears, this one might. But, it's also a chance to reminisce, to review the good times as well as the bad, and to talk about how he or she has coped in the past and what can be done to cope now. Of course, if there's any chance that your loved one will return home or move to an assisted living facility, don't dispose of his or her things. Many families have hastily sold an older person's home, furnishings, and possessions when he or she became ill because they assumed that their loved one wouldn't be coming home. This leaves the older person who recovers from illness with nowhere to go. It's so much harder to start all over again than it is to return to familiar surroundings, especially for frail older people.

Talk About Concerns

Making the decision to place a loved one in a nursing facility calls for great sensitivity on your part and that of other family members. Listen to the older person's concerns. Try not to let your own feelings get in the way of being available and willing to hear about the older person's fears. He or she may be upset, frightened, even tearful. The natural reaction is to reassure the person that it's not going to be so bad, it really will be fine, and so on. Premature or false assurance isn't what the person needs and may discourage any further expression of fears or concerns. What is needed is an understanding, sympathetic listener, one who can allow the person to say whatever is on his or her mind, one who can laugh and cry with the loved one as they all embark on this major life change.

When you talk with your loved one about the transition from the community or the hospital into a long-term care facility, resist the temptation to make false promises. For example, don't promise that you'll visit every day if you can't do it. Do promise to visit however often it's realistic for you to do, whether it's every week, every month, or every holiday—whatever you're realistically able to do. Encourage the person to talk about the advantages of going into a nursing facility; some are listed earlier in the chapter, but personalize them if you can.

If the older adult in your life is so ill that you can't talk about the transition and his or her concerns, you can still hold the person's hand, tell him or her what's happening, describe the nursing facility you've chosen, and assure the person that you'll continue to be concerned and involved. By conveying your love, you will have accomplished the most important part of preparing the person to enter a nursing facility.

Help During the First Few Days or Weeks

Instead of staying away the first few days or weeks as some facilities actually suggest, try to spend some extra time helping your loved one adjust to his or her new environment. Seeing a familiar person in new surroundings reduces the strangeness and eases the transition for the person.

During your early visits, explore the nooks and crannies of the facility and find those that will especially please your loved one. You can suggest appropriate activities from those that the facility offers, and even attend some with the person. Encouraging contact with other residents is another way you can be helpful, but don't push your loved one too hard during the first week or two. Some people prefer to take their time, and most of us want to make our own choices regarding new friends. Some people need time to mourn the loss of their home, independence, and cherished possessions.

ACTIVE VISITING

It's essential that someone visit the older person regularly to ensure his or her welfare and to convey the family's continuing love and concern. This is active visiting.

James Fisher wrote, "If ever one needs a guardian angel, it's when he relies on others for everyday needs." Whether you call that individual a guardian angel, an active visitor, or an advocate, every resident needs one. If you can't visit regularly, consider hiring a qualified care manager to do this for you. Pastors, friends, neighbors, and relatives of other residents of the nursing facility also may be able to fill the role of active visitor.

Why is this guardian angel/active visitor/advocate so important? Many residents are unable to speak for themselves. Frequently, they're unaware of their rights or how to assert them. Some are afraid to speak up for fear of retribution from staff. This fear isn't always unfounded, and, if expressed, it should be thoroughly investigated, not dismissed. Even when residents are willing to speak up, they may be overwhelmed by the process of defending themselves and need help.

Despite regulations to the contrary, access to the outside world is limited by residents' own frailties and by facility practices (telephone access in particular may afford no privacy at all). Also, when older, frail residents do speak up, often their words are ignored or discounted. Of course this shouldn't happen, but it does, so the active visitor often must speak on behalf of or in addition to his or her loved one.

Assertiveness and Advocacy

Being an advocate for a loved one may be a new role for you. It can be difficult to approach busy nurses, doctors, and facility administrators with your concerns, but if you don't, who will? Three common and generally ineffective reactions to authority figures are avoidance, awe, and anger:

> Avoidance: Many people are afraid that their approach will be rebuffed. Others dislike confrontation and postpone it as long as possible. Often, the problem gets worse while they procrastinate.
>
> Awe: Health care professionals have a certain aura about them that makes it especially difficult to question their actions. But you need to remember—they're only human. Some are better at their jobs than others, and anyone can make a mistake.
>
> Anger: If you're really upset, frustrated, or feel powerless, you may overreact. Although anger sometimes brings about the desired response the first or second time it's used, you can't use it every time a problem occurs.

Assertiveness is more effective than avoidance, awe, or anger. A direct, calm, honest expression of your concerns is hard to ignore, and it doesn't make people defensive the way that anger does. When you're assertive, you're standing up for the rights of your loved one without violating other people's rights.

Lawrence Horowitz described the ideal advocate as "someone who can love you and feel for you, but not be paralyzed by the emotion of the moment." The ideal advocate cares passionately and persists until a problem is resolved. At the same time, the most effective advocate is someone who can analyze the situation intelligently and be objective as he or she determines where the problem lies.

When Being Assertive Doesn't Work

If your assertive approach doesn't bring about the needed improvement in care, speak to the physician in charge of your loved one's care. If this doesn't work, bring your complaint to the local office of the state agency that regulates nursing facilities or to the local ombudsman's office, which will investigate your complaint, negotiate a resolution if possible, or refer it to the proper authorities if necessary.

LEAVING THE NURSING FACILITY

People do leave nursing facilities. Many residents, especially those who receive active rehabilitative therapy, improve rapidly and are able to go home. Often, they're so relieved to be going home that they fail to prepare sufficiently for their transition to the community. Among other things, they may not choose an appropriate home health care agency, and home health care is so important to the recovery process (see Chapter 16 for more information on choosing a home health care agency or home health caregiver). If they choose appropriately, they can prevent returning to the nursing facility or to the hospital, which can be demoralizing.

Sometimes, the facility simply isn't appropriate for the individual. It may have been a poor choice in the first place or the person's situation may have changed. Although a transfer to another facility is difficult for everyone, it may be necessary for the welfare of your loved one. If this does happen, preparing your loved one for the transfer is just as important as it was when he or she was first placed in a facility.

Placing your loved one in a nursing facility may be one of the most important actions you take as a caregiver. This major decision is worthy of everyone's careful thought and consideration, not only when it happens but also as you observe how well it's working out for you and your loved one. Remember, although your role as a caregiver will change dramatically when placement occurs, it certainly doesn't end. Many family members feel that they can be better caregivers after their loved one is placed in a facility because they're now able to direct all of their energies to what paid staff can't do: provide the love and support that the person needs, maybe more than at any other time in his or her life.

18 Coping When Your Loved One Dies

There will come a time when all of the physical and mental care-giving energies that you've so intensely focused on the older adult in your life are no longer needed. That time is when your loved one dies. A flurry of emotions rushes forth: grief and loss, personal satisfaction in having helped him or her, and sometimes a sense of relief that your life, which to some extent has been on hold, can resume.

You and probably many others gave your utmost to help your loved one have the best quality of life that his or her cir-cumstances allowed. While the older adult in your life was alive, you juggled commitments and responsibilities for self, spouse/partner, children, and sometimes grandchildren. That put you in a very large boat called the "sandwich generation," a generation of people caught between caring for their aging parents and their own children. You've always been there to sort out any problems and/or concerns, and you tried to do the best you knew how at the time. You may have neglected your own health and well-being while you tried to provide the kind of care that honored the com-mitment you made to the person.

Maybe that person was a sister or brother, someone with whom you've shared special times. This relationship and the bond are very different from those between you and your parents or you and your spouse. This person's death will bring an end to that spe-cial bond.

The grief and loss that you feel are normal. After all, you put a lot of time, physical and emotional energy, and personal re-sources into caregiving. The person's death brings all of that to an end. But don't feel guilty if you feel a sense of emptiness when your loved one dies. Some people aren't sure what they should feel when their role is suddenly taken away. There are many similarities to what some people feel when they retire from work or to the "empty nest syndrome." The worker suddenly stops working and wonders what his or her worth is to him- or herself, other people, and society. The mother or father wonders what to do when the children "leave the nest" and don't need her or him as much.

This feeling of emptiness, which some people feel especially in the early days and weeks after their loved one dies, may be coupled with guilt. You may find yourself wondering, did I do enough? Why did I do "X" instead of "Y"? Why didn't I do _____? instead of focusing on all of the things you did. During this time of bereavement, it's important to let yourself "hear" other people when they talk about the loving care you gave the older adult in your life. You're too close to the situation to be objective about your caregiving. You also need to talk with family, significant others, and friends about your loved one and the experiences you shared. In doing so, you may achieve a more honest perspective of how you cared for the person. It's all too common for us to be the worst judges of our own attributes. We need to be able to let others help us become aware of our strengths as well as our weaknesses.

Right after you lose the person, when your grief is the most intense, you may get solace from reflecting on your relationship with him or her. Try to focus on the positive aspects of the person and of you and of your relationship. This approach lets you view yourself and of your loved one as caring people, even though there may have been times of anger, frustration, and hurt. Bringing up memories of difficult times serves no useful purpose. What's important to realize is that perfection in relationships may be a goal in life, but usually it isn't achievable.

Try to focus on the knowledge that you were there when he or she needed you, even if sometimes you felt like you wanted to be somewhere else. Remember how you put his or her care above that of others. There's satisfaction in helping to make the last days, months, or years of the older adult in your life a caring time. As you reflect on your role as a caregiver to this person, you may recall times when you felt exhausted, frustrated, guilty, and/or angry, and then the person would say or do something—a smile, a sigh of pleasure when made comfortable, or a spontaneous hug as you came close, with a whisper of "thank you" or "I love you"—and those negative feelings would melt away. True, that's small reward, but rewards that enabled you to bring more energy to your caregiving.

Your role as caregiver may have ended, but your being a caring person lives on. We hope that this book has helped you to travel more easily, in the words of the author of Ecclesiastes, in the worst of times and the best of times, as you care and give care to the older adult in your life.

References

Chapter 3

Barer, B.M., & Johnson, C.L. (1990). A critique of the caregiving literature. *Gerontologist, 30*(1), 26–29.

de Vinck, C. (1994, June 17). Father time. *The Wall Street Journal,* p. A14.

Framo, J.L. (1992). *Family-of-Origin Therapy: An Intergenerational Approach* (p. 7). New York: Brunner/Mazel.

Greenberg, J.S., & Becker, M. (1988). Aging parents as family resources. *Gerontologist, 28*(6), 786–791.

Hargrave, T.D., & Anderson, W.T. (1992). *Finishing Well: Aging and Reparation in the Intergenerational Family.* New York: Brunner/Mazel.

Pearlin, L.J., Mullan, J.T., Semple, S.J., & Skaff, M.M. (1990). Caregiving and the stress process: An overview of concepts and their measures. *Gerontologist, 30*(5), 583–594.

Whitaker, C.A. (1976). A family is a four dimensional relationship. In P.J. Guerin (Ed.), *Family Therapy* (pp. 188–192). New York: Gardner Press.

Whitbeck, L., Hoyt, D.R., & Huck, S.M. (1994). Early family relationships, intergenerational solidarity and support provided for parents by their adult children. *Journal of Gerontology: Social Sciences, 49*(2), 585–594.

Chapter 4

Canary, D.J., & Stafford, L. (1994). *Communication and Relational Maintenance.* San Diego: Academic Press.

Framo, J.L. (1992). *Family-of-Origin Therapy: An Intergenerational Approach.* New York: Brunner/Mazel.

Friedman, M.M. (1992). *Family Nursing: Theory and Practice.* Norwalk, CT: Appleton & Lange.

Gottman, J.M., & Carrere, S. (1994). Why can't men and women get along? Developmental roots and marital inequities. In D.J. Canary & L. Stafford (Eds.), *Communication and Relational Maintenance.* San Diego: Academic Press.

Hargrave, T.D., & Anderson, W.T. (1992). *Finishing Well: Aging and Reparation in the Intergenerational Family.* New York: Brunner/Mazel.

Kaye, J., & Robinson, K.M. (1994). Spirituality among caregivers. *Image, 26*(3), 218–221.

Paris, T., & Paris, E. (1992). *"I'll Never Do to My Kids What My Parents Did to Me!"* Los Angeles: Lowell House.

Tannen, D. (1986). *That's Not What I Meant! How Conversational Style Makes or Breaks Relationships.* New York: Ballantine Books.

Tannen, D. (1990). *You Just Don't Understand: Women and Men in Conversation* (pp. 158–159). New York: Ballantine Books.

Wilmot, W.W. (1994). Relationship rejuvenation. In D.J. Canary & L. Stafford (Eds.), *Communication and Relational Maintenance.* San Diego: Academic Press.

Chapter 7

Alexopouas, G.S., Barnett, S.M., Young, R.C., Kakuma, T., Feder, M., Einhorn, A., & Rosenthal, E. (1996). Recovery in geriatric depression. *Archives of General Psychiatry, 53,* 305–312.

Bernstein Lewis, C. (1995). Sexuality and the elderly. In C. Bernstein Lewis (Ed.), *Aging: The Health Care Challenge: An Interdisciplinary Approach to Assessment and Rehabilitative Management of the Elderly* (3rd ed., pp. 330–353). Philadelphia: F.A. Davis.

Bowling, A., & Browne, P.D. (1991). Social networks, health, and emotional well-being among the oldest old in London. *Journal of Gerontology, 46*(1), 20–32.

Clayson, J. (1999, June). Mental health for elders: Depression poses special problems for aged. Available: http://abcnews.go.com/onair/CloserLook/wnt990608_elderly.html

Fishman, S. (1992). Relationships among an older adult's life review, ego integrity, and death anxiety. *International Journal of Psychogeriatrics, 4*(2), 267–277.

Gilewski, M.J., Farberow, N.L., Gallagher, D.E., & Thompson, L.W. (1991). Interaction of depression and bereavement on mental health in the elderly. *Psychology of Aging, 6*(1), 67–75.

Husaini, B.A., Moore, S.T., Castor, R.S., & Neser, W. (1991). Social density, stressors, and depression: Gender differences among the black elderly. *Journal of Gerontology, 46*(5), 236–242.

Kennedy, G.J., Kelman, H.R., & Thomas, C. (1991). Persistence and remission of depressive symptoms in late life. *American Journal of Psychiatry, 148*(2), 174–178.

Krause, N., Jay, G., & Liang, J. (1991). Financial strain and psychological well-being among the American and Japanese elderly. *Psychology of Aging, 6*(2), 170–181.

Lewinsohn, P.M., Rhode, P., Seeley, J.R., & Fischer, S.A. (1991). Age and depression: Unique and shared effects. *Psychology of Aging, 6*(2), 247–260.

Locker, D., Liddell, A., & Burman, D. (1991). Dental fear and anxiety in an older adult population. *Community Dental Oral Epidemiology, 19*(2), 120–124.

Newmann, J.P., Engel, R.J., & Jensen, J.E. (1991). Age differences in depressive symptom experiences. *Journal of Gerontology, 46*(5), 224–235.

No sex please, we're over 60. (1988, January). *Nursing Times,* 34–35.

Oxman, T.E., & Baynes, K. (1994). Boundaries between normal aging and dementia. In V.O.B. Emery & T.E. Oxman (Eds.), *Dementia: Presentations, Differential Diagnosis, and Nosology.* Baltimore: The Johns Hopkins University Press.

Powers, C.B., Wisocki, P.A., & Whitbourne, S.K. (1992). Age differences and correlates of worrying in young and elderly adults. *Gerontologist, 32*(1), 82–88.

Steiner, D., & Marcopulos, B. (1991). Depression in the elderly. Characteristics and clinical management. *Nursing Clinics of North America, 26*(3), 585–600.

Taber's Cyclopedic Medical Dictionary. (1997). (18th ed., p. 128). Philadelphia: F.A. Davis.

Wilson. H.S., & Kneisl, C.R. (1996). *Psychiatric Nursing* (5th ed.). Menlo Park, CA: Addison-Wesley.

Chapter 8

Ebersole, P., & Hess, P.A. (1994). *Toward Healthy Aging: Human Needs and Nursing Response* (p. 145). St. Louis: Mosby–Year Book.

Matteson, M.A., McConnell, E.S., & Linton, A.D. (Eds.). (1996). *Gerontological Nursing: Concepts and Practice* (2nd ed.). Philadelphia: W.B. Saunders.

Watson, R.R. (1994). *Handbook of Nutrition in the Aged.* Boca Raton, FL: CRC Press.

Chapter 9

Abrams, W.B., Beers, M.H., & Berkow, R. (Eds.). (1995). *The Merck Manual of Geriatrics* (2nd ed.). Whitehouse Station, NJ: Merck & Co. (You can read this manual online at http://www.merck.com/pubs/mm_geriatrics; the manual is written for health care professionals but many nonprofessionals have found it handy. You may find *The Merck Manual of Medical Information, Home Edition* helpful as well. http://www.merck.com/pubs/mmanual_home/)

Chrischilles, E.A., Foley, D.J., Wallace, R.B., Lemke, J.H., et al. (1992). Use of medications by persons 65 and over: Data from the established populations for epidemiologic studies of the elderly. *Journal of Gerontology, 47*(5), M137–M144.

Deglin, J.H., & Vallerand, A.H. (1991). *Davis's Drug Guide for Nurses* (3rd ed.). Philadelphia: F.A. Davis.

Ebersole, P., & Hess, P.A. (1994). *Toward Healthy Aging: Human Needs and Nursing Response* (pp. 307–342). St. Louis: Mosby–Year Book.

Gilbert, A., Luszcz, M., & Owen, N. (1993). Medication use and its correlates among the elderly. *Australian Journal of Public Health, 17*(1), 18–22.

Gittelman, D.K. (1993). Chronic salicylate intoxication. *Southern Medical Journal, 86*(6), 683–685.

Ham, R.J., Holtzman, J.M., Marcy, M.L., & Smith, M.R. (1983). *Primary Care Geriatrics* (pp. 9, 198–199, 225–230). Boston: PSG.

Lamy, P.P. (1981). Special features of geriatric prescribing. *Geriatrics, 36*(12), 42–49.

Matteson, M.A., & McDonnell, E.S. (1997). *Gerontological Nursing: Concepts and Practice.* Philadelphia: W.B. Saunders.

McHenry, L.M., & Salerno, E. (1992). *Pharmacology in Nursing.* St. Louis: Mosby–Year Book.

Michocki, R.J., Lamy, P.P., Hooper, F.J., & Richardson, J.P. (1993). Drug prescribing for the elderly. *Archives of Family Medicine, 2*(4), 441–444.

Murai, A., & Matsumoto, M. (1993). Present status of elderly patients at geriatric outpatient clinics in terms of number of clinics consulted and number of drugs taken. *Nippon Ronen Igakkai Zasshi, 30*(3), 208–211.

Pollow, R.L., Stoller, E.P., Forster, L.E., & Duniho, T.S. (1994). Drug combinations and potential for risk of adverse drug reaction among community-dwelling elderly. *Nursing Research, 43*(1), 44–49.

Simons, L.A., Tett, S., Simons, J., Lauchlan, R., et al. (1992). Multiple medication use in the elderly. Use of prescription and non-prescription drugs in an Australian community setting. *Medical Journal of Australia, 157*(4), 242–246.

Stuck, A.E., Beers, M.H., Steiner, A., Aronow, H.U., et al. (1994). Inappropriate medication use in community-residing older persons. *Archives of Internal Medicine, 154*(19), 2195–2200.

Taber's Cyclopedic Medical Dictionary (14th ed.). (1983). Philadelphia: F.A. Davis.

Tideiksaar, R. (1998). *Falls in Older Persons: Prevention and Management* (2nd ed.). Baltimore: Health Professions Press.

Watanabe, R.K., Gilbreath, K., & Sakamoto, C.C. (1994). The ability of the geriatric population to read labels on over-the-counter medication containers. *Journal of the American Optometric Association, 65*(1), 32–37.

Chapter 10

http://www.aad.org. (World Wide Web site of the American Academy of Dermatology) http://www.jas.tj/skincancer/.

National Institute of Diabetes & Digestive & Kidney Diseases. (1997, November). *Take Care of Your Feet for a Lifetime: A Guide for People with Diabetes* (NIH Publication No. 98-4285). Bethesda, MD: National Diabetes Information Clearinghouse.

National Institute on Aging. (1999). *Age Page: Skin Care and Aging.* http://www.nih.gov/nia/health/pubpub/skin.htm.

Chapter 11

Burgio, K.L., Ives, D.G., Locher, J.L., & Arena, V.C. (1994). Treatment seeking for urinary incontinence in adults. *Journal of the American Geriatrics Society, 42,* 208–212.

Burgio, K., Matthews, K.A., & Engel, B.T. (1991). Prevalence, incidence and correlates of urinary incontinence in healthy, middle-aged women. *Journal of Urology, 146,* 1255–1259.

Division of Chronic Disease Control and Community Intervention, National Center for Chronic Disease Prevention and Health Promotion, Centers for Disease Control. (1991). Urinary incontinence among hospitalized persons aged 65 years and older—United States, 1984–1987. *Morbidity and Mortality Weekly Report, 40,* 433–436.

Fischbach, F.T. (1995). *A Manual of Laboratory and Diagnostic Tests* (5th ed., pp. 167–168). Baltimore: Lippincott Williams & Wilkins.

Herzog, A.R., & Fultz, N.H. (1990). Prevalence and incidence of urinary incontinence in community-dwelling populations. *Journal of the American Geriatrics Society, 38,* 273–281.

Mitteness, L.S. (1990). Knowledge and beliefs about urinary incontinence in adulthood and old age. *Journal of the American Geriatrics Society, 38,* 374–378.

Noelker, L. (1987). Incontinence in elderly cared for by family. *Gerontologist, 27,* 194–200.

Palmer, M.H., German, P.S., & Ouslander, J.G. (1991). Risk factors for urinary incontinence one year after nursing home admission. *Research in Nursing Health, 14,* 405–412.

Chapter 14

Burke, M.M., & Walsh, M.B. (1992). *Gerontologic Nursing: Care of the Frail Elderly*. St. Louis: Mosby–Year Book.

Cervantes, E., Heid-Grubman, J., & Schuerman, C.K. (1995). *The Paraprofessional in Home Health and Long-Term Care: Training Modules for Working with Older Adults*. Baltimore: Health Professions Press.

Ebersole, P., & Hess, P. (1994). *Toward Healthy Aging: Human Needs and Nursing Response* (4th ed.). St. Louis: Mosby–Year Book.

Ferrini, A.F., & Ferrini, R.L. (1993). *Health in the Later Years* (2nd ed.). Madison, WI: Brown & Benchmark Publishers.

Fox, H. (1978). The client who generates frustration. In J. Haber, A.M. Leach, S.M. Schudy, & B.F. Sideleau (Eds.), *Comprehensive Psychiatric Nursing* (pp. 263–279). New York: McGraw-Hill.

Harris, J.L., & Rawlins, R.P. (1993). Anger. In R.P. Rawlins, S.R. Williams, & C.K. Beck (Eds.), *Mental Health–Psychiatric Nursing: A Holistic Life-Cycle Approach* (pp. 207–223). St. Louis: Mosby–Year Book.

Hogstel, M.O. (1994). *Nursing Care of the Older Adult* (3rd ed.). Albany, NY: Delmar Publishers.

Holmberg, S.K. (1993). Somatization. In R.P. Rawlins, S.R. Williams, & C.K. Beck (Eds.). *Mental Health–Psychiatric Nursing: A Holistic Life-Cycle Approach* (pp. 382–411). St. Louis: Mosby–Year Book.

Homma, A., Ishii, T., & Niina, R. (1994). Relationship of behavioral complications and severity of dementia in Japanese elderly persons with dementia. *Alzheimer's Disease and Associated Disorders, 8*(Suppl. 3), 46–53.

Kelly, E.M. (1978). The client who generates fear. In J. Haber, A.M. Leach, S.M. Schudy, & B.F. Sideleau (Eds.). *Comprehensive Psychiatric Nursing* (pp. 247–262). New York: McGraw-Hill.

Miller, C.A. (1995). *Nursing Care of Older Adults: Theory and Practice* (2nd ed.). Philadelphia: Lippincott.

Needham, J.F. (1994). *Plans of Care for Specialty Practice: Gerontology Nursing*. Albany, NY: Delmar Publishers.

Raskind, M.A. (1993). Geriatric psychopharmacology: Management of late-life depression and the noncognitive behavioral disturbances of Alzheimer's disease. *Psychiatric Clinics of North America, 16*(4), 815–827.

Rawlins, R.P. (1993). Hope–hopelessness. In R.P. Rawlins, S.R. Williams, & C.K. Beck (Eds.), *Mental Health–Psychiatric Nursing: A Holistic Life-Cycle Approach*. St. Louis: Mosby–Year Book.

Shultz, C.M. (1993). Dependence-independence. In R.P. Rawlins, S.R. Williams, & C.K. Beck (Eds.), *Mental Health–Psychiatric Nursing: A Holistic Life-Cycle Approach*. St. Louis: Mosby–Year Book.

Suit, L.B. (1993). Guilt. In R.P. Rawlins, S.R. Williams, & C.K. Beck (Eds.), *Mental Health–Psychiatric Nursing: A Holistic Life-Cycle Approach*. St. Louis: Mosby–Year Book.

Swanson, A.R. (1978). The client who generates depression. In J. Haber, A.M. Leach, S.M. Schudy, & B.F. Sideleau (Eds.), *Comprehensive Psychiatric Nursing* (pp. 306–324). New York: McGraw-Hill.

Zamora, L.C. (1978). The client who generates anger. In J. Haber, A.M. Leach, S.M. Schudy, & B.F. Sideleau (Eds.), *Comprehensive Psychiatric Nursing* (pp. 280–305). New York: McGraw-Hill.

Chapter 15

American Association of Retired Persons. (1993). *All About AARP.* Washington, DC: Author.

Health Care Financing Administration. Information on Medicare. (http://www.hcfa.gov/medicare/mcarcnsm.htm)

Horowitz, L.C. (1988). *Taking Charge of Your Medical Fate.* New York: Random House.

Nickens, T. (1995, April 1). Clean up your acts, state tells 12 HMOs. *The Miami Herald.*

Rogers, P. (1995, March 20). HMO hustle: Sales process rife with lies, other woes. *The Miami Herald.*

Skala, K. (1991). *American Guidance for Seniors.* Falls Church, VA: American Guidance, Inc.

Smith, S. (1995, February 16). Learn lingo, assess your needs before deciding on health plan. *The Miami Herald.*

Chapter 16

American Association of Retired Persons. (1992). *A Handbook About Care in the Home.* Washington, DC: Author.

Dee-Kelly, P.A., Heller, S., & Sibley, M. (1994). Managed care: An opportunity for home care agencies. *Nursing Clinics of North America, 29*(3) 471–481.

Hankwitz, P.E. (1991). Quality assurance in home care. *Clinics in Geriatric Medicine, 7*(4) 847–861.

O'Donnell, K.P., & Sampson, E.M. (1991). Home health care: The pivotal link in the creation of a new health care delivery system. *Journal of Health Care Finance, 21*(2) 74–86.

Sheldon, P., & Bender, M. (1994). High-technology in home care: An overview of intravenous therapy. *Nursing Clinics of North America, 29*(3) 507–519.

Shellenbarger, S. (1995, April 5). A worker's guide to finding help in caring for an elder. *The Wall Street Journal.*

Chapter 17

Fisher, J. (1991). *Nursing Home Options.* Santa Barbara, CA: Kimberly Press.

Horowitz, L. (1998). *Taking Charge of Your Medical Fate.* New York: Random House.

State Long-Term Care Ombudsman Program. (1993). *Florida Ombudsman Certification Training Manual.* Tallahassee: Author.

List of Associations and Resources[1]

ACTION
1100 Vermont Avenue, NW
Washington, DC 20525
Telephone: (202) 606-4855
Senior Corps, (800) 424-8867: An agency of the federal government that sponsors volunteer programs conducted by older adults; the Senior Companion program is one of the programs.

Aging Network Services
4400 East-West Highway, Suite 907
Bethesda, MD 20814
Telephone: (301) 657-4329
Good long-distance caregiving services

Alzheimer's Association
919 North Michigan Avenue, Suite 1000
Chicago, IL 60611
Telephone: (800) 272-3900; TDD: (312) 335-8882
World Wide Web site: www.alz.org
24-hour toll-free hotline

Alzheimer's Disease Education and Referral Center
Post Office Box 8250
Silver Spring, MD 20907-8250
Telephone: (301) 495-3311
Information service: (800) 438-4380

---

[1] Because website addresses change frequently, some of the addresses provided here may no longer be valid. If you get a 404 message, try one of the Internet search engines to search for the organization by name.

American Academy of Dermatology
930 North Meacham Road
Schaumburg, IL 60173
Telephone: (847) 330-0230
World Wide Web site: www.aad.org

American Academy of Ophthalmology
Post Office Box 7424
San Francisco, CA 94120-7424
Telephone: (415) 561-8500
World Wide Web site: www.eyenet.org
National Eye Care Project Helpline, (800) 222-3937, hours M–F
8 A.M.–4 P.M.: puts disadvantaged people ages 65 or older in touch
with a local ophthalmologist

American Association of Homes and Services for the Aging
901 E Street, NW, Suite 500
Washington, DC 20004-2037
Telephone: (202) 783-2242
World Wide Web site: www.aahsa.org
Free information on long-term care and housing for older adults

American Association of Retired Persons (AARP)
601 E Street, NW
Washington, DC 20049
Telephone: (800) 424-3410 (main number)
Telephone: (800) 523-5800 (health insurance)
Telephone: (800) 456-2277 (pharmacy service)
World Wide Web site: www.aarp.org
AARP is the nation's leading organization for people ages 50 and
older. It serves their needs and interests through information and
education, advocacy, and community services that are provided
by a network of local chapters and experienced volunteers
throughout the country. The organization offers members a wide
range of special benefits and services. Booklet: "Dangerous Products, Dangerous Places"

American Cancer Society (ACS)
Telephone: (800) 227-2345
World Wide Web site: www.cancer.org
Materials available: Numerous free brochures, information on services. The ACS breast cancer network, alternative therapies, detection and prevention guidelines, and patient and family information

American Council of the Blind
1155 15th Street, NW, Suite 1004
Washington, DC 20005
Telephone: (800) 424-8666, (202) 467-5081
World Wide Web site: http://acb.org
Information and referral service (800) 424-8666 (hours M–F 3 P.M.– 5:30 P.M.); distributes a variety of free educational materials and publishes *Braille Forum* for blind and visually impaired people

American Dental Association
211 East Chicago Avenue
Chicago, IL 60611
Telephone: (312) 440-2593
World Wide Web site: www.ada.org
Distributes free educational material on tooth decay, dentures, diet, and mouth care

American Diabetes Association
1660 Duke Street
Alexandria, VA 22314
Telephone: (703) 549-1500
Information service: (800) 232-3472
World Wide Web site: www.diabetes.org

American Dietetic Association
216 West Jackson Boulevard, Suite 800
Chicago, IL 60606
Telephone: (312) 899-0040
World Wide Web site: www.eatright.org

American Foundation for the Blind
11 Penn Plaza
New York, NY 10001
Telephone: (212) 502-7600
Telephone: (800) 232-5463 (information hotline, hours M–F
8:30 A.M.–4:30 P.M.)
World Wide Web site: www.afb.org

American Heart Association
7272 Greenville Avenue
Dallas, TX 75231
Telephone: (214) 373-6300
World Wide Web site: www.amhrt.org

American Heart Stroke Connection
Telephone: (800) 553-6321 (information service)
Provides information on stroke and offers referrals to stroke support groups

American Lung Association
1740 Broadway
New York, NY 10019-4374
Telephone: (800) LUNG-USA (586-4872) and (212) 315-8700
World Wide Web site: www.lungusa.org

American Medical Association
515 North State Street
Chicago, IL 60610
Telephone: (312) 464-5000
World Wide Web site: www.ama-aasn.org
Many local medical associations provide physician referral services; provides good publications on prescription and over-the-counter medications, and a handbook of first aid and emergency care

American Optometric Association
243 North Lindbergh Boulevard
St. Louis, MO 63141
Telephone: (314) 991-4100
World Wide Web site: www.aoanet.org

American Parkinson's Disease Association
1250 Hylan Boulevard, Suite 4B
Staten Island, NY 10305-1946
Telephone: (718) 981-8001
World Wide Web site: www.apdaparkinson.com
Information hotline, (800) 223-2732, refers callers to local chapters around the country; patient education materials available

American Pharmaceutical Association
2215 Constitution Avenue, NW
Washington, DC 20037
Telephone: (202) 628-4410
World Wide Web site: www.aphanet.org
Publishes the National Medical Awareness Test and the Self-Medication Awareness Test

American Podiatric Medical Association
9312 Old Georgetown Road
Bethesda, MD 20814-1698
Telephone: (301) 571-9200
World Wide Web site: www.apma.org
Foot Care Information Center, (800) 366-8227. Free public information available on foot care; you can also obtain information to locate a podiatrist for consultation by calling the main number.

American Psychological Association
750 First Street, NE
Washington, DC 20002-4242
Telephone: 202-336-5500
World Wide Web site: www.apa.org
State chapters help individuals locate a psychologist for consultation; brochures available to public about mental health

American Red Cross
18th and D Streets, NW
Washington, DC 20006
Telephone: (202) 737-8300
World Wide Web site: www.redcross.org
Free pamphlets: *Better Eating for Better Health* and *The Lowdown on High Blood Pressure: Know the Facts*; available from your local Red Cross chapter

American Tinnitus Association
Post Office Box 5
Portland, OR 97207-0005
Telephone: (503) 248-9985
World Wide Web site: www.ata.org
Association-sponsored self-help groups offer information, support, and referrals to community services and resources.

Arthritis Foundation
1314 Spring Street, NW
Atlanta, GA 30309
Telephone: (404) 872-7100
Information Service: (800) 283-7800
World Wide Web site: www.arthritis.org
Chapters nationwide offer health education programs

Better Hearing Institute
Post Office Box 1840
Washington, DC 20013
Telephone: (703) 642-0580
Hearing Helpline, (800) EAR-WELL (327-9355)
World Wide Web site: www.betterhearing.org

Children of Aging Parents
1609 Woodbourne Road, Suite 302-A
Levittown, PA 19057
Telephone: (215) 945-6900
Nonprofit organization provides information and emotional support to caregivers of older adults

Consumer Product Safety Commission
Office of Information & Public Affairs
4330 East-West Highway
Bethesda, MD 20814-4408
Telephone: (301) 504-0990
World Wide Web site: www.cpsc.gov
Consumer Product Safety Hotline, (800) 638-2772;
(800) 638-8270 (TDD)
Free publication: *Home Safety Checklist for Older Consumers*

Elder Health Program
School of Pharmacy, University of Maryland at Baltimore
20 North Pine Street
Baltimore, MD 21201
Telephone: (410) 706-3011
Free information about older people and medications

Medic Alert Foundation
2323 Colorado Avenue
Turlock, CA 95382-2018
Telephone: (800) IDALERT (800-432-5378)
Information Service, (800) 344-3226
World Wide Web site: www.medicalert.org
Nonprofit organization provides an emergency medical identification system (bracelet or pendant) for people with hidden or special medical problems that aren't readily apparent.

National Association of Area Agencies on Aging
927 15th Street, NW, Suite 600
Washington, DC 20005
Telephone: (202) 296-8130
Publishes the *Directory of State and Area Agencies on Aging*

National Association for Continence
Post Office Box 8310
Spartanburg, SC 29305-8310
Telephone: (800) BLADDER (800-252-3337) and (864) 579-7900
World Wide Web site: www.nafc.ioffice.com
Patient advocacy group; serves as a clearinghouse of information and resources for people with bladder and bowel control problems and their families

National Association of the Deaf
814 Thayer Avenue
Silver Spring, MD 20910
Telephone: (301) 587-1788 (voice), (301) 587-1789 (TDD)
World Wide Web site: www.nad.org

Nonprofit organization maintains a complete listing of organizations that provide services to people who are deaf or hard of hearing and their families.

National Association for Hispanic Elderly (Asociacion Nacional por Personas Mayores)
1452 West Temple Street, Suite 100
Los Angeles, CA 90026
Telephone: (213) 487-1922
From the Administration on Aging website: "Project Aliento seeks to make the aging network accessible to Hispanic elderly and their families and to broaden the base of agencies and groups involved in providing services to Hispanic elderly. It demonstrates a model of home- and community-based long-term care for Hispanic elderly by developing linkages between the formal and informal long-term-care systems."

National Association for Home Care
228 Seventh Street, SE
Washington, DC 20003
Telephone: (202) 547-7424
World Wide Web site: www.nahc.org
Material available to the public on how to select a home health care agency; www.nahc.org/Tango/HClocator/locator.html is their Home Care/Hospice Agency Locator, which contains the most comprehensive database of more than 22,500 home care and hospice agencies

National Association of Social Workers
750 First Street, NE, Suite 700
Washington, DC 20002-4241
Telephone: (800) 638-8799 and (202) 408-8600
World Wide Web site: www.naswdc.org
The NASW helps people locate licensed social workers in their area.

National Cancer Institute
Public Inquiries Office
31 Center Drive, MSC 2580
Building 31, Room 10A03
Bethesda, MD 20892-2580
Telephone: 301-435-3848
World Wide Web site: www.nci.nih.gov
Cancer Information Service, (800) 4-CANCER (800-422-6237)
NCI provides accurate, up-to-date information about cancer and cancer-related resources in local areas. A variety of publications are available on cancer prevention, early detection, diagnosis, treatment, and survivorship.

National Committee for Quality Assurance
2000 L Street, NW, Suite 500
Washington, DC 20036
Telephone: (202) 955-3500
World Wide Web site: www.ncqa.org

National Council on Patient Information and Education
666 Eleventh Street, NW, Suite 810
Washington, DC 20001
Telephone: (202) 347-6711
Nonprofit organization committed to improving communication between health care professionals and patients about prescription medicines

National Diabetes Information Clearinghouse
Post Office Box NDIC
9000 Rockville Pike
Bethesda, MD 20892
Telephone: (301) 654-3327

National Eye Institute
2020 Vision Place
Bethesda, MD 20892-3655
Telephone: (301) 496-5248
World Wide Web site: www.nei.nih.gov

Free brochures available on cataracts, glaucoma, age-related macular degeneration, and diabetic retinopathy. Through its new National Eye Health Education Program (NEHEP), NEI conducts large-scale public and professional education programs in partnership with national organizations.

National Heart, Lung, and Blood Institute
Information Office, Building 31, Room 4A21
31 Center Drive
Bethesda, MD 20892
Telephone: (301) 496-4236
World Wide Web site: nhlbi.nih.gov
Publishes (among other titles) *A Handbook of Heart Terms; How Doctors Diagnose Heart Disease; Heart Attacks; Chronic Obstructive Pulmonary Disease; The Human Heart, A Living Pump*

National Hispanic Council on Aging
2713 Ontario Road, NW
Washington, DC 20009
Telephone: (202) 265-1288
World Wide Web site: www.nih.gov/nia/related/aoaresrc/dir/158. htm
The Council develops and publishes educational materials that are culturally and linguistically appropriate for older Hispanics.

National Hospice Organization
1901 North Moore Street, Suite 901
Arlington, VA 22209
Telephone: (703) 243-5900
Hospice hotline, (800) 658-8898
World Wide Web site: www.nho.org

National Information Center on Deafness
Gallaudet University
800 Florida Avenue, NE
Washington, DC 20002
Telephone: (202) 651-5051 (voice), (202) 651-5052 (TDD)
Fact sheets available on hearing loss and aging

National Institute on Aging
Public Information Office
9000 Rockville Pike
Building 31, Room 5C27
Bethesda, MD 20892
Telephone: (301) 496-1752
World Wide Web site: www.nih.gov/nia
Free publications available in English and Spanish on a variety of topics, including nutrition, medication, safety, exercise, and Alzheimer's disease

National Institute of Arthritis and Musculoskeletal and Skin Diseases
Information Office
9000 Rockville Pike
Building 31, Room 4C05
Bethesda, MD 20892
Telephone: (301) 496-8188
Free publications: *Medicine for the Layman: Arthritis, Medicine for the Layman: Osteoporosis,* and others

National Institute of Diabetes and Digestive and Kidney Diseases
Information Office
9000 Rockville Pike
Building 31, Room 9A04
Bethesda, MD 20892
Telephone: (301) 496-3583
World Wide Web site: www.niddk.nih.gov
Free publications on noninsulin-dependent diabetes, understanding urinary tract infections, foot care for diabetics, and many others

National Institute of Mental Health
Information Resources and Inquiries Branch
5600 Fishers Lane, Room 15C-05
Rockville, MD 20857
Telephone: (301) 443-4513
World Wide Web site: www.nimh.nih.gov

Free publications include *Useful Information on Alzheimer's Disease, Plain Talk About Handling Stress, If You're Over 65 and Feeling Depressed,* and many others

National Institute of Neurological Disorders and Stroke
Information Office
9000 Rockville Pike
Building 31, Room 8A06
Bethesda, MD 20892
Telephone: (301) 496-5751
World Wide Web site: www.ninds.nih.gov
Free publications include *Medicine for the Layman: Brain in Aging and Dementia and Fact Sheet,* and *Smell and Taste Disorders*

National Insurance Consumer Helpline
Telephone: (800) 942-4242
Help in choosing a health insurance plan that will meet your loved one's needs

National Organization for Rare Disorders, Inc. (NORD)
Post Office Box 8923
New Fairfield, CT 06812-8923
Telephone: (800) 999-6673, in Connecticut (203) 746-6518; Fax: (203) 746-6481
World Wide Web site: www.rarediseases.org
NORD is a federation of voluntary health organizations dedicated to helping people with rare "orphan" diseases and assisting the organizations that serve them. NORD is committed to the identification, treatment, and cure of rare disorders through programs of education, advocacy, research, and service.

National Parkinson Foundation, Inc. (NPF)
1501 Northwest 9th Avenue/Bob Hope Road
Miami, FL 33136
Telephone: (800) 327-4545 and (305) 547-6666
World Wide Web site: www.parkinson.org
A variety of free publications, in both English and Spanish, are available, and numerous articles, books, and videos are offered at low cost or via small donation to NPF.

National Safety Council
444 North Michigan Avenue
Chicago, IL 60611
Telephone: (800) 621-7619 (ext. 6900)
Pamphlets: *Preventing Falls—A Safety Program for Older Adults, Falling—The Unexpected Trip, Your Home Safety Checklist,* and *Ladder Safety*

The Simon Foundation
Box 835-F
Wilmette, IL 60091
Telephone: (800) 23-SIMON (800-237-4666)
World Wide Web site: www.simonfoundation.org
Nonprofit, educational organization that provides information about and products for urinary incontinence to professionals and the public; numerous publications and a newsletter (*The Informer*) available

Skin Cancer Foundation
245 Fifth Avenue, Suite 2402
New York, NY 10016
Telephone: 800-754-6490
World Wide Web site: www.skincancer.org
Nonprofit, educational organization that provides information about this most common malignancy through public education programs and continuing medical education; the foundation publishes *The Skin Cancer Foundation Catalog,* a 20-page, illustrated descriptive guide to educational brochures, newsletters, books, manuals, journal, audiovisuals, and posters.

United Ostomy Association
36 Executive Park, Suite 120
Irvine, CA 92714
Telephone: (800) 826-0826
World Wide Web site: www.uoa.org
Private, nonprofit organization that provides information about ostomies to the public and offers supportive services to people with an ostomy and their families; local chapters throughout the

U.S.; the United Ostomy Association is a member of the National Health Council and a charter member of the International Ostomy Association

U.S. Food and Drug Administration (FDA)
Consumer Affairs Office
5600 Fishers Lane, HFE 88
Rockville, MD 20857
Telephone: (301) 443-3170
World Wide Web site: www.fda.gov
Free information about the safe use of medicines

Vestibular Disorders Association
Post Office Box 4467
Portland, OR 97208-4467
Telephone: 503-229-7705 (answering machine)
World Wide Web site: www.teleport.com/~veda
Nonprofit organization providing information and support in English and Spanish for people with vertigo, dizziness, and balance disorders.

And Don't Forget . . .

Depression in Later Life: Recognition and Treatment, is available for $1.50 (check or money order) from the Oregon State University Extension Service, #PNW347, Publication Orders, Department P, Agriculture Communications, Administration Services Room A422, Corvallis, OR 97331-2119.

Healthy Aging, which is recommended by the Administration on Aging, includes information about nutrition, exercise, mental health, and more. To request a copy, send a check or money order for $1.50 and a self-addressed, stamped envelope to ETNET, Post Office Box 7536, Department P, Wilton, CT 06897.

For more information about sleep disorders, www.sleepnet.com/asda.htm provides a list of American Sleep Disorders Association Accredited Member Centers and Laboratories.

Index

Page numbers followed by *f* indicate figures; those followed by *t* indicate tables.

333